Learning the Truth about Me

Always Remember, Never Forget Healing comes after Doing what God teaches us to do.

Because of Christ
Carole L. May

Learning the Truth about Me

Let the Light Shine In

Carole L. May

Definition of Cardinal
"Chief, principal, preeminent or fundamental."

The Bible represents cardinal truth.

Scripture quotations in this publication appear from the following Bible versions:

ERV quotations taken from Holy Bible: Easy-to-Read Version. Copyright 2006 by World Bible Translation Center, Inc., and used by permission.

ICB quotations taken from the International Children's Bible, New Century Version (Anglicized Edition). Copyright 1991 by Authentic Media. Use by permission.

NASB quotations taken from the NEW AMERICAN STANDARD BIBLE. Copyright 1960, 1962, 1963, 1968, 1971, 1972, 1973, 1975, 1977, by the Lockman Foundation. Used by permission.

NIV quotations taken from Holy Bible, New International Version®, NIV® Copyright © 1973, 1978, 1984, 2011 by Biblica, Inc.® Used by permission. All rights reserved worldwide.

NKJV quotations taken from the New King James Version®. Copyright © 1982 by Thomas Nelson. Used by permission. All rights reserved.

Please note underlined words within the Bible verses are placed there by the author for purpose of emphasis.

Italicized words within Bible verses or definitions are in the source document.

Copyright © 2015 Carole L. May
All rights reserved.

ISBN: 1505631432
ISBN 13: 9781505631432

Dedication

This book is dedicated to every hurting heart whether big and tall or short and small.

May the *peace of mind* God makes available to all mankind become a part of *your* inner being.

The teachings within will guide you to Christ. He will teach you how to live in accordance with God's will now. Doing this will ensure that you will have a home with Him throughout eternity.

And may God be glorified!

Acknowledgments

The Holy Spirit has been the Director of this book. The times are numerous when His thoughts have been given in the middle of the night for the purpose of sharing them with the reader.

>May God Be Honored
>May God Be Glorified!

Expressed Appreciation

All the people God has put into my life have taught me various things in various ways. They are too numerous to mention, but because of the additional insight they have provided, the goal of this book has been to present this material in a simple, basic format in an effort to lead each of us into a greater understanding of God's will for our lives.

God has, indeed, blessed me with some of the dearest friends man can have. Expressed appreciation to Pat Criscito for her valued counsel as an experienced author; Terrie Stilwell for her never-ending guidance and support in Christ; our Saturday Morning Ladies' Bible Class for its continuous encouragement to complete this project; Mary Ward, Gina Browne', Brandon Browne', Marie Fowler, and Barbara Walker for their patience while proofreading. Thank you, one and all.

Disclaimer

It is very important to this author to offer this disclaimer to the readers of this publication.

This material is *not* being presented from the standpoint of being a "preacher of the Gospel." Rather, it has been prepared by one who has been made aware of over 50 suicide attempts or completions within the past three and one-half years.

My heart grieves every time awareness of another occurs. Our world is losing hope. The <u>truth</u> is the only hope that will bring refreshment to the breaking hearts of the world comes through a growing personal knowledge and application of the Word of God to daily living.

Yes, He is the only one who can provide a "way of escape" for us. Likewise, you and I are the only ones that can develop *Same Page Thinking* with Him as we listen to and follow His teachings. When this is done, He can and will bring many blessings and healing into the lives of the brokenhearted—far beyond what we ever thought possible!

It is my prayer that this book will be a blessing in the lives of many. Perhaps it will be an encouragement to your personal life. Equally important, if you personally know people who are dealing with deep anger, depression or suicidal thoughts, please share it with them. Depending upon their physical or emotional states, it may not be wise to leave this material with them to read for themselves. It may prove to be overwhelming. Therefore, it may be best to use it as a tool to help them by sharing what you have learned with them one-on-one. Through this avenue of approach, you will bring a greater degree of hope into their lives simply by *taking the time* to contribute to the fulfillment of their emotional needs.

The insight God has shared with me *must* be shared with you. Please share what you learn with others. Together, through Christ, we can overcome.

Onward

to

Higher Ground

Table of Contents

Dedication... v
Acknowledgments....................................... vii
Expressed Appreciation ix
Disclaimer xi
Introduction... xix
The Knots Prayer..................................... xxxv
Something To Consider............................. xxxvii
Section One   **Basic Truths....................... 1**
Prelude 3
Chapter One
    We Must Simply Understand These Truths
    Without Them, Nothing Makes Sense................... 9
Chapter Two
    Where Did the Bible Come From? 14
Chapter Three
    Understanding What the Bible Truly Is 18

Section Two　　　God's Plan for Us to Have
　　　　　　　　　　Two Sets of Parents New
　　　　　　　　　　Thought? Read On **41**

Prelude 43

Chapter One
　First Parents We Became Aware Of. 47

Chapter Two
　Introducing Our Spiritual Parents
　Part One　Our Spiritual Father. 53
　Part Two　Introducing God's Spiritual Parenting Partner. . . 63

Chapter Three
　Multiple *P*s Seen in Creation 90

Chapter Four
　God's One-on-One Parenting 95

Chapter Five
　Our Responsibility as Children of God 103

Section Three　　　Understanding My Frame. **107**

Prelude 109

Chapter One
　Opening Our Eyes, What Do We See? 111

Chapter Two
　And Looking Inside? 120

Chapter Three
　Continuing On! I Have an Even Greater Connection to My
　Father. 138

Section Four	**Satan Runs Interference with God's Plan for Man**	**145**
Prelude		147
Chapter One		
What Not to Believe		157
Chapter Two		
Satan's Approach through Eve		164
Section Five	**The Great Physician's Prescription**	**173**
Prelude		175
Chapter One		
Choosing the Right Doctor		176
Chapter Two		
How to Build a Meaningful Life		179
Section Six	**The Rampant Growth of Sin**	**195**
Prelude		197
Chapter One		
It Exploded like Wildfire		200
Chapter Two		
Spiritual Killers		222
Chapter Three		
Independence		225
Chapter Four		
Negative Thinking		233
Chapter Five		
Being A Workaholic		239

Chapter Six
> Materialism 246

Chapter Seven
> Competition, Man's Distorted View. 257

Chapter Eight
> How Effective Have Satan's Schemes Been?. 261

Section Seven   It Was Because of This 283

Prelude 285

Chapter One
> Assuming Is Dangerous. 287

Section Eight   Understanding the Trinity. 297

Prelude 299

Chapter One
> God, The Father 303

Chapter Two
> Jesus Christ, The Son Of God 310

Chapter Three
> The Holy Spirit. 321

Section Nine   How to Build a Spiritual Life. 327

Prelude 329

Chapter One
> Fear 330

Chapter Two
> Trust In God. 336

Chapter Three
   Faith 341
Chapter Four
   Prayer. 350

Section Ten   **God's Desire for Man** **365**

Prelude 367
Chapter One
   Understanding The Need FOR Baptism By Immersion . . . 369
Chapter Two
   Examples Of Baptisms In The New Testament 380
Chapter Three
   As The Result Of Baptism 389
Chapter Four
   My New Home On Earth. 393
Chapter Five
   My New Family On Earth. 401

Section Eleven   **How to Overcome Evil**
                         with Good **407**

Prelude 409
Chapter One
   How To Help Turn The Tide. 410
Chapter Two
   Forgiveness
   It Is Both Possible And Necessary 419

Section Twelve   How To Develop Mental Peace. . . . **431**

Prelude 433

Chapter One
    Never Forget This Truth. 434

Chapter Two
    God's Recipe for Recovery. 436

Chapter Three
    Heaven Will Be My Home For Eternity 439

Appendices 445

The Ugly Truth We Can No Longer Deny or Ignore 447

Other Factors To Be Considered. 453

My Personal Plea. 475

Introduction

A Message from My Heart to Yours

It is this writer's firm belief that much of today's spiritual teaching is presented in a manner that is difficult for many to understand—especially if they, like me, grew up in a home that did not offer Bible-based spiritual guidance. Without this, it is very difficult for individual family members to develop an understanding of their purpose in life or identify with their value in the sight of God.

When lack of spiritual knowledge prevails, man fails to realize one of God's Priorities is to protect His children spiritually so we can return to heaven to live with Him. The only way His goal will become reality is for us to allow Him to guide us through words of *solid truth* for the purpose of providing the tools needed to build a *solid foundation* upon which to build a meaningful, purpose-filled life. His love for us will not allow Him to guide us any other way. A loving father does not lie to his children. Because *there are no lies mixed in with Bible truth*, it is possible for us to gain greater insight into our purpose for living. As a result, peace of mind and hope for a brighter future will develop within us.

Everyone deeply desires and searches for these priceless assets. Evidence of our world's need for them cannot be disputed. Daily realizations of turmoil and restlessness are demonstrated in countless ways because the foundational teaching identifying our purpose for living has not been established within our mind-set.

After being personally affected by ten attempted or completed suicides in recent years (in addition to a murder-suicide), my prayer to God became…

> "Show me through Scripture what the core issue is. Why are so many people trying to take their own lives?"

His immediate answer was very clear!

> "Individual people do not understand their individual value in My sight. Without identifying with value, they have no purpose. Without purpose, they have no reason to live."

A lot of thought has been given to His response. Does this apply only to those who are trying to end their lives? Or does it also apply to a large number of people in our world today who merely exist rather than living a meaningful life? How many of us really understand our individual value in His sight?

Therefore, it is important to identify with our God-given value. Before physical birth, all people were created in His "image" and "likeness"—no exceptions! This inborn reflection of spiritual purity was placed within us by our Heavenly Father. Therefore, we are a part of Him. *As our Spiritual Father, one of His priorities is to help us understand how important we are to Him!*

Another of His priorities is to teach His children how to honor Him by reflecting this same image and likeness to those around us. The only way this goal can be achieved is to provide proper nutrition to our spiritual soul. In the same way our physical bodies require an ongoing supply of daily food our soul requires daily nourishment based upon Bible-based truth. God's Word is the only source capable of filling this need.

New understanding will come through meditation and prayer. As spiritual nourishment is fed to the human heart and mind, a positive illustration of God's love for individual people will develop. As growth occurs, the need for ongoing nurturing of our souls and quenching of spiritual thirst will become a daily realization.

Through this process, our *true* value in His sight will be revealed and *felt!* Whether or not this realization becomes foundational to our spiritual growth will depend upon our response to His teachings, which He always speaks in love.

Listening to Him and doing what He says are ways of expressing our love for Him to Him. An added benefit is that we will be protecting ourselves from spiritual harm throughout life. Then and only then will our individual spiritual needs be satisfied as God intends.

Why is strong emphasis being placed upon this thought? Our hearts and minds are like leaky baskets. Regardless of how hard we try to fill them with spiritual food, only a small portion is retained at one time. Many of the vital nutrients needed for daily living leak out. Thus, our spiritual hearts and minds need constant refueling.

If we, as individuals, would clearly understand and accept our Father's multiple efforts to guide us, our world would be a much better place!

If a solid foundation for spiritual growth is to be achieved, we must gain an understanding of what prevents its development. This will come as we gain insight into where and how false concepts of religious teaching originate. Many of them begin under the umbrella of <u>RATIONALISM.</u> Certainly this is a major factor leading to the prevention of our seeing Bible truth. What does rationalism mean?

1. The principle or practice of accepting reason as the only authority in determining one's opinions or course of action.
2. Pertaining to philosophy:
   The doctrine that knowledge comes wholly from pure reason without aid from the senses.

3. Pertaining to theology:

    The doctrine that rejects revelation and the supernatural and makes reason the sole source for religious truth.[1]

Several false teachings have developed through the use of rationalism. Just a few examples include we are of no value to God before becoming a Christian; we are born with a sinful nature; we are nothing more than filthy rags in the sight of God; we can be done without or God will not hear the prayers of a sinner.

These erroneous concepts are the result of false assumptions or Bible verses not being understood within the context in which they were written. A greater understanding of what "context" means is given in section one, chapter three.

The only tool that will help us to identify any error taught is to read the complete teaching surrounding the verses. Lifting one or two verses out of the whole and building a false teaching upon them brings forth the many confusing viewpoints presented in our religious world today. Can we now see the importance of keeping God's teachings within the setting in which they were written?

Countless beliefs flourish as the result of our not knowing God's Word or blowing off the teachings therein. For example, are we paying attention to this warning?

> [8] Be sure that no one leads you astray with false ideas and words that mean nothing. Those ideas come from men.

> They are the worthless ideas of this world. They are not from Christ.
>
> Colossians 2:8 (ICB)

This verse certainly describes the results of using "rationalism" as our spiritual guide. Do we now have a better understanding of why it is important for us as individual people to examine God's truth-filled Word for ourselves rather than parroting as truth what others may teach? This is absolutely necessary if we are ever going to be freed from spiritual confusion. A solid foundation cannot be built upon anything other than truth!

As long as humanity continues to use manmade "wisdom" in his search for truth, false teaching will prevail. With the wrong foundation,

* Will we be able to gain an understanding of where we fit into God's Plan?
* Are we going to be motivated to read the Bible if we believe it is only going to emphasize how "filthy" or "useless" we are with no hope of growing beyond those feelings?

Continuing on, we will soon realize the influence a false belief system has had upon our personal lives as well as the religious world today.

INTRODUCTION

Furthermore, when mankind is stripped of hope, do we not feel doomed? Is it possible to identify one factor that leads to the development of this feeling? Yes! The Bible explains:

> [4] The god of this age has blinded the minds of unbelievers, so that they cannot see the light of the gospel that displays the glory of Christ, who is the image of God.
> II Corinthians 4:4 (NIV)

Until the end of time, Satan's never-ending efforts will be to redirect man's thinking away from God. Consequently, if you and I allow him to be successful within our personal lives, we will be blinded to *God's truth.*

Overall, Satan has been *very* successful in his efforts to ground mankind in *negative thinking* toward God.

As a result, our doubt of His love for us increases, joy is minimized, and fear and anger set in.

Therefore, *it is imperative that we allow the Bible to nourish our thirsty souls.* Without understanding His love for us, it is possible that we will view God as being some type of dictator or people hater. Tragic indeed! Certainly this is <u>not</u> God's will!

Perhaps one of the most damaging false teachings is that God chooses who will live with Him for eternity. This is a belief held in the minds of many. If it were true, would that not place Him in a position of playing favorites?

On the other hand, it is important to understand there are several examples of God choosing people for various purposes. For instance, He told the Israelites,

> [7] I will make you my own people, and I will be your God
>
> Exodus 6:7 (ICB)

> [6] You are holy people. You belong to the Lord your God. He has chosen you from all the people on the earth. You are his very own.
>
> Deuteronomy 7:6 (ICB)

It is important to understand that God is addressing a *group* of people when He refers to them as "you." Other Scriptures that reference God and a chosen group of people include Isaiah 65:9, Jeremiah 7:23, and Ezekiel 36:28.

Before moving forward, it is important to notice another example of man being given the option of choosing for himself who he will serve as an individual.

> [14] Then Joshua spoke to the people. He said, "Now you have heard the Lord's words. So you must respect the Lord and serve him fully and sincerely. Throw away the false gods that your people worshipped. That happened on the other side of the Euphrates River and in Egypt. Now you must serve the

INTRODUCTION

Lord. ¹⁵ But perhaps you don't want to serve the Lord. You must choose for yourselves today. You must decide whom you will serve. You may serve the gods that your people worshipped when they lived on the other side of the Euphrates River. Or you may serve the gods of the Amorites who lived in this land. As for me and my family, we will serve the Lord."

Joshua 24:14-15 (ICB)

⁓⊙⌒

Speaking to a mixed group of Jews and Gentiles,
³⁴ Then Peter began to speak: "I now realize how true it is that God does not show favoritism

Acts 10:34 (NIV)

These examples are illustrations of "choice" being given to individual people. The phrases "accepts from every nation" (*group*) and "the one" (*individual* people within those nations) indicate an *individual* choice to fear God and do what is right.

Now let's take a closer look into Scripture to gain a better understanding of <u>**God's viewpoint.**</u> First, it is important to understand these truths"

"...People judge by what is on the outside, but the Lord looks at the heart..."

I Samuel 16:7b (ERV)

⁓⊙⌒

³⁰ Only you know what people are really thinking, so only you can judge them fairly.

II Chronicles 6:30 (ERV)

God had made a covenant with the Israelites. The Bible explains what it was:

> King Josiah told all the leaders of Judah and Jerusalem to come and meet with him. ² Then the king went up to the LORD's Temple. All the people of Judah and the people who lived in Jerusalem went with him. The priests, the prophets, and all the people—from the least important to the most important—went with him. Then he read the *Book of the Agreement*. This was the *Book of the Law* that was found in the Lord's Temple. Josiah read the book so that all the people could hear it.
>
> ³ The king stood by the column and made an agreement with the LORD. He promised to follow the LORD and to obey his commands, the laws, and his rules. He promised to do this with all his heart and soul. He promised to obey the agreement written in this book. All the people stood to show that they promised to follow the agreement.
>
> II Kings 23:1-4 (ERV)

Now it is important to understand the choice made by the Israelites a few generations later:

> This is the message from the Lord: ² "Jeremiah, listen to the words of this agreement and tell them to the people living in Jerusalem and the rest of Judah. ³ Tell them that this is what the Lord, the God of Israel, says: 'Bad things

will happen to anyone who does not obey this agreement. ⁴ I am talking about the agreement I made with your ancestors when I brought them out of that furnace[a] called Egypt.' At that time I told them, 'Listen to me and obey all the commands I give you. Then you will be my people and I will be your God.'

⁵ "I did this to keep the promise that I had made to your ancestors. I promised to give them a very fertile land—a land flowing with milk and honey. And you are living in that country today."

I answered, "Amen, Lord."

⁶ The Lord said to me, "Jeremiah, tell this message in the towns of Judah and in the streets of Jerusalem: 'Listen to the words of this agreement, and then obey these laws. ⁷ I gave a warning to your ancestors at the time I brought them out of the land of Egypt. I have warned them again and again to this day. I told them to obey me. ⁸ But your ancestors did not listen to me. They were stubborn and did what their own evil hearts wanted. The agreement says that bad things will happen to them if they don't obey. So I made all the bad things happen to them. I commanded them to obey the agreement, but they did not.'"

Jeremiah 11:1-3 (ERV)

Later Jeremiah tells us
   ⁹ "Nothing can hide its evil as well as the human mind.
   It can be very sick,
   and no one really understands it.
   ¹⁰ But I am the Lord,
   and I can look into a person's heart.
   I can test a person's mind and decide what each one should have.

> I can give each person the right payment for what they do.
>
> Jeremiah 17:9-10 (ERV)

God makes it very clear who He wants to be saved!
> ¹¹ For the grace of God has appeared that offers salvation to all people.
>
> Titus 2:11 (NIV)

Again, it is important to focus on the words "the one" (singular) and "all" (plural). These words exclude no one!

With these teachings before us, it is much easier to understand that God's choice is based upon our choice. Are we going to choose to serve Him according to His commandments? It is now time for *all of us to choose* whom we will serve!

In today's world of confusion, rush and hush, whirlwind schedules, and more, it can be very challenging to allow oneself to think about "me." In fact, many times we push away this mental process because we are fearful or consider it to be "selfish" or "egotistical." What a tragedy!

On a broader scale, if we ever recognized it in the first place, have we lost sight of the basic truth that it is *very important* for each one of us to take time to think about <u>me and my value</u> as a person in the sight of God? Have we ever given thought regarding <u>my purpose</u> for living and where <u>my life</u> is going?

Without this self-evaluation (regardless of race, creed or color), will there be any motivation to work toward overcoming anger, confusion, discouragement and depression in my quest for a better future?

It is important to understand the urgency of developing a vision for a better life and allowing it to dominate rather than allowing the devil to continually rob us of the daily joys of living as the result of a negative mindset.

If we believe we are *not* included in the "chosen few," hope for a meaningful, peace-filled life is immediately taken from us. Then desperation sets in! Without hope, the <u>*feelings*</u> we have within become anchored in depression, anger, feelings of "not being good enough," "not being wanted," or other thoughts leading to mental despair. They become more deeply rooted with the passing of each day.

Is this speculation or do we see evidence of it in every sector of today's world?

We see more than evidence—we are bombarded with *its reality* on a daily basis. It comes in the form of wars, mass shootings, murder, suicide, abortions and divorce to name only a few of the endless cruel, brutal acts that are imposed upon humanity by mankind. Unfortunately, this happens so frequently that it is accepted as commonplace—just a "normal" part of life.

This certainly ought not to be. It is not God's will! For people who have been schooled in negative thinking all of their lives, it is quite possible they do not realize a *positive* side even exists. Therefore, an inward feeling of discontent develops as the result of accepting what the world has programmed us to believe rather than God's truth! Consequently, peace of mind is impossible to achieve.

Are we beginning to both *see* and *feel* the need for change in our knowledge base regarding our value as individual people? It is certainly necessary if a better quality of life is to be enjoyed!

It is not wrong to have a positive self-image. The Apostle Paul explains:

> [3] For by the grace given to me I say to every one of you: Do not think of yourself more highly than you ought, but rather think of yourself with sober judgment.
> Romans 12:3 (NIV)

Certainly we are to have a positive image of self because God created us! However, it becomes a prideful issue when our focus is to glorify ourselves rather than honoring Him.

Therefore, it is with these thoughts in mind that *Learning the Truth about Me* has been prepared in an effort to provide a clearer understanding of God's Plan for us. Hopefully, it will be helpful in bridging the gap between the confusion and broken-heartedness suffered in life and the peace of mind God desires for us.

The *sole* purpose of this publication is to share, from my heart to yours, new learning to guide our thinking regarding our own self-images and purposes in life. It is possible to achieve a much higher quality of life. However, it cannot and will not be gained without the foundation of our personal belief systems being challenged, rebuilt where needed, and solidly anchored upon Bible truth. If lives are to be changed, this challenge must be accepted by each individual. Nobody can do it for us.

As we pursue Bible *truth*, points of comparison will be established that will allow us to compare God's truth with our current spiritual beliefs. Then we will have a clear vision of where changes must be made if we are to be pleasing to God.

 is critically important that our soul is firmly anchored in healthy, uplifting, spiritually nourished soil! Without truth, we will continue to experience a "cheated life."

Isn't a "Quality Life" embedded with meaning and purpose far more desirable? This is not to be interpreted as a life that will be laden with physical riches and abundance of possessions. On the contrary, it is the peace of mind that comes through living life in accordance with God's will.

So, in reality, does it not come down to choice? Are we going to continue thinking negatively with no hope for a brighter future? Or are we so sick and tired of "just existing" that we have now come to the point in life that we are willing to actively *seek* and *put into practice* a better way of living?

If we *accept* what we learn, *believe* it to be true, *allow* it to grow within the soil of our heart, and then *obey* the commandments given, the forthcoming fruit will develop into joy as the result of an everlasting peace of mind thought never to be possible.

Again, this truth must be emphasized. These blessings are only available through knowledge of and obedience to God's teaching.

As we move forward with this new hope, it is important that we focus on the truth that the Bible is God's message to *all* of mankind. It provides rock solid proof of <u>our value in His sight</u>. This will help us to better understand who we are, why we were born, and how to build a meaningful relationship with Jesus to ensure our eternal salvation.

Come along now as we walk this journey together for the purpose of learning what real truth is. In turn, it will lead us to the *full life* that both God and I desire here on earth and throughout eternity.

May God Be Glorified!

Carole L. May

References

[1] *Webster's New World Dictionary of the American Language*, David B. Guralnik, Editor in Chief; second edition; Simon and Schuster; 1982, p. 1179

THE KNOTS PRAYER

Dear God:
    Please untie the knots that are in
        my mind,
            my heart and
                my life.

Remove the
    have nots,
        the can nots and
            the do nots
                that I have in my mind.

Erase the
    will nots,
        may nots,
            might nots
                that may find a home in my heart.

Release me from
    the could nots,
        would nots and
           should nots
              that obstruct my life.

And most of all, Dear God,
    I ask that you remove from
        my mind,
           my heart and
              my life

    all of the 'am nots' that I have allowed to hold me back, especially the thought that I am not good enough.
                    Amen

            Author Known to God

SOMETHING TO CONSIDER

What is this thing called "religion"
of which so many talk?
Is it just talk, or is there something deeper,
more meaningful—perhaps a path for us to walk?

In answer to this question, many will reply,
"God is dead—so what difference does it make!"
"Believe what you like—it makes no difference to God."
"Life on earth is hell!"
"One religion is just as good as another."

With all of these thoughts, conflicting though they be,
is it possible to make sense out of religion
in a way that would be helpful to you and me?

So how do we resolve this dilemma—gain peace of mind?
There is only one way.

Turn to the Book, which is filled with answers
left there for me to find.
Yes, that book is called the Bible—the Book Divine.

For without it, all else remains "opinion."
No direction. No guidance. No real truth.
No answers to my issues of life.
So it is with excitement and glee
that I can read its message, knowing
God is interested in me!

It is important to remember,
the Bible was written in a way
that removes confusion and uncertainty
regarding His will for my life today.

So what is the missing link?
Perhaps I have not cooperated with His Plan
by taking time to read the Bible—and think.

Above all the other needs of life,
each of us must feed the spirit within by
reading, studying, meditating upon, and obeying the Word of
God.

SOMETHING TO CONSIDER

<u>Why?</u>
His will for me and my life is written upon the pages of His book.
Therefore, it is to very important that I take more than a casual look.
Then my perception of His Word will be embedded more accurately within me, relieving my misery and strife.
It helps me to think more positively about my existence.
It is truly "God's Road Map" to heaven—
without it, I will be lost.
The very destiny of my soul will depend upon
my response to this message.
So I must take a more serious look and study it, regardless of the cost!
Within this special book,
I Timothy 5:4 and James 1:26–27
tell us some of God's view.
Reading these will perhaps show that His teaching
may not agree with me and you.
So let's clear up the confusion and turn to God's Word.
This is the only truth that will last.
Why?
He wants what is best for you and me while here on earth.
He wants us to choose to live with him throughout eternity!

SECTION ONE

BASIC TRUTHS

Prelude

You may be asking, "What is a prelude?"

One definition provided by *Webster's Electronic Dictionary, 1828 Edition:*

> Something introductory or that shows what is to follow; something preceding which bears some relation or resemblance to that which is to follow [1]

This is the exact reason for sharing the basic information needed upon which to build a truly meaningful life. Without the right foundation, our lives can easily come crashing down around us. As a result, we become generally discontent with life, angry, depressed, or suicidal.

Truly, this is not God's will. Therefore, we will be moving forward toward the goal of learning how to gain the desired peace of mind.

Learning the Truth about Me is different in many ways. How? It is not just another self-help book. Within its pages, many solid

Bible-based truths will be established for the sole purpose of helping all of mankind to understand that, individually, we are a

VBPP—Valuable, Beautiful, Precious Person

in the

Sight of God!

—NO EXCEPTIONS—

This includes everyone!

Because "God" has been mentioned, please don't lay these teachings aside because a non-thinking, coldhearted, or uncaring person in your past life has not lived a life in keeping with Christianity. This type of thinking carries a high risk factor of developing cold-heartedness as the result of believing "religion is not for me."

Regardless of the roots from which negative thinking has grown, it is important to move forward with the understanding that the purpose of this writing is not to preach, but rather teach truths that will rebuild our spirits at the core level. Whether or not this goal is achieved will basically depend upon individual choice—believe or reject what is presented. Oh, how difficult this choice may be if life's experiences have taught us *not* to trust or believe in anyone or anything other than ourselves!

Almost on a daily basis we hear discussions of gun control. How many times do we consider the need for "heart control"? Controlling our hearts through the teachings of God's Word would eliminate any need for guns being used as weaponry against violence.

Prelude

The greatest need in our world today is Bible-based truth!

A cloudy, undefined approach to Christianity is not the solution to life's problems. It does not provide positive direction for man. Only solid, firmly anchored truth from God's Word can be trusted. It will provide the answer to any issue we may face in life. Onward as we pursue it.

Let's begin with an accurate understanding of truth. Does it have an elusive meaning to different people? Or is its true meaning built upon a much more solid foundation? Without answering this question, more and more confusion will enter the world on a daily basis. Therefore, let's improve life by gaining a clear understanding of what truth is. The Bible gives a straightforward definition:

> [17] Sanctify them by the truth; your word is truth.
>
> John 17:17 (NIV)

Now let's turn our attention to understanding the Greek definition of truth:

> "the truth, as taught in the Christian religion, respecting God and the execution of his purposes through Christ, and respecting the duties of man," [2]

Further insight is gained through understanding the meaning of sanctify.

"to cleanse from corruption; to purify from sin; to make holy by detaching the affections from the world and its defilements, and exalting them to a supreme love to God."[3]

The purpose of Wisdom's instruction given to the VBPPeople God created is to teach us how to live within the guidelines of truth. Obeying her guidance will keep us from sinning.

> ¹ My son, do not forget my teaching,
>   but keep my commands in your heart,
> ² for they will prolong your life many years
>   and bring you peace and prosperity.
>   Proverbs 3:1-2 (NIV)

> ³ Don't depend on your leaders for help.
>   Don't depend on people, because they cannot save you.
> ⁴ People die and are buried.
>   Then all their plans to help are gone.
> ⁵ It is a great blessing for people to have the God of Jacob
>   to help them.
>   They depend on the LORD their God.
>   Psalms 146:3–5 (ERV)

As we depend upon the Lord for truthful teaching, we will learn there is a difference between believing Him and believing *in* Him. What is the difference—believing what He says or simply believing *in* His existence?

PRELUDE

A very clear connection between "disobedience" and "unbelief" is shown through Scripture:

> [16] For who, having heard, rebelled? Indeed, *was it* not all who came out of Egypt, *led* by Moses? [17] Now with whom was He angry forty years? *Was it* not with those who sinned, whose corpses fell in the wilderness? [18] And to whom did He swear that they would not enter His rest, but to those who did not obey? [19] So we see that they could not enter in because of unbelief.
>
> Hebrews 3:16–19 (NKJV)

If we have experienced difficulty in believing the Bible, it is important that our belief system be restructured at the very core level of our inner being. When we *allow* this to happen, any sense of hopelessness, depression, or brokenheartedness commonly felt among us will be healed. This will take time, but healing will come.

The hope and motivation needed for a more meaningful, peace-filled life will develop as we allow God to be the *leader*, as we learn to believe, trust and follow Him.

Embracing Jesus, believing Him, and responding to His teachings are a *must* if the brokenhearted are to be healed.

Properly nurturing this seed of hope with truth will be our pursuit. We can depend upon God's Word to do this.

As we move forward, it is important for the first-time Bible reader to understand the information that follows quotations from Scriptures. Using Genesis 1:1 as an example:

- * "Genesis" is the name of the book in the Bible.
- * "1:" indicates the chapter within Genesis.
- * ":1" indicates the verse within the chapter.

Until one becomes more familiar with the Bible, it may be necessary to refer to the entire list of books given within the first few pages.

The books will be divided into the Old Testament (OT) and New Testament (NT). There are thirty-nine in the Old Testament and twenty-seven in the New Testament, making a total of sixty-six books in God's authorized Word.

References

[1] *Webster's,* 1828, Volume 2

[2] biblehub.com, Greek #225, Definition 2c

[3] *Webster's* 1828, op. cit, Definition 5

Chapter One

We Must Simply Understand These Truths
Without Them, Nothing Makes Sense

Up to this point, multiple references to God, the Bible, and our need for spiritual growth have been made. This has been done with intent. Why?

Simply stated, without our knowledge of God's Word, we will *never* learn our true value as individual people.

One of the saddest truths in the world today is that God's leadership has been shunned from the beginning of time. This is true because man has not focused upon Bible truth. Consequently, because of the lack of knowledge, all too often, man has been "turned off" from religion. Certainly, this is not surprising.

There are several factors that can influence our thinking. Here are a few.

Some have been trained throughout childhood to become an atheist or agnostic. What do these words mean?

- Atheist   A person who believes there is no God.[1]
- Agnostic   A person who believes that the human mind cannot know whether there is a God or an ultimate cause, or anything beyond material phenomena.[2]

Another major factor for religious confusion is recent information taken from the Internet. There are approximately twenty-one major religions in today's world.[3] Additionally, this number has developed into 41,000 denominations.[4]

With these stats before us, it is certainly understandable how our thinking regarding spiritual matters can and does become confused and distorted. Obviously all of this develops as the result of divisions and dissensions in the religious world. Trying to sort out "truth" from error as the result of too many doctrines becomes overwhelming.

Because real truth is not widely known many adverse factors enter into man's thinking. Consequently, the quest for greater insight is discouraging. We find ourselves asking, "Is it even possible to find truth?"

Yes, it is but this can only be done through a positive response through an open mind to God's teachings presented in the Bible. These include:

[17] I urge you, brothers and sisters, to watch out for those who cause divisions and put obstacles in your way that

are contrary to the teaching you have learned. Keep away from them.

Romans 16:17 (NIV)

[10] I appeal to you, brothers and sisters, in the name of our Lord Jesus Christ, that all of you agree with one another in what you say and that there be no divisions among you, but that you be perfectly united in mind and thought.

I Corinthians 1:10 (NIV)

The Apostle Paul's instruction to Timothy:
[2] Tell everyone God's message. Be ready at all times to do whatever is needed. Tell people what they need to do, tell them when they are doing wrong, and encourage them. Do this with great patience and careful teaching.
[3] The time will come when people will not listen to the true teaching. But people will find more and more teachers who please them. They will find teachers who say what they want to hear. [4] People will stop listening to the truth. They will begin to follow the teaching in false stories.

II Timothy 4:2-4 (ERV)

Others are turned away because they are "reading the lives of people" who claim to be Christian but their "talk" does not match their "walk." Even though this is very discouraging to the onlooker, we cannot allow it to deter us from looking further and examining God's Word—*and following Him!*

Additional discouraging beliefs among mankind regarding God's Holy Word may include it is not relevant to everyday living in today's world; it is too difficult for man to understand; our parents and grandparents taught us everything we need to know about God; what was good enough for them is good enough for me, or it is nothing but rules and regulations to be followed that take all the fun out of living.

These mindsets provide a very negative view! Whether we agree or not, the reality is that embracing any of them will continue to rob us of the peace of mind available through God's Word.

Now it is time for us to consider much more positive truths that are uplifting to the body, mind, and soul. To achieve this higher goal, we must simply read and follow the instructions laid before us in the Word of God rather than pointing fingers toward others in an effort to justify our personal behaviors.

Therefore, with intent and purpose, let's stop and focus on establishing a foundation of truth upon which to build a better life as the result of viewing the Bible in a more positive mind-set.

References

(1) *Webster's*, 1982; p. 87

(2) Ibid., p. 27

(3) Taken from http://answers.yahoo.com/question/index?qid=1005120500015

(4) Taken from http://en.wikipedia.org/wiki/List_of_Christiandemoninations

Chapter Two

Where Did the Bible Come From?

Let's answer that question by asking another. "How do we know George Washington was president of the United States?"

Although none of us know this to be true as the result of having lived during the time he was actually in office, do we still believe this to be true? Yes! We accept it as fact because it has been recorded in history books for decades. We have simply accepted what we have been taught.

Another thought to illustrate the point: Why do we accept the teaching that 1 + 1 = 2? Who said so?

We accept these teachings as truth simply because we had faith in the teacher and the fact that the same teachings have been presented for years. Because the teachings have not changed, our confidence has increased, which gives us more reason to believe what is being taught.

Accepting them as truth has opened the door for more learning far beyond what we thought possible at the time.

Unfortunately, the same cannot be said with regard to Bible teaching. Through the years many teachings have been presented as truth, when in reality, they have been changed by man. Nonetheless, they cannot be supported through Scripture. We have already learned that God's Word represents truth.

Therefore, to filter out truth from man-made teachings (false doctrine), it becomes very important that it be firmly established through close examination of God's Word. Only in this way can a greater confidence and belief in Him become our foundation for daily living.

To achieve this goal, let's examine what the Bible teaches regarding its origination. How do we know *it* is true? How do we know *it* can be depended upon?

> This passage explains Luke's purpose for writing.
> [1] Most Honorable Theophilus:
> Many others have tried to give a report of the things that happened among us to complete God's plan. [2] What they have written agrees with what we learned from the people who saw those events from the beginning. They also served God by telling people his message. [3] I studied it all carefully from the beginning. Then I decided to write it

down for you in an organized way. ⁴ I did this so that you can be sure that what you have been taught is true.

Luke 1:1–4 (ERV)

Listen to the Apostle Peter as he writes:

¹⁶ We told you about the power of our Lord Jesus Christ. We told you about his coming. The things we told you were not just clever stories that people invented. No, we saw the greatness of Jesus with our own eyes. ¹⁷ Jesus heard the voice of the great and glorious God. That was when he received honor and glory from God the Father. The voice said, "This is my Son, the one I love. I am very pleased with him." ¹⁸ And we heard that voice. It came from heaven while we were with Jesus on the holy mountain.
¹⁹ This makes us more sure about what the prophets said. And it is good for you to follow closely what they said, which is like a light shining in a dark place. You have that light until the day begins and the morning star brings new light to your minds. ²⁰ Most important of all, you must understand this: No prophecy in the Scriptures comes from the prophet's own understanding.

II Peter 1:16–20 (ERV)

Please do not cheat yourself by not accepting these Bible teachings. As you learn to trust them, you will gain confidence in the Scriptures as being God's Word. Then, as the result of believing and putting into practice what is learned, the spiritual food needed daily to sustain your inner being at the core level will be received.

On the other hand, this question is asked of those who choose not to believe. "Why are you willing to accept teaching from the world regarding secular subjects, which are basically accepted through man's faith in man, but not willing to accept teachings from the Bible?"

You alone can answer this question.

Overwhelming documentation through the Dead Sea Scrolls and ongoing archeological diggings continue to uphold Bible teachings.

Chapter Three

Understanding What the Bible Truly Is

Where are we to begin? Having an open mind willing to accept God's truth that may present new thoughts is critically important to our spiritual survival.

There is another very important caution that must be given to those seeking God's truth. If the correct meaning of Bible verses is to be gleaned, it is absolutely mandatory that they be read and kept in the "context" in which they were written.

Context is another word that needs to be defined if clear understanding is to be gained:

> "...the whole situation, background, or environment relevant to a particular event, personality, creation, etc."[1]

The following example is a clear demonstration of why keeping Bible teachings within their proper contexts is so critically important lest false doctrine creeps in.

What is false doctrine? It is any teaching that is presented as truth but delivers a different message than what the Bible actually teaches.

For example, some have been taught that we are nothing more than "filthy rags" in the sight of God. Isaiah 64 is used as the foundation of this teaching. Needless to say, it is not a very encouraging message and allows no motivation to pursue a closer relationship with Our Creator.

For the purpose of learning truth, let's read the facts as recorded in the Bible.

> [1] Oh, that you would rend the heavens and come down,
> that the mountains would tremble before you!
> [2] As when fire sets twigs ablaze
> and causes water to boil,
> come down to make your name known to your enemies
> and cause the nations to quake before you!
> [3] For when you did awesome things that we did not expect,
> you came down, and the mountains trembled before you.

> ⁴ Since ancient times no one has heard,
>   no ear has perceived,
> no eye has seen any God besides you,
>   who acts on behalf of those who wait for him.
> ⁵ You come to the help of those who gladly do right,
>   who remember your ways.
> But when we continued to sin against them,
>   you were angry.
> How then can we be saved?
> ⁶ All of us have become like one who is unclean,
>   and all our righteous acts are like filthy rags;
> we all shrivel up like a leaf,
>   and like the wind our sins sweep us away.
>
> Isaiah 64:1–6 (NIV)

Clearly these people had chosen *not* to follow God's teachings.

Another helpful tool to gain proper understanding is to learn definitions of the words used here. To begin, let's define the word "become" used in Isaiah 64. *Webster* defines it as:

(1) to come to be
(2) to grow to be; change or develop into by growth[2]

It is important to notice that "come to be" indicates present tense. Therefore, with relationship to this Scripture, the people had changed from being pleasing to God into a group that was "unclean" in His sight.

Why? This was true because the lifestyles exhibited between times of worship did not reflect the same spiritual appearance seen on the day of worship. Therefore, He considered their <u>deeds</u> to be as filthy rags.

It is very important to understand there is a difference between the two thoughts. It is very dangerous for us to retain this type of mind-set from a spiritual viewpoint because it strips us of any motivation to move forward. Therefore, clarification is necessary.

The thought that we are a filthy rag in the sight of God can mentally strip us of all hope—especially if we lean toward a negative mind-set. Many times truly filthy rags are thrown away as garbage. Sometimes they are even burned because of the stench produced. On the other hand, the thought of us being unclean as the result of our sins gives hope because through personal choice we can confess our sins, repent of them, ask God's forgiveness, and be cleaned up through obedience to His teachings. Thereby, we will be made acceptable in His eyes once again.

By comparing man's interpretation with Bible truth, we can rightly conclude that teaching man is a filthy rag in the sight of God is not accurate teaching of Bible truth.

Now, with this *correct* teaching clearly before us, let's take a few moments to THINK a bit deeper! Doing this will help us to recognize whether or not a teacher is teaching a false doctrine as the result of taking one or more statements out of context.

Although it is not always a safe tool, there are times when logic can be used while studying the Bible. Some teachings presented by man simply are *not* logical.

For example—how can it be concluded that we are nothing but filthy rags in the sight of God without implying that He also is a filthy rag? If true, it would certainly not be reflective of the "image" and "likeness" of God in which we were born. Both teachings *cannot* be true!

So, what lessons are to be learned from Isaiah 64? At least three points are to be remembered:

* God helps those who are trying to live right by remembering His ways.
* However, he becomes angry when we deliberately sin against Him.
* A spiritual change in the sight of God occurs when we stop doing right and turn to sin. He does not accept our personal choice.

The only way truth can be confirmed is to follow Luke's counsel:

> [11] The people in Berea were more open-minded than those in Thessalonica. They were so glad to hear the message Paul told them. They studied the Scriptures every day to make sure that what they heard was really true. [12] The result was that many of them believed, including many important Greek women and men.
>
> Acts 17:11–12 (ERV)

To those familiar with God's Word, these instructions and illustrations may appear to be unnecessary or even childish.

However, for those who have received no spiritual guidance in life, they may prove to be very helpful. Do you consider the Bible to be nothing more than a rigid book of rules and regulations that prevents us from having fun? If so, it is my prayer that these new concepts may bring new insight and a *ray of hope* into your life. You will then be introduced to the possibility of a brighter future as the result of gaining a more healthy understanding regarding the value of God's Word.

In an effort to achieve this goal, it is necessary that we take time to look through "the eyes of God" bring into the light healthier concepts. Then, as our viewpoint changes, we will begin to realize the rules and regulations or commands we thought to be a burden have been given to us by our Heavenly Father for the purpose of helping us to identify those daily satanic threats against our spiritual well-being. The following insight illustrates this point perfectly.

> The word command, as well as commandment, is used to translate the Hebrew word mits'vah but does not properly convey the meaning of mits'vah. The word command implies words of force or power as a General commands his troops. The word mits'vah is better understood as a directive. To see the picture painted by this word it is helpful to look at a related word, tsiyon meaning a desert or a landmark. The Ancient Hebrews were a nomadic people who traveled the deserts in search of green pastures for their flocks. A nomad uses the various rivers, mountains, rock outcroppings, etc. as landmarks to give them their direction. The verb form of mits'vah is tsavah meaning to direct one on a journey. The mits'vah of the Bible are not

commands, or rules and regulations, they are directives or landmarks that we look for to guide us. The word tsiyon meaning landmark is also the word translated as Zion, the mountain of God but, not just a mountain, it is the landmark.[3]

⁷ The law of the Lord is perfect
  refreshing the soul.
The statutes of the Lord are trustworthy,
  making wise the simple.
⁸ The precepts of the Lord are right,
  giving joy to the heart.
The commands of the Lord are radiant,
  giving light to the eyes.
⁹ The fear of the Lord is pure,
  enduring forever.
The decrees of the Lord are firm,
  and all of them are righteous.
Psalms 19:7–9 (NIV)

Clearly, these words of insight speak volumes regarding God's love for mankind. Only a truly loving God would make it possible for us to learn His directives through the Bible for the purpose of gaining and maintaining spiritual completeness leading us to heaven where He wants us to be throughout eternity.

What is the Bible?

Basic **I**nstruction **B**efore **L**eaving **E**arth

Why is this important?

Jesus' Teaching Will Judge People
⁴⁴ Then Jesus said loudly, "Everyone who believes in me is really believing in the one who sent me. ⁴⁵ Everyone who sees me is really seeing the one who sent me. ⁴⁶ I came into this world as a light. I came so that everyone who believes in me will not stay in darkness.

⁴⁷ "I did not come into the world to judge people. I came to save the people in the world. So I am not the one who judges those who hear my teaching and do not obey. ⁴⁸ But there is a judge for all those who refuse to believe in me and do not accept what I say. The message I have spoken will judge them on the last day. ⁴⁹ That is because what I taught was not from myself. The Father who sent me told me what to say and what to teach. ⁵⁰ And I know that whatever he says to do will bring eternal life. So the things I say are exactly what the Father told me to say."

John 12:44–50 (ERV)

---

¹² Blessed is the one you discipline, Lord,
  the one you teach from your law;
¹³ you grant them relief from days of trouble,
  till a pit is dug for the wicked.
¹⁴ For the Lord will not reject his people;
  he will never forsake his inheritance.
¹⁵ Judgment will again be founded on righteousness,

and all the upright in heart will follow it.
Psalms 94:12–15 (NIV)

Foundational to our study, we *must listen* to the words spoken in the Bible, *believe* and *obey* them if we are to be allowed to partake in eternal life with Him. Clearly, *the Lord is trying to teach us how deeply our Heavenly Father desires to have a one-on-one relationship with you and me!* That is LOVE—true love! This, my friend, is God!

Thus, because of His love, God made provision for the Bible to be preserved throughout all generations for the purpose of guiding mankind through life on earth in a manner that will provide everyone with a full life and peace of mind. This will only come through submission to His teachings of truth. Without this guidance, we will remain hopeless. Desperation will continue to reside within us.

Again, this ought not to be—it is *not* God's Plan for Man!

Also, foundational to our study, it is very important to understand that without His Word, the only other alternative for man is to try to find his own way. God's teaching is very clear.

[12] There is a way that people think is right, but it leads only to death.
Proverbs 14:12 (ERV)

¹⁵ Fools always think their own way is best, but wise people listen to what others tell them.

           Proverbs 12:15 (ERV)

───※───

²⁴ A person's steps are directed by the Lord.
How then can anyone understand their own way?

           Proverbs 20:24 (NIV)

With these thoughts in mind, can we now begin to see the importance of replacing any and all negative concepts of the Bible with more foundational truth? In an effort to do this, let's consider applying some practical, common terms from everyday life to God's Word. Hopefully, this will aid us in moving forward to a better understanding of Scripture.

First, consider this. A wise first-time traveler would be very foolish to even consider the thought of leaving San Diego, California for Bangor, Maine, without a road map and very detailed planning for the purpose of ensuring his safe arrival—especially if there were a million-dollar inheritance waiting for him at the end of the journey. With financial motivation, he would, without a doubt, seek out the most accurate map available and give attention to every detail during his entire travel to ensure safe arrival!

Now accept this truth! The reward God has planned for those who choose to follow Him is far more valuable than any million-dollar inheritance available to man. Perhaps your immediate thought is that you, as a Christian, are not worthy of heaven.

Satan would love for every follower of God to continue believing this lie. However, God's Word teaches the truth:

> [3] We ought always to thank God for you, brothers and sisters, and rightly so, because your faith is growing more and more, and the love all of you have for one another is increasing. [4] Therefore, among God's churches we boast about your perseverance and faith in all the persecutions and trials you are enduring.
> [5] All this is evidence that God's judgment is right, and as a result you will be counted worthy of the kingdom of God, for which you are suffering.
> II Thessalonians 1:3–5 (NIV)

Every individual must have a mind-set to live as closely as possible in accordance with the Lord's teaching. The Bible is the *only road map* leading to heaven. Anyone desiring safe arrival will be willing to follow Jesus as He leads His followers along the right path.

Truly, Jesus' leadership is the *only leadership* that can be trusted! He provides this insight:

> [13] "You can enter true life only through the narrow gate. The gate to hell is very wide, and there is plenty of room on the road that leads there. Many people go that way. [14] But the gate that opens the way to true life is narrow.

And the road that leads there is hard to follow. Only a few people find it.
Matthew 7:13-14 (ERV)

And how do we find the gate? Again, Jesus said,
⁹ I am the gate; whoever enters through me will be saved. They will come in and go out, and find pasture.
John 10:9 (NIV)

Because life's road leading to heaven is hard, it is critically important for us to have a true understanding of why Jesus *must* be our leader as we travel life's road together! Continual guidance, encouragement, and comfort will be needed day by day. *Even though it is seldom easy to follow Jesus by standing for truth, it is much easier than suffering the consequences after falling into a pit of total darkness as the result of following Satan.*

The Old Testament offers great words of encouragement! Feast your soul upon these words of *solid direction based upon truth!*

⁸ The Lord says, "I will teach you
 and guide you in the way you should live.
 I will watch over you and be your guide.
⁹ Don't be like a stupid horse or mule that will not come to you
 unless you put a bit in its mouth and pull it with reins."
¹⁰ Many pains will come to the wicked,

BASIC TRUTHS

but the LORD's faithful love will surround those who trust in him.

Psalms 32:8–10 (ERV)

Here comes the "steak dinner" from His Word! Understanding the Hebrew definition of <u>trust</u> brings a *huge* ray of *hope* and *light* to those who believe Him.

> To attach oneself, to trust, confide in, feel safe, be confident, secure...the basic idea is associated with firmness or solidity. The word expresses the sense of well-being which results from knowing that the "rug won't be pulled out from under you"...The folly of relying upon any other type of security is strongly contrasted with depending upon God alone...This type of hope is a confident expectation, not a constant anxiety. We can truly relax when we know Who is in control.[4]

As we continue to expand our views of the Bible, let's think of it as a <u>*dictionary*</u>. Its purpose is to help us understand meanings of unfamiliar words. The following is just a small listing of words that the Bible clearly defines based upon truth. It explains who God, Wisdom, and Jesus are; the functions of the Holy Spirit; and the role each of them fulfills.

Additionally, the learning offered expands to include the true understanding of love, truth, belief, pure religion and what will happen at the end of time.

These are but a few of the insights offered by the Bible.

Clearly the Bible reveals a <u>security code</u>. Those who live in a "gated community" understand the importance of knowing the correct gate code that will allow them to pass from the outside (where no security is offered) to inside the gate where a more safe environment supposedly exists. *The security code" identified within the Bible offers absolute security to those who choose to put His teachings into practice.*

Wise counsel is recorded in the book of Proverbs for the purpose of encouraging us to gain proper understanding regarding spiritual matters.

---

⁵ Trust the Lord completely, and don't depend on your own knowledge.

Proverbs 3:5 (ERV)

---

¹³ Those who find wisdom are fortunate; they will be blessed when they gain understanding.

Proverbs 3:13 (ERV)

Those who have a *healthy fear for the Lord* are willing to accept His Terms of entrance with the determination to remain "inside the gate." Then, when these teachings are fully embraced, eternal life filled with peace and contentment in the presence of God is assured.

Another interesting concept to consider is the Bible could also be referred to as a _recipe book_. Why? It teaches us how to develop "*Same-Page Thinking*" with God. In other words it reveals to us the characteristics God teaches His followers to have in their individual lives so they can be identified as Bible-defined Christians. Additionally, we are taught how to become "representatives of" or "ambassadors for" Christ in the world through our lifestyles and teaching. Here is but a small example of this truth:

> [5] May the God who gives endurance and encouragement give you the same attitude of mind toward each other that Christ Jesus had, [6] so that with one mind and one voice you may glorify the God and Father of our Lord Jesus Christ.
> [7] Accept one another, then, just as Christ accepted you, in order to bring praise to God.
> Romans 15:5–7 (NIV)

> [1] Therefore if you have any encouragement from being united with Christ, if any comfort from his love, if any common sharing in the Spirit, if any tenderness and compassion, [2] then make my joy complete by being like-minded, having the same love, being one in spirit and of one mind.
> Philippians 2:1-2 (NIV)

¹ Therefore, since we have so great a cloud of witnesses surrounding us, let us also lay aside every encumbrance and the sin which so easily entangles us, and let us run with endurance the race that is set before us, ² fixing our eyes on Jesus, the author and perfecter of faith, who for the joy set before Him endured the cross, despising the shame, and has sat down at the right hand of the throne of God.

Hebrews 12:1-2 (ERV)

⁸ Finally, all of you, be like-minded, be sympathetic, love one another, be compassionate and humble. ⁹ Do not repay evil with evil or insult with insult. On the contrary, repay evil with blessing, because to this you were called so that you may inherit a blessing.

I Peter 3:8-9 (NIV)

Another term that could easily be applied to the Bible is *a maintenance manual*. God's Word instructs us to "maintain" many things in this life. First and foremost He teaches us how to maintain a relationship with Him. This certainly includes but is not limited to maintaining our righteousness before Him, justice, the rights of the poor and oppressed, our love for God, discretion, love, and justice in the courts.

If heaven is to be our eternal home, the importance of maintaining the condition of our soul simply must not be overlooked.

Indeed, it is a dominant theme throughout Scripture—how to cleanse and maintain it as the result of being reconciled back to Our Creator through Christ.

Because the words "reconcile" or "reconciliation" will be used several times, it is important for us to understand their meanings. This is important because, without them, the message to be received will be meaningless. In relationship to Jesus, it means:

> "to conciliate anew; to call back into union and friendship the affections which have been alienated; to restore to friendship or favor after estrangement; as to *reconcile* men or parties that have been at variance."[5]

We will learn how the pure relationship we had in the sight of God at birth was disturbed, how to restore it and then maintain the *same* cleanliness that we had at the beginning of our earth life. Without *doing* what He has taught, we have no hope for true peace of mind here on earth or throughout eternity. Indeed, His instruction is a priceless asset!

Still another term that can be applied to the Bible is *a report card*. Just as report cards are received from educational institutions reflecting our progress or failure in the classroom, the Bible reveals to us both our strong and weak points and how to work toward further spiritual growth based upon God's teaching while living on earth.

One more descriptive term that could be used is a *medical guide*. This is absolutely true. As we will learn, the Bible reveals how to add health to your bones, overcome mental health issues, and grow past deadly anger issues, which are so very destructive to the human body and relationships.

Here are two examples:

> [7] Don't trust in your own wisdom, but fear and respect the Lord and stay away from evil. [8] If you do this, it will be like a refreshing drink and medicine for your body.
> Proverbs 3:7-8 (ERV)

> [20] My son, pay attention to what I say. Listen closely to my words. [21] Don't let them out of your sight. Never stop thinking about them. [22] These words are the secret of life and health to all who discover them. [23] Above all, be careful what you think because your thoughts control your life.
> Proverbs 4:20-23 (ERV)

It is important not to overlook the truth that the Bible is also a *filter*. It has a very special purpose! It separates the desirable Bible-based, God-spoken truth from the undesirable beliefs that are anchored in and promoted by the teachings of man. An example of this truth has already been revealed through the comparison of man's teaching regarding "filthy rags" with Bible truth as given in Isaiah 64.

Teachings that are not anchored within the truth of Scripture *cannot* be trusted! The prophet Isaiah gives us this counsel:

> [22] Stop trusting other people to save you. Do not think too highly of them; they are only humans who have not stopped breathing yet.
>
> Isaiah 2:22 (ERV)

After thinking about these various nouns that describe God's Word, hopefully the *relevance of the Bible* comes into clear view. Thus, to be certain we are traveling the right road, it is critically important that we know God's Word so we can be *assured* we have the correct knowledge base. Without this, we will be unable to identify teachings that are not in keeping with His will. Then, and only then, will we have the spiritual foundation that ensures our entrance into heaven for eternity.

Now it is time to listen as we read the Bible's definition of God's Word. The Apostle Paul spoke these words to Timothy:

> [13] But evil men and impostors will proceed *from bad* to worse, deceiving and being deceived. [14] You, however, continue in the things you have learned and become convinced of, knowing from whom you have learned *them*, [15] and that from childhood you have known the sacred writings which are able to give you the wisdom that leads to salvation through faith which is in Christ Jesus. [16] All Scripture is inspired by God and profitable for teaching, for reproof, for

correction, for training in righteousness; [17] so that the man of God may be adequate, equipped for every good work.
II Timothy 3:13–17 (NASB)

These five verses are packed with a wealth of information. They include Paul's warning of imposters distorting the truth; Bible students can have confidence in what has been learned from God; knowing the Scriptures provides the student with wisdom leading to salvation; how wisdom is developed; the origination of Scriptures; and their purpose in addition to how they are to be used.

Because the Greek meaning of the words defining Scriptures varies greatly from any dictionary definition, it is critically important that we gain deeper understanding as they apply to Bible truth.

* <u>teaching</u>:
  properly *applied*-teaching; Christian doctrine (teaching) as it especially extends to its necessary *lifestyle* (applications).[6]
* <u>reproof</u>:
  inner conviction focuses on God *confirming His inbirthing of faith* ("the internal *persuasion* from Him").[7]

- * correction:
  properly, suitable because *straight*, i.e., *restored to its (original) proper condition*; hence, *correction* (referring to something that is aptly "*straightened out*").⁽⁸⁾
- * training:
  properly, *instruction* that *trains* someone to reach full development (maturity).⁽⁹⁾
- * in righteousness:
  properly, *judicial approval* (the *verdict* of *approval*); in the NT, *the approval* of God ("divine approval").⁽¹⁰⁾

Nothing of value in this life is free—and so it is with our eternal salvation. Yes, what God offers is free—it cannot be bought. However, in order to receive it, man must be willing to invest his time and energy learning how to become a follower of Jesus. Then only through submission to His plan will we be allowed to enter heaven. *This is the price we must be willing to pay.*

Now it is time to move forward as we actively engage in learning positive messages of truth from His Word. As you read, pray for guidance and understanding while thinking and meditating upon the powerful messages. Through submission and obedience to Him, your personal spiritual growth and security will be assured!

References

(1) *Webster's, 1982*, op cit., p. 307

(2) Ibid., p. 125

(3) Ancient Hebrew Word Meanings, Command—mitsvah by Jeff A. Benner; http://www.ancient-hebrew.org

(4) *Hebrew-Greek Key Word Study Bible*, New American Standard Bible, Lexical Aids to the Old Testament; Spiros Zodhiates, Editor, Item 982, p. 1714. Permission granted by AMG Publishers)

(5) *Webster's, 1828, Volume 2*

(6) Biblehub.com, Greek #1319

(7) Ibid., Greek #1650

(8) Ibid., Greek #1882

(9) Ibid., Greek #3809

(10) Ibid., Greek #1343

Section Two

God's Plan for Us to Have Two Sets of Parents

New Thought? Read On

Prelude

In the same manner that God's plan for the physical home includes dual parenting (male and female), the same principle applies to our *spiritual parenting*. Is the suggestion that the Bible describes *two* spiritual parents a new thought for you? Perhaps. Therefore, let's dig deeper into Scripture for the purpose of establishing this thought as a *rock-solid truth!*

Are you wondering why emphasis is being placed upon the importance of developing a solid foundation that, by God's design, He has a spiritual parenting partner? Yes, we have *dual* Spiritual Parents!

To help us establish this truth, it is important to understand why the book of Proverbs is included in the Bible. They were written

> [2] for gaining wisdom and instruction;
>   for understanding words of insight;
> [3] for receiving instruction in prudent behavior,
>   doing what is right and just and fair;

⁴ for giving prudence to those who are simple,
   knowledge and discretion to the young—
⁵ let the wise listen and add to their learning,
   and let the discerning get guidance—
⁶ for understanding proverbs and parables,
   the sayings and riddles of the wise.
Proverbs 1:2–6 (NIV)

Proverbs chapters 1, 3, 8 and 9 are great places to begin gaining wisdom and instruction along with words of understanding and insight. For example:

⁷ The fear of the LORD is the beginning of knowledge,
   but fools despise wisdom and instruction.
Proverbs 1:7 (NIV)

***

This counsel is followed by Wisdom's special invitation:

⁸ Listen, my son, to your father's instruction
   and do not forsake your mother's teaching.
Proverbs 1:8 (NIV)

Clearly, a father, mother, and son constitute a *family*.

Using human logic, the immediate assumption could be that the word "your" used in this verse refers to our physical parents. Let's challenge our thinking by asking, "Are we being counseled to listen to them?" As we enter into these thought processes, it is important to both ask and answer these questions:

* Is a child to obey a physical father if he instructs his child to "Drink this beer; it won't hurt you"?
* Likewise, should the child follow the example of a demeaning mother who uses bad language when speaking about others—including her children?
* Additionally, some physical parents choose to abandon their children.

With these thoughts in mind, would God instruct us to follow their lead? Following any human—regardless of who they are—will not provide the role model and instruction needed to protect the "image" and "likeness" of God originally placed within us. Consequently, we may be led away from the truth of God's Word and, thereby, be robbed of the desired lifestyle leading to peace of mind regardless of how weary our hearts may be.

Therefore, it is important to understand the adjective "your" used in Proverbs 1:8 indicates personal possession!

So, if reference is not being made to our physical parents, what is really being taught? Is indication not given to the thought that God put into place two *spiritual* parents in addition to our two *physical* parents? Yes! How can we be sure?

The *true* answer can only be found through a close examination of God's teaching.

Onward

to

Higher Ground

Chapter One

First Parents We Became Aware Of

Every living person came into this life as the result of the same birth process designed by God to populate the earth through man and woman. His intent for the home was (and still is) to have both a father and mother working together for the purpose of guiding and training their children as they follow the spiritual plan *designed by God.*

Unfortunately, there are several <u>man-made</u> formats present in today's world that bring heartache and havoc rather than peace and heartfelt security into the hearts of children. They include being conceived out of wedlock—many not knowing who their parents are—oh, the pain and questions that may remain; being raised within the environment of same-sex marriage; living on the streets because of a broken home; being rotated in and out of the foster care environment because of greed or inabilities to care for children—thus the child's needs remain unfulfilled; being removed from foster or adoptive parents and returned to an abusive home; single-parent homes by choice, not as the result of death of a parent; divorce and remarriage; influences resulting from a parent's war or military responsibilities; devastation imposed upon a family as the result of long-distance absence of a parent due to demands placed upon him or her by an employer; the list goes on and on—seemingly endless.

There is still another gut-wrenching factor that can bring complete emotional devastation into the home. What is it--the death of one or both of our physical parents. All too often this happens before children have reached the degree of maturity that allows them to understand life or live alone. Needless to say, after the fact, there are many challenges to be met by the remaining parent or members of the extended family. In the absence of a support system, many children become wards of the state.

The truth is, regardless of the age of the surviving children, the separation from Mom, Dad, or both through death or other circumstances of life leaves a huge emotional hole in the heart. Perhaps those affected *feel* or *think* the remaining void can never be filled.

Why is this true? In a healthy, God-designed home, Dad is the one depended upon for giving strength and support. Also, he is the one who establishes the guidelines for the home. Not only does he put them in place, but he *conveys* them to the entire

First Parents We Became Aware Of

family. In short, he is a healthy communicator, and there is no doubt that he represents both love and "final authority" to his family!

Family members know this is true not because he is a controller or dictator. Rather, he is motivated by *love for his family*. His goal is not only to provide for their *needs* while on earth but also train them how to live for eternity.

Just knowing the authoritative guidelines of a loving father are in place and enforced for the purpose of protecting every member of his family (both physically and spiritually) gives a deep sense of safety and inner peace. Even though unpleasant disciplinary consequences follow when his guidelines are disobeyed, the children have deep reassurance in *knowing* that they are loved.

Very often, in a healthy home Mom is the one who provides moral, physical, spiritual, and emotional guidance, while Dad works to provide for the family's needs. She does this in submission to his leadership. Indeed, God-designed parenting is a team effort that works very well when put into action.

The words written above describe our physical parents. Have you ever asked yourself, "In the eyes of God, who are they?" Interesting question, isn't it? The answer: In His eyes, our physical parents are, like us, His offspring—owned by Him. He sent them a gift from heaven! The gift given was *me*—in newborn form.

When you send a gift through the mail, what are the two most important pieces of information required on the package?

God's Plan for Us to Have Two Sets of Parents...

Yes, the address to which it is being sent and, equally important, the sender's returns address. This information is critically important to ensure the safe return of the gift to the sender in the event that the package cannot be delivered.

The same principle applies to <u>me</u>. How? Although you and I were given to our physical parents as a gift from God, an invisible return address was placed on each one of us! It says, "Sent by God—return to heaven!"

After your birth, your parents referred to you as "their child" because it was through them that you were brought into the world. Therefore, *they* claim ownership of *you*. Why? *You* are a part of *them*. In fact, it may not be uncommon for an onlooker to comment that you are the "spittin' image" of one of your parents. This is verbal affirmation indicating that you bear genetic resemblances to family members.

Another truth remains. You, as a babe, came forth from your Mom's womb as the result of Dad's sperm and Mom's egg being united. However, does that mean that *she* (or even Dad) gave the resulting fetus the ability to grow therein? Does that mean they *own* you? Of course not! The union of the sperm and egg, the growth that followed, and the birth of the child were all results of a more powerful influence in existence—GOD! Her womb served only as the "housing" where this growth took place. This is true of every human on earth. Our parents' claim to ownership is of an *earthly* nature.

As a child, it was and still is very important to our mental health and physical security to *know* we *belong* to someone. Certainly, we need to know to whom we belong! Without this core information, we can become depressed and disheartened leading to feelings of abandonment very early in life.

A small but deep-cutting, harmful powerful example of this comes when a child is told he or she is no longer wanted by either of his or her physical parents. To say that havoc results in the child's heart is an incomprehensible understatement! The child is devastated, heartbroken to the very core—desperate to understand the meaning of life as the heart cries out, "I want to be important to somebody!"

Indeed, every living person is important to the One who *really* owns us—God! It is because our world, as a whole, does not recognize this truth that we suffer deep, needless pain trying to identify with someone who really cares.

Guidance and comfort to work through and overcome this type of inner pain can only be provided by our Heavenly Parents. It is through establishing a trust in them that the child will learn the in-depth care and concern they have for his or her personal well-being.

So let's search further to bring peace of mind to everyone in need of this reassurance. Remember, the only place to find *genuine peace is through Bible-truth!* Therefore, let's pursue the answer to these vitally important questions,

* "To whom do I *really* belong?"
* "Why was I born?"
* "What is my purpose for living?"

The answers to these will be taken from the Bible—the only source of truth explaining the existence of man and his purpose here on earth. Whether or not this information is accepted is man's choice. Nonetheless, remember with every choice comes a consequence. Please, make the right choice. Believe the truths presented in the Word of God.

Chapter Two

Introducing Our Spiritual Parents
Part One
Our Spiritual Father

This is our first introduction to God, our Heavenly Father:

> [1] In the beginning God created the heavens and the earth.
>
> Genesis 1:1 (NIV)

Have you ever asked yourself, "Why was the earth created?"

In a God-centered home, it is the responsibility of the father to provide housing for his family. Within that house, it is not uncommon for parents—especially when expecting their first child—to gather into one room everything that will be needed to care for their child *before* his or her arrival. This designated area is referred to as the babe's nursery. It has been provided because parents want everything to be "just right." They want their offspring to have a cheerful, healthy environment in which to grow and develop.

And why are physical parents this way? *It is but one of many ways that they reflect the "likeness" of God.* He created the world—His Nursery—before man came into existence for the exact same purpose! God wanted everything to be "just right" so that His offspring would have everything necessary to sustain their lives while living on earth! Nothing would be too good for them.

The Bible's account of creation is recorded in Genesis—the first book of the Bible—beginning with the first chapter.

While reading, notice the foundational support and continuity each day of creation gave to the following day! For example, it would be impossible for plant life to grow without the existence of land, water, sun, and moon having been created first. Indeed, attention was given to every minute detail—nothing happened as the result of an accident. Everything created had a purpose.

Keeping these thoughts in mind, <u>it is important to focus on the true story of creation.</u>

> [2] Now the earth was formless and empty, darkness was over the surface of the deep, and the Spirit of God was hovering over the waters.

³ And God said, "Let there be light," and there was light. ⁴ God saw that the light was good, and he separated the light from the darkness. ⁵ God called the light "day," and the darkness he called "night." And there was evening, and there was morning—the first day.

⁶ And God said, "Let there be a vault between the waters to separate water from water." ⁷ So God made the vault and separated the water under the vault from the water above it. And it was so. ⁸ God called the vault "sky." And there was evening, and there was morning—the second day.

⁹ And God said, "Let the water under the sky be gathered to one place, and let dry ground appear." And it was so. ¹⁰ God called the dry ground "land," and the gathered waters he called "seas." And God saw that it was good.

¹¹ Then God said, "Let the land produce vegetation: seed-bearing plants and trees on the land that bear fruit with seed in it, according to their various kinds." And it was so. ¹² The land produced vegetation: plants bearing seed according to their kinds and trees bearing fruit with seed in it according to their kinds. And God saw that it was good. ¹³ And there was evening, and there was morning—the third day.

¹⁴ And God said, "Let there be lights in the vault of the sky to separate the day from the night, and let them serve as signs to mark sacred times, and days and years, ¹⁵ and let them be lights in the vault of the sky to give light on the earth." And it was so. ¹⁶ God made two great lights—the greater light to govern the day and the lesser light to govern the night. He also made the stars. ¹⁷ God set them in the vault of the sky to give light on the earth, ¹⁸ to govern the day and the night, and to separate light from darkness.

And God saw that it was good. [19] And there was evening, and there was morning—the fourth day.

[20] And God said, "Let the water teem with living creatures, and let birds fly above the earth across the vault of the sky." [21] So God created the great creatures of the sea and every living thing with which the water teems and that moves about in it, according to their kinds, and every winged bird according to its kind. And God saw that it was good. [22] God blessed them and said, "Be fruitful and increase in number and fill the water in the seas, and let the birds increase on the earth." [23] And there was evening, and there was morning—the fifth day.

[24] And God said, "Let the land produce living creatures according to their kinds: the livestock, the creatures that move along the ground, and the wild animals, each according to its kind." And it was so. [25] God made the wild animals according to their kinds, the livestock according to their kinds, and all the creatures that move along the ground according to their kinds. And God saw that it was good.

Genesis 1:2-25 (NIV)

Why is This Important to Me?

Certainly this is a valid question. If life is going to make any sense at all, it must be answered from a Biblical viewpoint. To achieve this goal we must finish the story of creation.

Therefore, God verbalized His plan.

[26] Then God said, "Let us make mankind in our image, in our likeness, so that they may rule over the fish in the sea and the

birds in the sky, over the livestock and all the wild animals, and over all the creatures that move along the ground."

Genesis 1:26 (NIV)

Thus it became a reality.

²⁷ So God created mankind in his own image,
in the image of God he created them;
male and female he created them.

Genesis 1:27 (NIV)

Now for the purpose of helping us to gain a much deeper understanding of why God created the earth, a visual contrast between Genesis 1:26-27 and this illustration is being offered:

²⁶ The Go s "Let us e our ge, our l e ess, so th t they y rule over the f sh the se the b r s the s y, over the l vestoc ll the w l ls, over ll the cre tures th t ove lo g the grou"
²⁷ So Go cre te h s ow ge,
the ge of Go he cre te the;
le fe le he cre te the .

Now, as they appear here, do these verses make sense? Absolutely not! The *only* change made was the removal of the letters "m, a, n, k, i, and d" used to spell the word "mankind." When they are put back into their proper places, the powerful meaning of its message is restored. Without the complete message being used to establish a point of comparison, this one is meaningless.

After considering this illustration, are you

- * Wondering why is this important to me?
- * Why should I care how or why the earth was created?

Answers to these questions can be gained by asking three more.

- * Am I not part of mankind?
- * Without the earth being in existence before I was born, where would I live?
- * What would I eat?

Hopefully, through this illustration, we will gain a much deeper appreciation of God's love for us clearly demonstrated long before we were born.

The Importance God Places upon Me as a Person

It is important to notice God's observation regarding what had been created each day. He saw "It was good."
Genesis, 1:10, 12, 18, 21, and 25

Listen closely as we learn the Hebrew meaning of the word "good." (Hebrew was the language used when writing the Old Testament.) Read carefully:

"good" means "excellent of its kind[1]

This was God's evaluation of the creation of the earth.

Although we may *never* completely understand what it means to be created in the "image" and "likeness" of God, these definitions will provide great insight. They are based upon Bible truth.

"Image" means *image, likeness*, of resemblance, of God's making man in his own image[2]
"Likeness" means "likeness, similitude" [3]

But wait, there is still more! It is important to compare God's commentary after the creation of the earth with His evaluation after man's creation. Notice *His* viewpoint!

[31] God saw all that he had made, and it was very good. And there was evening, and there was morning.
Genesis 1:31 (NIV)

"Very" means "good exceedingly" [4]

After the creation of the earth, man was the *only addition* after which God said His creation was "very good."

Bringing these word meanings together describes the image and likeness all of mankind sends forth to the world *at birth!*

"Man is an image, likeness, resemblance of God that is exceedingly good."

With this insight it now becomes much easier to understand why mankind is important in the sight of God.

Is it possible to learn more about who God is? Certainly this is an intelligent question that deserves a Bible-based answer.

Considerably more learning will be offered as we move forward but, for now, please accept these words from Scripture. They provide some insight regarding the *personality* of God. Hopefully, they will be helpful in building a degree of *trust* in Him.

> [6] And he passed in front of Moses, proclaiming, "The Lord, the Lord, the compassionate and gracious God, slow to anger, abounding in love and faithfulness, [7] maintaining love to thousands, and forgiving wickedness, rebellion and sin. Yet he does not leave the guilty unpunished; he punishes the children and their children for the sin of the parents to the third and fourth generation."
>
> Exodus 34:6–7 (NIV)

> [18] The Lord is near to the brokenhearted
> And saves those who are crushed in spirit.
>
> Psalms 34:18 (NASB)

¹⁷ The sacrifice that God wants is a humble spirit.
God, you will not turn away someone who comes with a humble heart and is willing to obey you.

Psalms 51:17 (ERV)

¹⁷ He will respond to the prayer of the destitute;
he will not despise their plea.

Psalms 102:17 (NIV)

³ He heals the brokenhearted
and binds up their wounds.

Psalms 147:3 (NIV)

Hopefully, through these Bible-based verifications of God's love for all mankind, everyone can begin to understand we are, indeed, important to GOD, Our Creator!

With this reassuring knowledge, what reason can man possibly have for not being drawn closer to truly believing the *absolute* truth recorded in God's Word?

More truths are given through the following Scriptures. Truly they illustrate how much attention to detail God gave to the creation of every individual *before* we were born!

David said:

¹⁵ You could see my bones grow as my body took shape,
  hidden in my mother's womb.
¹⁶ You could see my body grow each passing day.
  You listed all my parts, and not one of them was missing.
Psalms 139:15-16 (ERV)

³⁰ God even knows how many hairs are on your head.
Matthew 10:30 (ERV)

All of this and more is included within *my framework* designed by my Heavenly Father.

To say these are all of the manifestations of God's concern for me is a gross understatement!

Are there even words to describe His love for us?

References

[1] Biblehub.com, Greek #2896, Definition #3
[2] Ibid., Greek #6754, Definition #2
[3] Ibid., Greek #1823, Definition #1
[4] Ibid., Greek #3966, Definition #2a

Chapter Two

Part Two
Introducing God's Spiritual Parenting Partner

To deepen our understanding of this concept, a comparison between two translations of Proverbs 1:8 is being provided:
New International Version (NIV)

> [8] Listen, my son, to your father's instruction
> and do not forsake your mother's teaching.

King James Translation (KJV)

> [8] My son, hear the instruction of thy father, and forsake not the law of thy mother:

It is very important to both realize and understand that this is the very first counsel given to the "son" by his "mother."

Before going further, definitions for the words "father" and "mother" as they are used in Proverbs 1:8 are needed.

Father means "chief."

Mother means "mother as the bond of the family" [1]

With "law of thy mother" in mind, reading it closely may bring better understanding to the role God gives to Wisdom, His spiritual parenting partner.

Torah (Law)
By Jeff A. Benner

The Hebrew word "Torah" is usually translated into the English word "Law". Because of this translation there is a great misunderstanding of what "Torah" truly is. "TORAH IS NOT LAW". When we use the word "law" we assume a certain meaning and concept of the word that is not present in the Hebrew Scriptures.

Let us start by looking at the Etymology of the Hebrew word Torah so that we may better understand its true definition. The word Torah comes from the Hebrew root word

PART TWO INTRODUCING GOD'S SPIRITUAL PARENTING PARTNER

"Yarah", a verb which means "to flow or throw something". This can be a flowing of an arrow from an archers bow, or the flowing of a finger to point out a direction. Nouns are derived from the verb by making one or two changes to the verb root. In this case the Y (yud) is replaced by an O (vav) and an M (mem) is added at the front of the word to form the noun "Moreh". A Moreh is "one who does the flowing". This can be an archer who flows an arrow, or a teacher who flows his finger to point out way the student is to go in the walk of life. Another noun is formed the same way except that a T (tav) is placed at the front of the word instead of an M and we have the word "Torah". Torah is "what is flowed by the Moreh". This can be the arrow from the archer or the teachings and instructions from the teacher.

A hebraic definition of Torah is "a set of Instructions, from a father to his children, violation of these instructions are disciplined in order to foster obedience and train his children". Notice how the word "Torah" is translated in the New International Version translation in the following passages.

"Listen, my son, to your father's instruction and do not forsake your mother's teaching [Torah]." (Proverbs 1:8)

"My son, do not forget my teaching [Torah], but keep my commands in your heart". (Proverbs 3:1)

The purpose of a parents Torah is to teach and bring the children to maturity. If the Torah is violated out of disrespect or defiant disobedience, the child is punished. If the child desires to follow the instructions out of a loving obedience but falls short of the expectations, the child is commended for the effort and counseled on how to perform the instructions better the next time. Unlike Torah, law is a set of rules from a government and binding on a community. Violation of the rules require punishment. With this type of law, there is no room for teaching, either the law was broken with the penalty of punishment or it was not broken. God, as our heavenly Father, gives his children his Torah in the same manner as parents give their Torah to their children, not in the manner as a government does to its citizens;

"Blessed is the man you discipline, O LORD, the man you teach from your Torah" (Psalms 94:12) [2]

Hold on to these thoughts because they will prove to bring great insight as our learning continues.

It cannot be denied that God put many plans into place before the creation of man for the purpose of spiritually protecting His offspring. The Garden of Eden was designed for our sustenance while living on earth (Genesis 1), the plans He had made for our individual lives before we were born (Ephesians 2:10), and His plan making it possible for us to live with Him throughout eternity are three that quickly come to mind. Also included in those same plans was <u>*perfect parenting*</u> for all mankind.

Let us move onward as we continue to build upon this Bible-based truth.

God Authorized the Existence of His Spiritual Parenting Partner

Where Did Wisdom, Our Spiritual Mother, Come From?

²² "The LORD possessed me at the beginning of His way,
Before His works of old.
²³ "From everlasting I was established,
From the beginning, from the earliest times of the earth.
                                    Proverbs 8:22-23 (NASB)

GOD'S PLAN FOR US TO HAVE TWO SETS OF PARENTS...

AUTHORITY GIVEN TO WISDOM

15 "By me kings reign,
And rulers decree justice.
16 "By me princes rule, and nobles,
All who judge rightly.

Proverbs 8:15-16 (NASB)

WISDOM'S RESUME
TIMEFRAME GIVEN

24 "When there were no depths I was brought forth,
When there were no springs abounding with water.
25 "Before the mountains were settled,
Before the hills I was brought forth;
26 While He had not yet made the earth and the fields,
Nor the first dust of the world.
27 "When He established the heavens, I was there,
When He inscribed a circle on the face of the deep,
28 When He made firm the skies above,
When the springs of the deep became fixed,
29 When He set for the sea its boundary
So that the water would not transgress His command,
When He marked out the foundations of the earth.

Proverbs 8:24–29 (NASB)

How Wisdom Honored God, Her Creator

[30] Then I was beside Him, *as* a master workman;
And I was daily *His* delight,
Rejoicing always before Him,
[31] Rejoicing in the world, His earth,
And *having* my delight in the sons of men.

Proverbs 8:30–31 (NASB)

Wisdom Explains some of Our Spiritual Father's Strengths of Character

[6] For the LORD gives wisdom;
From His mouth *come* knowledge and understanding.
[7] He stores up sound wisdom for the upright;
He is a shield to those who walk in integrity,
[8] Guarding the paths of justice,
And He preserves the way of His godly ones.

Proverbs 2:6–8 (NASB)

---

[5] Trust in the LORD with all your heart
And do not lean on your own understanding.
[6] In all your ways acknowledge Him,
And He will make your paths straight.

Proverbs 3:5–6 (NASB)

―⁂―

¹⁹ The LORD by wisdom founded the earth,
By understanding He established the heavens.
²⁰ By His knowledge the deeps were broken up
And the skies drip with dew.

Proverbs 3:19–20 (NASB)

Insights into Our Spiritual Parents' Strengths of Character

Getting to Know the Lord

³² For the devious are an abomination to the LORD;
But He is intimate with the upright.
³³ The curse of the LORD is on the house of the wicked,
But He blesses the dwelling of the righteous.
³⁴ Though He scoffs at the scoffers,
Yet He gives grace to the afflicted.

Proverbs 3:32-34 (NASB)

―⁂―

¹⁰ The fear of the LORD is the beginning of wisdom,
And the knowledge of the Holy One is understanding.

Proverbs 9:10 (NASB)

Part Two Introducing God's Spiritual Parenting Partner

<u>Getting to Know Wisdom</u>

> ⁷ "For my mouth will utter truth;
> And wickedness is an abomination to my lips.
>
> Proverbs 8:7 (NASB)

> ¹² "I, wisdom, dwell with prudence,
> And I find knowledge *and* discretion.
> ¹³ "The fear of the Lord is to hate evil;
> Pride and arrogance and the evil way
> And the perverted mouth, I hate.
>
> Proverbs 8:12–13 (NASB)

If understanding is to be gained, clear communication is mandatory. Wisdom clearly exemplifies this truth as she speaks to God's offspring. There is no "scratching of the head" trying to figure out what she means. Certainly it is true that she does not play word games! Neither is there any doubt that her love for man is the motivation for speaking to us *with frankness.* Her goal is to teach us how to protect our souls for eternity. Therefore, she makes every effort to gently instruct and persuade mankind in righteous living.

It is important to understand the words in Proverbs chapters 1, 3, 8 and 9 were spoken by Wisdom, not written by Solomon. His proverbs begin with chapter 4. As this study continues, this truth will be established.

How to Protect Our Soul within Us

One very important observation is to be made here. Notice the parenting style.

Often children will ask their physical parents "why" when they are given an instruction. Many times the answer is, "Because I said so." Many times that type of answer leaves the child frustrated. It can easily be interpreted as the parent's effort to control.

This is not true of our spiritual parents. As these verses are read, notice Wisdom is very careful to explain *why* we, as people created by God, are to avoid certain behaviors. However, when the choice is made to reject their instructions, we are only hurting ourselves.

Let's begin as we apply this observation.

Wisdom Speaking

Notice the personal reference:

> ¹ My son, do not forget *my* teaching,
> But let your heart keep *my* commandments;

Part Two Introducing God's Spiritual Parenting Partner

<u>Why?</u>
² For length of days and years of life
And peace they will add to you.

Proverbs 3:1-2 (NASB)

<u>Now notice Wisdom redirects the focus toward God as a separate being</u>:

³ Do not let kindness and truth leave you;
Bind them around your neck,
Write them on the tablet of your heart.

<u>Why?</u>

⁴ So you will find favor and good repute
In the sight of God and man.

Proverbs 3:3-4 (NASB)

⁷ Do not be wise in your own eyes;
Fear the LORD and turn away from evil.

<u>Why?</u>

⁸ It will be healing to your body

GOD'S PLAN FOR US TO HAVE TWO SETS OF PARENTS...

And refreshment to your bones.
Proverbs 3:7-8 (NASB)

⁹ Honor the LORD from your wealth
And from the first of all your produce;

<u>Why</u>?
¹⁰ So your barns will be filled with plenty
And your vats will overflow with new wine.
Proverbs 3:9-10 (NASB)

¹¹ My son, do not reject the discipline of the LORD
Or loathe His reproof,
¹² For whom the LORD loves He reproves,
Even as a father *corrects* the son in whom he delights.
Proverbs 3:11-12 (NASB)

WISDOM'S PUBLIC SPEECH
(Notice the *female* pronouns used)
WISDOM WARNS AGAINST REJECTING HER

¹ Does not wisdom call,
And understanding lift up her voice?

² On top of the heights beside the way,
Where the paths meet, she takes her stand;
³ Beside the gates, at the opening to the city,
At the entrance of the doors, she cries out:
⁴ "To you, O men, I call,
And my voice is to the sons of men.
⁵ "O naive ones, understand prudence;
And, O fools, understand wisdom.

> Proverbs 8:1-5 (NASB)

Notice to whom Wisdom is speaking. She changes her focus from "my son" to "men, sons of men, naive ones and fools." Certainly she has gone public with her plea!

²⁰ Wisdom shouts in the street,
She lifts her voice in the square;
²¹ At the head of the noisy *streets* she cries out;
At the entrance of the gates in the city she utters her sayings:
²² "How long, O naive ones, will you love being simple-minded?
And scoffers delight themselves in scoffing
And fools hate knowledge?

> Proverbs 1:20-22 (NASB)

³⁵ The wise will inherit honor,

But fools display dishonor.
Proverbs 3:35 (NASB)

Preparation made by Wisdom

¹ Wisdom has built her house,
She has hewn out her seven pillars;
² She has prepared her food, she has mixed her wine;
She has also set her table.
Proverbs 9:1–2 (NASB)

Invitation

³ She has sent out her maidens, she calls
From the tops of the heights of the city:
⁴ "Whoever is naive, let him turn in here!"
To him who lacks understanding she says,
⁵ "Come, eat of my food
And drink of the wine I have mixed.
⁶ "Forsake *your* folly and live,
And proceed in the way of understanding."
Proverbs 9:3–6 (NASB)

General Truths Regarding Wisdom

Wisdom's Purpose

<u>To women Wisdom says:</u>

¹² To deliver you from the way of evil,
From the man who speaks perverse things;
¹³ From those who leave the paths of uprightness
To walk in the ways of darkness;
¹⁴ Who delight in doing evil
And rejoice in the perversity of evil;
¹⁵ Whose paths are crooked,
And who are devious in their ways;

<u>To men Wisdom says:</u>

¹⁶ To deliver you from the strange woman,
From the adulteress who flatters with her words;
¹⁷ That leaves the companion of her youth
And forgets the covenant of her God.

<u>Why?</u>

¹⁸ For her house sinks down to death
And her tracks *lead* to the dead;
¹⁹ None who go to her return again,
Nor do they reach the paths of life.

Proverbs 2:12–19 (NASB)

---

¹⁷ "I love those who love me;
And those who diligently seek me will find me.

Proverbs 8:17 (NASB)

Choices Given to Man by Wisdom

¹ My son, if you will receive my words
And treasure my commandments within you,
² Make your ear attentive to wisdom,
Incline your heart to understanding;
³ For if you cry for discernment,
Lift your voice for understanding;
⁴ If you seek her as silver
And search for her as for hidden treasures;

Result

⁵ Then you will discern the fear of the LORD
And discover the knowledge of God.
Proverbs 2:1–5 (NASB)

---

¹³ How blessed is the man who finds wisdom
And the man who gains understanding.

Why is this true?

Again, notice the pronouns indicating female gender.

[14] For her profit is better than the profit of silver
And her gain better than fine gold.
[15] She is more precious than jewels;
And nothing you desire compares with her.
[16] Long life is in her right hand;
In her left hand are riches and honor.
[17] Her ways are pleasant ways
And all her paths are peace.
[18] She is a tree of life to those who take hold of her,
And happy are all who hold her fast.

Proverbs 3:13–18 (NASB)

Choices Given
Not Demanding that We Obey

Referring to verses 3:13–18 above,

[21] My son, let them not vanish from your sight;
Keep sound wisdom and discretion,
[22] So they will be life to your soul
And adornment to your neck.
[23] Then you will walk in your way securely
And your foot will not stumble.
[24] When you lie down, you will not be afraid;
When you lie down, your sleep will be sweet.
[25] Do not be afraid of sudden fear
Nor of the onslaught of the wicked when it comes;
[26] For the Lord will be your confidence
And will keep your foot from being caught.

Proverbs 3:21-26 (NASB)

GOD'S PLAN FOR US TO HAVE TWO SETS OF PARENTS...

⊙⊙

³⁶ "But he who sins against me injures himself;
All those who hate me love death."
Proverbs 8:36 (NASB)

Personal Benefits Received When We Choose to Listen

<u>Why should we listen?</u>

⁶ "Listen, for I will speak noble things;
And the opening of my lips *will reveal* right things.
⁷ "For my mouth will utter truth;
And wickedness is an abomination to my lips.
⁸ "All the utterances of my mouth are in righteousness;
There is nothing crooked or perverted in them.
⁹ "They are all straightforward to him who understands,
And right to those who find knowledge.
Proverbs 8:6–9 (NASB)

⊙⊙

³² "Now therefore, *O* sons, listen to me,
For blessed are they who keep my ways.
³³ "Heed instruction and be wise,
And do not neglect *it*.
³⁴ "Blessed is the man who listens to me,

Watching daily at my gates,
Waiting at my doorposts.
³⁵ "For he who finds me finds life
And obtains favor from the Lord.

        Proverbs 8:32–35 (NASB)

༺✦༻

Why should we follow Wisdom's guidance?

⁹ Then you will discern righteousness and justice
And equity *and* every good course.

        Proverbs 2:9 (NASB)

༺✦༻

¹¹ "For wisdom is better than jewels;
And all desirable things cannot compare with her.

        Proverbs 8:11 (NASB)

༺✦༻

¹⁴ "Counsel is mine and sound wisdom;
I am understanding, power is mine.

        Proverbs 8:14 (NASB)

༺✦༻

¹⁸ "Riches and honor are with me,

Enduring wealth and righteousness.
¹⁹ "My fruit is better than gold, even pure gold,
And my yield *better* than choicest silver.
²⁰ "I walk in the way of righteousness,
In the midst of the paths of justice,

Proverbs 8:18–20 (NASB)

How will I gain Wisdom?

¹⁰ For wisdom will enter your heart
And knowledge will be pleasant to your soul;
¹¹ Discretion will guard you,
Understanding will watch over you.

Proverbs 2:10–11 (NASB)

Final Result!

²⁰ So you will walk in the way of good men
And keep to the paths of the righteous.
²¹ For the upright will live in the land
And the blameless will remain in it.

Proverbs 2:20–21 (NASB)

Wisdom's Guidance When Interacting With Our Fellow Man

²⁷ Do not withhold good from those to whom it is due,
When it is in your power to do *it*.
²⁸ Do not say to your neighbor, "Go, and come back,
And tomorrow I will give *it*,"
When you have it with you.
²⁹ Do not devise harm against your neighbor,
While he lives securely beside you.
³⁰ Do not contend with a man without cause,
If he has done you no harm.
³¹ Do not envy a man of violence
And do not choose any of his ways.

Why?

³² For the devious are an abomination to the LORD;
But He is intimate with the upright.
Proverbs 3:27-32 (NASB)

Benefits of Redirecting Thoughts of a Wise Man

With Regard to Others

⁸ Reprove a wise man and he will love you.
⁹ Give *instruction* to a wise man and he will be still wiser,
Teach a righteous man and he will increase *his* learning.
Proverbs 9:8–9 (NASB)

Personal Positive Benefits

¹⁰ The fear of the LORD is the beginning of wisdom,
And the knowledge of the Holy One is understanding.
¹¹ For by me your days will be multiplied,
And years of life will be added to you.
¹² If you are wise, you are wise for yourself.

Negative consequences if not done

And if you scoff, you alone will bear it.
Proverbs 9:10-12 (NASB)

Painful Consequences If We Reject Wisdom

As this section is read, it is important to realize that it was written by Wisdom. Also, notice the personal pronouns—"I," "me," and "my." This indicates a second authoritative being other than God.

PART TWO INTRODUCING GOD'S SPIRITUAL PARENTING PARTNER

The next five verses helps us to understand Solomon did not write them. How can we be certain? God does not give authorization to any human to laugh at another's calamity or mock someone in distress. However, He does give it to *Wisdom,* His spiritual parenting partner, our spiritual mother.

[24] "Because I called and you refused,
I stretched out my hand and no one paid attention;
[25] And you neglected all my counsel
And did not want my reproof;
[26] I will also laugh at your calamity;
I will mock when your dread comes,
[27] When your dread comes like a storm
And your calamity comes like a whirlwind,
When distress and anguish come upon you.
[28] "Then they will call on me, but I will not answer;
They will seek me diligently but they will not find me,

Result:

[29] Because they hated knowledge
And did not choose the fear of the LORD.
[30] "They would not accept my counsel,
They spurned all my reproof.
[31] "So they shall eat of the fruit of their own way
And be satiated with their own devices.
[32] "For the waywardness of the naive will kill them,

And the complacency of fools will destroy them.

Proverbs 1:24–32 (NASB)

Solution

²³ "Turn to my reproof,
Behold, I will pour out my spirit on you;
I will make my words known to you.

Proverbs 1:23 (NASB)

Result

³³ "But he who listens to me shall live securely
And will be at ease from the dread of evil."

Proverbs 1:33 (NASB)

Wisdom's Warnings not to Associate with Sinners

¹⁰ My son, if sinners entice you,
Do not consent.
¹¹ If they say, "Come with us,
Let us lie in wait for blood,
Let us ambush the innocent without cause;
¹² Let us swallow them alive like Sheol,
Even whole, as those who go down to the pit.

Proverbs 1:10–12 (NASB)

How Followers of Satan Deceive

¹³ We will find all *kinds* of precious wealth,
We will fill our houses with spoil;
¹⁴ Throw in your lot with us,
We shall all have one purse,"
¹⁵ My son, do not walk in the way with them.
Keep your feet from their path.

Proverbs 1:13–15 (NASB)

And, in keeping with her character, Wisdom offers insight how— not demanding but gently instructing with truth

¹⁶ For their feet run to evil
And they hasten to shed blood.
¹⁷ Indeed, it is useless to spread the *baited* net
In the sight of any bird;
¹⁸ But they lie in wait for their own blood;
They ambush their own lives.
¹⁹ So are the ways of everyone who gains by violence;
It takes away the life of its possessors.

Proverbs 1:16–19 (NASB)

WARNINGS AGAINST FOLLOWING FOLLY

<u>Her Personality</u>

> [13] The woman of folly is boisterous,
> *She is* naive and knows nothing.
> [14] She sits at the doorway of her house,
> On a seat by the high places of the city.
>
> Proverbs 9:13–14 (NASB)

Notice to whom FOLLY is calling--those who are trying to walk on the straight path!

> [15] Calling to those who pass by,
> Who are making their paths straight:
> [16] "Whoever is naive, let him turn in here,"
> And to him who lacks understanding she says,
> [17] "Stolen water is sweet;
> And bread *eaten* in secret is pleasant."
> [18] But he does not know that the dead are there,
> *That* her guests are in the depths of Sheol.
>
> Proverbs 9:15–18 (NASB)

Part Two Introducing God's Spiritual Parenting Partner

Onward
to
Higher Ground

~~~

References

(1) biblehub.com/hebrew/517.htm

(2) http://www.ancient-hebrew.org/12_torah.html

Chapter Three

Multiple Ps Seen in Creation

Some extremely valuable Bible-based truths have been presented thus far. More will come. For now, let's meditate upon what we have learned for the purpose of developing a much deeper appreciation for God and creation.

One purpose for doing this is to remove any doubt regarding God's Power and the value He places upon man. Think on these things.

Some Scriptures outside of Genesis will be used to support the information presented.

Characteristic	**Scripture Reference**
* *Presence of Spiritual Beings*	
God	Genesis 1:1 (NIV)
Holy Spirit	Genesis 1:2 (NIV)

Multiple Ps Seen in Creation

* *Partnership between*
  God and Wisdom   Proverbs 8:22-31 (NIV)
  God's creation and the earth   Genesis 1:3-28 (NIV)
* *Power*
  God created   Genesis 1:1 (NIV)
  He said   Genesis 1:3 (NIV)
  He saw   Genesis 1:4 (NIV)
  He separated   Genesis 1:4 (NIV)
  He called   Genesis 1:5 (NIV)
  He made   Genesis 1:7 (NIV)
  He gathered   Genesis 1:9 (NIV)
  He set   Genesis 1:17 (NIV)
  He blessed   Genesis 1:22 (NIV)
* *Precise Planning*
  Nothing but darkness existed   Genesis 1:2 (NIV)
     before God created the earth
  He
     spoke light into existence   Genesis 1:3 (NIV)
     separated light from darkness   Genesis 1:4 (NIV)
     separated water from above and   Genesis 1:6-7 (NIV)
        below the expanse of the sky
     separated the land from the seas   Genesis 1:9 (NIV)
  Land produced seed-bearing plants   Genesis 1:11-12 (NIV)
     and trees on the land according to
     their kind

    Sun and moon spoken into existence   Genesis 1:14-18 (NIV)
        to govern day and night
    He
        created sea life and birds   Genesis 1:20-21 (NIV)
        land produced living creatures,   Genesis 1:24:25 (NIV)
        livestock, and wild animals

* *Purpose*
    God wanted a family   Isaiah 45:18 (NIV)

* *Pattern*
    Man was the *only* one created   Genesis 1:26-27 (NIV)
        through the use of a pattern

* *Purity*
    Fruit of the Spirit   Galatians 5:22 (NIV)
        evident in the newborn

* *Perfection*
    His works are perfect   Deuteronomy 32:3-4 (NIV)

* *Pride*   Genesis 1:31 (NIV)
        All of creation was very good

* *Presents—Lots of Presents*
    "I give"   Genesis 1:29 (NIV)

* *Practicality*
    God provided   Genesis 1:29 (NIV)
        food for man and animals

- *Partnership* between
God and Man	Genesis 1:27 (NIV)
God, dust of the earth, and man	Genesis 2:7(a) (NIV)
God and our spirit	Genesis 2:7(b) (NIV)
God and our physical life	Genesis 2:7(c) (NIV)
God placed Adam in the Garden of Eden	Genesis 2:8 (NIV)
God gave Adam responsibility	Genesis 2:15 (NIV)
God allowed him to name the animals He had created	Genesis 2:19-20 (NIV)

- *Parental Protection*
Complete, genuine guidance	Proverbs 3:1-2 (NIV)
The Lord is patient with you	II Peter 3:9(b) (NIV)
His desire for our lives on earth	I Timothy 2:2 (NIV)
God wants all men to be saved	I Timothy 2:3 (NIV)
Do not do this or you will die	Genesis 2:17 (NIV)

- *Personal Interest and Involvement*
God's compassion on Adam because he was lonely	Genesis 2:18, 20(b) (NIV)

- *New partnerships developed between*
Adam and Eve	Genesis 2:21–22 (NIV)
Adam named his wife "Eve"	Genesis 3:20 (NIV)

- *Peace between God and Man*
God established the first home between male and female	Genesis 2:22, 25

* <u>*Priority*</u>
  God protected heaven from evil   Genesis 3:24 (NIV)

Reviewing these truths makes it very clear that, through *the eyes of God*, man was and still is His ultimate creation.

His desire and plan is to be the Perfect Parent for the purpose of guiding you and me away from those things that will harm us on an emotional, physical, mental, or spiritual level. There are no exceptions. You are invited to meditate upon on these truths.

Chapter Four

God's One-on-One Parenting

Obviously God knew the full potential to *"become"* that He had placed within Adam at the time he was created. Being the all-knowing, all-powerful, all-loving Father that He is, it was His intent to plant within Adam's heart the attitudes of mind that would assure him, "I can do this!"

Before Eve was made from Adam's rib, God's parenting was focused upon him for the purpose of instilling within him the self-confidence needed to become whatever God had planned for him as he moved forward in life. Without this, it would be impossible for Adam to experience the full life his Father desired for him.

How did God pursue His plan? As we examine insights revealed through Scripture, it will become clear how <u>God honored Adam</u> over and over again. Read, listen, and think upon these truths.

¹⁵ The LORD God took the man and put him in the Garden of Eden to work it and take care of it.
Genesis 2:15 (NIV)

Adam was definitely honored by God when He gave Adam the privilege of becoming the caregiver of the beautiful Garden of Eden. Because God had already planted within Adam the required skills to get the job done, He was confident Adam could meet the challenge. However, it was necessary for Adam to be given the opportunity to develop and strengthen those skills within himself. This confidence had to become deeply rooted within him if he was going to fulfill God's plan. During this process, two objectives would be gained:

* God's love for him would be reaffirmed; and
* Adam's trust in God would be strengthened.

There is a lesson to be learned by all of mankind. Because you and I have been created by the same God, it is important for each one of us to understand that He has given us creative talents in accordance with His will for our lives.

Despite this truth, how many of us truly identify with them? We are cheating both God and ourselves when this is not done. *Not identifying with and using the abilities given to us can easily become a major factor influencing depression!*

On the other hand, *God knows* that *all* people have the ability to become more than we are if we will only allow Him to develop us according to His plan!

Moving on, let's notice how God honored Adam through this warning:

> [16] And the LORD God commanded the man, "You are free to eat from any tree in the garden; [17] but you must not eat from the tree of the knowledge of good and evil, for when you eat from it you will certainly die."
>
> Genesis 2:16–17 (NIV)

He could have let Adam "find out the hard way." However, that attitude would not have exemplified God's love for man.

The word "die" within this verse does not refer to immediate death. How can we be certain? Genesis 5:5 reveals that Adam lived 930 years; therefore, we can be assured it does not refer to physical death.

Rather, it refers to man's spiritual death as the result of violating God's instructions. Anyone who follows this lifestyle will be separated from the presence of God forever! As we will learn, spiritual death is much more painful than any physical death one can imagine.

God continued to honor Adam:

> ¹⁹ Now the LORD God had formed out of the ground all the wild animals and all the birds in the sky. He brought them to the man to see what he would name them; and whatever the man called each living creature, that was its name. ²⁰ So the man gave names to all the livestock, the birds in the sky and all the wild animals.
>
> Genesis 2:19–20 (NIV)

It is important to *meditate* upon what we have just read.

Have you ever given thought to the question, "Why did God not change the name of any animal?"

Because God is the architectural designer of man's inner being, He *knows* how closely the emotional structure of humanity is connected to the soul. Therefore, He was not going to give Adam any reason to either *think* or *feel* that what he did was not good enough for his Father.

As a result of God's wise interaction with Adam, he definitely *felt* accepted as a child in the sight of God. What a fulfilling thought! An honor, indeed!

On the other hand, had God changed any name,

* Doubt would have been placed in Adam's mind regarding God's true acceptance of him. Consequently, Adam would have been damaged at a deep *emotional* level.
* Plus, the spiritual bond between the two of them would have been weakened.

God simply would not risk the development of spiritual anguish between Father and son. To do so would undermine His immediate plans and intent for Adam; the strengthening of Adam's spiritual connection to God; the development of Adam's leadership skills; and God's plans and intent for the entire male gender throughout the generations to come.

What would cause this to happen? Certainly Satan would take advantage of any negative thoughts or feelings Adam would have regarding his own abilities. Consequently, he could have easily given up thinking the task assigned was too difficult. This would offset all positive efforts God was trying to instill within him.

Another personal expression of His compassion for Adam is clearly expressed here:

> [18] The LORD God said, "It is not good for the man to be alone. I will make a helper suitable for him."
>
> Genesis 2:18 (NIV)

In response to this need, God honored Adam by providing him with a companion to be at his side. His companion was made from his very own rib.

> [21] So the LORD God caused the man to fall into a deep sleep; and while he was sleeping, he took one of the man's ribs and then closed up the place with flesh. [22] Then the LORD

God made a woman from the rib he had taken out of the man, and he brought her to the man.

Genesis 2:21-22 (NIV)

<u>Adam's response:</u>

[23] The man said,
"This is now bone of my bones
  and flesh of my flesh;
she shall be called 'woman,'
  for she was taken out of man."

Genesis 2:23 (NIV)

<u>God allowed him to name his companion:</u>

[20] Adam named his wife Eve, because she would become the mother of all the living.

Genesis 3:20 (NIV)

It is important to recognize all of the *personalization* between God and Adam, and Adam and Eve identified within the story of God's Creation. It is clearly demonstrated through the action verbs created, make, made, took, put, brought, and closed up.

Obviously, as the result of this husband and wife being uniquely created, extremely strong *physical* and *emotional* bonds would come into existence from the very beginning.

As the result of God's design, Adam would have a strong desire to love, cherish, and protect her. She was the most important *physical* possession he had. Certainly, his desire was to remain close to her in their state of perfect union.

As the result, the tremendously intimate connections between God and man, man and God, and husband and wife were reinforced.

It is important to stop and think for a moment. Let's ask ourselves, "Why did God honor Adam over and over again?"

It cannot be disputed that, from the very beginning, Adam had "head" knowledge regarding the existence of his Father. This came as the result of their one-on-one contact in the Garden. However, God knew that this would *not* be enough to sustain all of mankind throughout life.

In His infinite wisdom, God knew Adam's example would become the role model to be followed by *males* of the next generation. Their God-centered example would be passed down from generation to generation until the end of time.

Therefore, establishing and maintaining a strong one-on-one relationship with Adam was God's top priority. It would be needed if the male's multiple roles in life—leader of his wife as well as in the home, the Lord's church, the community, and the workplace—were to be fulfilled. Indeed, the path leading to achievement of these goals had to be clearly laid before him.

Therefore, without Adam realizing it, God was developing within him a "head" and "heart" knowledge of his Father. A combination of both would be needed if a strong emotional bond was to be developed between them. Without this bond, God knew the spiritual bond would degenerate.

It is true that if all of mankind in general is to have a truly meaningful relationship with God, the need for maintaining all aspects of our spiritual being must be recognized. It is not enough to only recognize the need. Every effort must be made to fulfill it by cooperating with God. If this truth is ignored, our souls will not be properly nourished. Without it, we will die spiritually!

Let's be open to God's guidance. May we allow him to feed us that which is so very important to our spiritual survival!

Onward

to

Higher Ground

Chapter Five

Our Responsibility as Children of God

Jesus' words teach us God's desire for our lives:

> [10] I have come that they may have life, and have it to the full.
>
> John 10:10 (NIV)

To help us achieve this goal, it is important to listen to God's counsel through Solomon:

> [23] Above all else, guard your heart,

Why?

> for everything you do flows from it.
>
> Proverbs 4:23 (NIV)

It is vitally important to notice the priority given—*above all else*—guard your heart! Head knowledge alone will *not* be adequate. How do we achieve the goal of guarding our hearts? Make the right choice to listen and follow His teachings. Over time gifts of hope, deep inner peace, and contentment will enter your heart as the result of *putting into practice* what is learned. It is only through the process of doing what has been suggested that we will develop the heart knowledge absolutely necessary for spiritual recovery. Far too often, there is a tremendous chasm within our soul because our spiritual foundation does not include *both* head and heart knowledge of Him. Therefore, they cannot work together. Consequently, we remain spiritually empty—away from God!

As we gain more truth and put it into practice, this chasm will be closed. The key to success in overcoming negative thoughts about God or life is following Him. By allowing His teachings to penetrate deep within our hearts, our faith will be made stronger as the result of experiencing God on a personal level. A positive mind-set will become a part of us as we draw closer to Him.

This is the Apostle Paul's prayer for all who choose to believe, trust, and follow Jesus. Paul says,

> [16] I ask the Father with his great glory to give you the power to be strong in your spirits. He will give you that strength through his Spirit. [17] I pray that Christ will live in your hearts because of your faith. I pray that your life will be strong

in love and be built on love. [18] And I pray that you and all God's holy people will have the power to understand the greatness of Christ's love—how wide, how long, how high, and how deep that love is. [19] Christ's love is greater than anyone can ever know, but I pray that you will be able to know that love.

<u>Why?</u>

> Then you can be filled with everything God has for you. [20] With God's power working in us, he can do much, much more than anything we can ask or think of.
>
> Ephesians 3:16–20 (ERV)

When we follow this path, these are but a few of the blessings we will receive.

In an effort to emotionally absorb some of the grace and mercy demonstrated through God's Word, it is important that we stop to meditate upon Paul's prayer.

* What is Paul asking God to give His followers?
* In response, what will He give?
* What is the Christian life to be built upon?
* How many people are included? Does that include you and me?
* Through this power, what will we be able to understand?
* How great is Christ's love?

Is it possible for us to know that love? How can we be certain?

In an effort to answer the last two questions, we must ask more:

Would Paul ask God to enable us to know God's love if we do not have the ability to accomplish the goal within us?

We must ask ourselves, "Am I willing to work hand-in-hand with God to achieve this goal?"

And what will happen as the result of allowing His power to work within me?

You are invited to come along now as we begin this exciting journey for the purpose of helping everyone—including you and me—to gain new hope and strength that will come as the result of making the *right* choice!

Onward

to

Higher Ground

Section Three

Understanding My Frame

Prelude

Have you ever given thought to "How I Am Made?" There are three DVDs—part one, *Planet Earth*; part two, *Animal Kingdom*; and part three, *Human Life*—contained in a set from the Moody Institute of Science.[1]

The knowledge gained from *Human Life* is nothing short of amazing. Perhaps it becomes more amazing and impressive when we stop to realize that this same process is what brought you and me into existence as a babe in physical form.

However, there is so much more to my "frame" than what is seen by the human eye. May this section provide greater insight and bring clearer understanding to what is *inside* my frame. By no means will this discussion be all-inclusive.

Come along now as we learn together.

References

[1] Link to DVD set, The Wonders of God's Creation:http://www.christianbook.com/the-wonders-of-gods-creation-3/9781575672489/pd/672480

Chapter One

Opening Our Eyes, What Do We See?

We have just learned the "frame" or pattern from which we were made—the "image" and "likeness" of God. What is a frame? What does it do? One purpose is to place a form around something within for the purpose of protection. Not only is this true of a house or a picture, but it is also true of our physical body.

Now it is important for us to understand, in part, what was included in "my frame" before coming to earth. What is tucked deep within?

To gain a solid knowledge base, let's start with Jesus' statement:

> [14] Jesus said, "Let the little children come to me, and do not hinder them, for the kingdom of heaven belongs to such as these."
>
> Matthew 19:14 (NIV)

Understanding My Frame

The Greek definition of "little child" gives great insight!

> A childling (of either sex), that is (properly) an infant, or (by extension) a half grown boy or girl; figuratively an immature Christian: (little, young) child, damsel.[1]

Did you notice the word "infant" used within this definition? Obviously, the two terms can be used interchangeably—an infant is a little child.

It will be very important to hold on to this truth as we continue.

To the best of his ability, David honors God by acknowledging his awareness of his Creator's work within him before he was born:

> [13] For you created my inmost being;
> you knit me together in my mother's womb.
> [14] I praise you because I am fearfully and wonderfully made;
> your works are wonderful,
> I know that full well.
> [15] My frame was not hidden from you
> when I was made in the secret place,
> when I was woven together in the depths of the earth.
> [16] Your eyes saw my unformed body;
> all the days ordained for me were written in your book
> before one of them came to be.
>
> Psalms 139:13–16 (NIV)

It is obvious that David had given deep thought to how God had "knit him together" before birth. Had David not embraced this thinking, he would not have come to this conclusion.

Do we recognize the same is true of all humanity—including ourselves? It does not matter whether or not I believe in God, the same is true of me. Therefore, it is important to recognize what is contained within "my frame."

Why should we search for answers? Why should we even try to gain deeper understanding of a subject that appears to have been ignored within the concept of spiritual teaching?

Excellent questions! The answers will be found as we continue to learn more about God and His will.

In today's world of "dash and go," it is quite likely very little thought or meditation is devoted to this type of thinking. However, does that mean that we should not examine the *reality* of truth for the purpose of gaining new insights, a deeper appreciation for God, and a greater strength, leading to a stronger faith as we draw closer to Him?

The Apostle Paul gave valuable guidelines when he wrote to the church in Ephesus:

> [18] I pray that the eyes of your heart may be enlightened in order that you may know the hope to which he has called you, the riches of his glorious inheritance in his holy people, [19] and his incomparably great power for us who believe. That power is the same as the mighty strength [20] he exerted when he raised Christ from the dead and seated him at his right hand in the heavenly realms.
>
> Ephesians 1:18-20 (NIV)

Because it is foundational to our growth, it is imperative that we open *our* spiritual eyes to truth regarding *our* origination (God). Then we must move forward to the hope of His calling, the riches of His glory, and the power of His greatness. This is Paul's desire for those who choose to follow God.

As you read Paul's description of the power God wants Christians to have, do you find it mind-boggling? Think about it—allow it to sink deep into your soul. This is God's desire—*to allow those who respond to His teachings to have the same power used when Christ was raised from the dead.* Certainly this power is not to be used to glorify self but to honor God as we follow Him throughout life.

In the light of truth, oh, how the world and the Lord's church would be strengthened if Christians worldwide would only claim this same power! This result will come when the eyes of our hearts are opened. Only then will our thinking regarding God change from negative to positive. It will develop into reality as the result of becoming anchored within the framework of Scriptures.

It is important to understand that these same insights and blessings are not promised to those who choose not to believe. As a consequence of their wrong choices, they will continue to "exist" through a "cheated life." However, it is possible to experience the full life Jesus intends. This can only come by following Him.

Now let's move forward and examine more truths regarding our inner being.

Not all of mankind shares the same ethnic background, talents, or quality of life. *However, lives—regardless of race, creed, or color—do share several commonalities.*

Let's look at just a few of them:

* The way the fetus is developed within the womb;
* Medical science estimates that the length of blood vessels in the average person is 60,000 miles,[2] and
* The way a healthy body transforms nutrients from food into energy.

There are far more components to man's structure than science will ever discover. Nobody on planet earth fully understands all aspects of our inner being.

In support of this truth, let's turn our attention to the outward reflections of God given through the newborn. These attributes are immediately seen on day one of life. They are clear evidence of the fruit of the Holy Spirit being present within the child.

> [22] But the fruit of the Spirit is love, joy, peace, forbearance, kindness, goodness, faithfulness, [23] gentleness and self-control. Against such things there is no law.
> Galatians 5:22-23 (NIV)

As these thoughts are considered, are they not clearly shown as part of the *child's personality at birth*? We may have reason to question this until deeper insight into the words' meanings is gained.

- Love: Affection, good-will, love, benevolence; of the love men to men; especially of that love of Christians toward Christians which is enjoined and prompted by their religion, whether the love be viewed as in the soul or as expressed[3] Undoubtedly, this is the love of the "immature Christian" (newborn) shining forth to the world.
- Joy: Joy, gladness[4]
- Peace: Peace between individuals[5]
- Forbearance: Patience, long suffering, slowness in avenging wrongs[6]
- Kindness: Benignity, a kind act or favor[7]
- Goodness: Uprightness of heart and life[8]
- Faithfulness: Fidelity, faithfulness, i.e. the character of one who can be relied on[9]
- Gentleness: Mildness of disposition, gentleness of spirit, meekness[10]
- Self-control: The virtue of one who masters his desires and passions, especially his sensual appetites[11]

Before moving on, observe this. As we just learned, part of the Greek definition of *love* is "that love of Christians toward Christians which is enjoined and prompted by their religion…" As an extension of God's love, the newborn shows it to all people!

Oh, how, we need to dwell upon and digest these Bible teachings. Doing so would help us to accept ourselves and others the way we are. Life would be so much simpler and more meaningful.

Now it is important that we stop to reflect upon *why* these attributes are present within from the time of birth.

Ultimately they show a portion of God's personality. Obviously, having these attributes within us from the beginning point of life is a wonderful gift from Him. Collectively they form the root system from which *healthy emotions* should grow. When properly nurtured, children will have the ability to both *feel* and *express* the thoughts and feelings within them. This is God's plan.

Some may have never considered the fruit of the Spirit to be connected to the emotional structure of man. However, scientific research has verified this to be true.

If you choose, you can gain insight into this research by doing an Internet search using these words: "How is patience connected to our emotions?" Enter the same question substituting the other attributes included within the fruit of the Spirit.

Very informative, isn't it! This is another demonstration of the truth spoken by David in Psalms 139:13–14.

Certainly it is important to take the time to meditate upon these thoughts. This will help us to understand that the teachings of God's Word are designed to protect us at an emotional level.

Hopefully, after gaining deeper insight, it will become easier to understand that our emotional structure is *directly* connected to our spiritual well-being. This truth will be discussed further in the following chapter.

Now, as we give thought to these God-given characteristics, can we clearly see that, unless the *newborn* has been adversely affected *in vitro* by physical abuse or other types of negative influences, *all* newborns reflect God to the world? Without a doubt, this can only be true because babes have been duplicated from the "pattern" used at creation. In a nutshell, they truly represent love!

Perhaps this new knowledge is both surprising and challenging because it may not have been part of previous teaching received through Bible classes or sermons. May this truth give each of us a stronger motivation to expand our knowledge base leading to a deeper knowledge of God, which will lead to true peace of mind.

Refresh your weary spirit through prayer and these positive thoughts.

Onward to Higher Ground

༺☙❧༻

References

(1) biblehub.com/greek/3813.htm

(2) 100 Interesting Facts About The Human Body; Fact #25; http://www.lifesmith.com/Berkeley%20Teaching/humanbody.htm

(3) *Greek-English Lexicon of The New Testament* translated, revised and enlarged by Joseph Henry Thayer, DD.; Baker Book House; 1977; p. 4, Item 26

(4) Ibid., p. 664-665, Item 5479

(5) Ibid., p. 182, Item 1515

(6) Ibid., p. 387, Item 3115

(7) Ibid., p. 672, Item 5544

(8) Ibid., p. 3, Item 19

(9) Ibid., p. 514, Item 4102

(10) Ibid., p. 535, Item 4236

(11) Ibid., p. 166–167, Item 1466

Chapter Two

And Looking Inside?

It is important for us to understand that "my frame" is basically composed of four parts—*spiritual, emotional, physical, and mental*. Each of the four represents separate—yet closely connected—forms of power and strength that God has placed within each of us for purposes of survival.

First, let's consider the spiritual portion of man. The truth has already been established that, because we are created in the "image" and "likeness" of God, *every person comes into this world as a spiritual being with an invisible connection to God. This connection is referred to as the "soul."* This direct contact is the hub, foundation, or "motherboard" of our very existence. Within it are indefinable and incredible strengths through which the threads of our "innermost being" are intertwined.

To further illustrate this truth, let's liken the "dragline-silk" component of a spider web to the "spiritual" part of man. This will give us a deeper understanding. The dragline can be seen. It is the part of the web that allows the spider to "hang" outside of the web and yet live. [1]

God's Word clearly explains how it is possible for the Christian to honor Him by hanging on to Him while living in this sinful world. It must begin with believing and trusting God.

And this is Bible truth! This Scripture confirms that small children are born with a *natural* belief in Jesus tucked within them:

> [6] "If anyone causes one of these little ones—those who believe in me—
>
> Matthew 18:6 (NIV)

The word "believe" means:

> "To have faith (in, upon, or with respect to a person or thing), that is, credit; by implication to entrust (especially one's spiritual well being to Christ): (believe(r), commit (to trust), put in trust with.[2]

Obviously for a child to believe, the belief had to be put into place by an outside influence. In this case, it was God. If the child's belief is going to develop into the "spiritual dragline" needed throughout life, continual nurturing must take place. How can this be done?

God gave each of us a jump start by planting His Word within us. Now we are being instructed to

> [21] Get rid of all moral filth and the evil that is so prevalent and humbly accept the word planted in you, which can save you.
> James 1:21 (NIV)

The Greek meaning for the word "planted" is:

properly, implant, bring into living union like with a successfully engrafted shoot; (figuratively) what is "planted" and hence "inborn, congenital, natural"...i.e. placed in ("established") which enables something to develop...used only in Js 1:21).[3]

Even though this definition may challenge our present understanding, it is important to meditate upon it. When something is "inborn" within us, it is not visible nor can it be removed. Nonetheless, it has a purpose. God placed or established His Word within us before birth so we can become successfully *engrafted*.

Engrafted into what? A vine.

What vine? Jesus explains:

> [5] I am the vine, you are the branches; he who abides in Me and I in him, he bears much fruit, for apart from Me you can do nothing.
> John 15:5 (NASB)

The Apostle Paul adds this insight:

> [17] For in the gospel the righteousness of God is revealed—a righteousness that is by faith from first to last, just as it is written: "The righteous will live by faith."
>
> Romans 1:17 (NIV)

Our "first" faith came from that which was engrafted in us. And, those who have been "trained in righteousness" and have lived the Christian life throughout their years on earth will have lived by faith until "the last."

Indeed, this is not something that I can do for you, nor can you for me. It is an individual choice.

Now, let us consider more attributes that are contained within our frames at birth. Certainly the healthy newborn child represents love to the world. *Everything* has a beginning. Therefore, the question is asked, "Where did love originate?"

> [8] Whoever does not love does not know God, because God is love.
>
> I John 4:8 (NIV)

What is the Bible's definition of love?

Love	**It**
is patient	does not envy
is kind	does not boast
keeps no record of wrongs	is not proud
rejoices with the truth	is not rude
always protects	is not self-seeking

always trusts	is not easily angered
always hopes	does not delight in evil
always perseveres	

II Corinthians 13:4–7 (NIV)

Most certainly a newborn cannot give something that is not in his or her possession. Therefore, where does a newborn's love come from? Let's put two and two together. God is love. We were created in the "image" and "likeness" of God at birth. As part of that we are born with the three characteristics mentioned in this verse!

> [5] The goal of this command is love, which comes from a pure heart and a good conscience and a sincere faith.
> I Timothy 1:5 (NIV)

Clear understanding of the meanings of these words is important. Greek definitions:

<u>pure</u>
properly, "without admixture", hence "clean" because unmixed (without undesirable elements); (figuratively) spiritually clean because purged (purified by God), i.e. free from the contaminating (soiling) influences of sin[4]
<u>heart</u>
"the affective center of our being" and the capacity of moral preference...; "desire-producer that makes us tick"..., i.e. our "desire-decisions" that establish who we really are[5]

conscience
properly, joint-knowing, i.e. conscience which joins moral and spiritual consciousness as part of being created in the divine image. Accordingly, all people have this God-given capacity to know right from wrong because each is a free moral agent)[6]
faith
properly, persuasion (be persuaded, come to trust); faith[7]

By bringing all of these definitions together collectively, it can be concluded that infants are born as "immature Christians" who reflect God's love through their pure hearts, clear consciences, and sincere faith. Consequently, they completely entrust their spiritual well-being to God and Jesus. This truth applies to all of us at birth. Wow, what a breath of fresh air!

This will remain true until children are taught to sin.

Immediately some may question the thought that a newborn is an immature Christian at birth. In this setting, *how can a baby be born anything other than an immature Christian* with these basic Christ-like characteristics tucked within his or her frame?

Another aspect of the human "frame" within is our *emotional* structure. On the surface, to accept the thought that emotions are an intricate part of our *spiritual* makeup may be challenging—even rejected by some. The fact that the word "emotion" is not found in the Bible may contribute to one believing that there is no place for emotion in Christianity. However, does the Bible support this theory?

To answer this question, let's focus on the subject of emotions for the purpose of learning the important part they contribute to our overall well-being in the sight of God.

Webster defines emotion as

1. a) strong feeling; excitement
   b) the state or capability of having the feelings aroused to the point of awareness
2. Any specific feeling; any of various complex reactions with both mental and physical manifestations, as love, hate, fear, anger, etc[8]

Although it has been clearly established that God and His Son are spiritual in nature, do we really think of them as being filled with "emotions" as well? Perhaps not. However, Scriptures reveal many examples of deep emotional responses within them. For example:

> [16] For God <u>so loved</u> the world that he gave his one and only Son, that whoever believes in him shall not perish but have eternal life.
>
> John 3:16 (NIV)

If love is not an emotion, what is it?

Counter to this,

* The Lord was *grieved* that he had had made man   Genesis 6:6 (NIV)

* His heart was *filled with pain* — Genesis 6:6 (NIV)
* God is a *jealous* God — Exodus 20:5 (NIV)
* Therefore, the Lord was *angry* with his people — Psalms 106:40 (NIV) Deuteronomy 4:21 (NIV)
* Jesus made a whip out of cords, and drove all from the temple area — John 2:15 (NIV)

Keeping these verses within their proper contexts helps us to have a better understanding of God's complete personality. Gaining this insight is absolutely critical lest we develop a false security based upon a false knowledge base! Without truth as a foundation, it is easy to develop an incomplete profile of who He really is.

If our concept of our spiritual Father is one of never being upset or never showing anger as the result of people's behavior, the need to restructure this thinking process is absolutely critical.

The following Scriptures will also help us to understand all people, at all levels in life during Bible times, expressed their emotions for various reasons:

* Jacob and Esau wept (grown men) — Genesis 33:4 (NASB)
* Joseph wept (a man in power) — Genesis 45:2 (NASB)

- * The king wept very bitterly II Samuel 13:36 (NASB)
   (result of vengeful murder)
- * Many religious leaders Ezra 3:12 (NASB)
   (sadness)
- * Apostle Peter Mark 14:72 (NASB)
   (guilt after denying Christ)
- * Jesus, Son of God Luke 19:41 (NASB)
   (sinful nature of people; John 11:35 (NASB)
   His compassion for them)
- * Jews weeping
   (death of Lazarus) John 11:33 (NASB)
- * Mary Magdalene John 20:11 (NASB)
   (at Jesus' grave)
- * Apostle Paul Acts 20:37 (NASB)
   (leaving those he would not see again)

Unlike most of us, these people kept in touch with the real person they were inside. What a great example! This certainly is another "breath of fresh air!"

Obviously, they were not plagued with the stigma society has placed upon man in our present world. Too often today's counsel includes, "Big boys don't cry," or "Wipe the tears from your pretty little face," "Suck it up," etc. As a result, the mental health of many has degenerated to a very low level. Unfortunately, these types of reprimands clearly demonstrate a lack of wisdom that can only be gained through Bible knowledge.

In an effort to offset some of this negativity, the following verse is being repeated to help us gain an even deeper understanding of the spiritual and emotional connection within us.

> ⁷ Then the Lord God formed a man from the dust of the ground and breathed into his nostrils the breath of life, and the man became a living being.
>
> Genesis 2:7 (NIV)

The Hebrew definition for "nostrils" is very interesting. It clearly supports the truth that our spirit and emotions are connected. The Hebrew word is "Aph"—a masculine noun.

> Refers to the breathing part of the body, specifically the nose, nostril or face. It is considered a vital part of the body. God made man a living being by breathing into his nostrils (Gen. 2:7). By the act of breathing, emotions can be expressed. In anger, the nose dilates and breathing becomes more intense. This word, therefore, is normally used to refer to the anger of men and of God. This anger is expressed in the appearance of the nostrils. The word gives specific emphasis to the emotional aspect of anger and wrath, whereas its synonyms relate other aspects.[9]

Certainly this is another very clear illustration of how "fearfully and wonderfully" we are made.

Additionally, the following Scriptures are only a few within the Bible that clearly illustrate the fact that our emotions are deeply intertwined among the spiritual, physical, and mental components within each of us.

---

² Your arrows have pierced me,
and your hand has come down on me.
³ Because of your wrath there is no health in my body;
there is no soundness in my bones because of my sin.
⁴ My guilt has overwhelmed me
like a burden too heavy to bear.

Psalms 38:2-4 (NIV)

<u>Illustrations of four components of man intertwining</u>:

- spiritual: "your arrows have pierced me"
  "your hand has come down on me"
  "because of your wrath
- physical: no health in my body"
- emotional: "there is no soundness in my bones because of my sin"
- mental: "guilt has overwhelmed me like a burden too heavy to bear"

⁷ Do not be wise in your own eyes;
Fear the LORD and turn away from evil.
⁸ It will be healing to your body
And refreshment to your bones.

        Proverbs 3:7–8 (NASB)

Illustrations:

mental:	"do not be wise in your own eyes;"
spiritual:	"fear the LORD and turn away from evil"
physical:	"it will be healing to your body"
emotional:	"and refreshment to your bones"

"Fear the Lord and stay away from evil" will not be written on any prescription pad within the medical community for recovery from a physical or emotional issue. Nonetheless, following God's counsel will lead to recovery.

※

¹⁵ But what can I say?
 He has spoken to me, and he himself has done this.
I will walk humbly all my years
 because of this anguish of my soul.
¹⁶ Lord, by such things people live;
 and my spirit finds life in them too.
You restored me to health
 and let me live.
¹⁷ Surely it was for my benefit
 that I suffered such anguish.

In your love you kept me
  from the pit of destruction;
you have put all my sins
  behind your back.

Isaiah 38:15-17 (NIV)

<u>Illustrations</u>:

- spiritual: "He has spoken to me, and he himself has done this."
- physical: "I will walk humbly all my years because of this anguish of my soul."

"You restored me to health and let me live."

- mental: "Lord, by such things people live; and my spirit finds life in them too."

  "Surely it was for my benefit that I suffered such anguish."
- emotional: "In your love you kept me from the pit of destruction; you have put all my sins behind your back."

This is another thought to be considered. Without knowing and recognizing what we are feeling within our spirit, it may be difficult to express our innermost needs to God. *Indeed, our prayer life can become inhibited as the result of not understanding how much He loves us and desperately wants a relationship with us.*

And Looking Inside?

If it is still difficult to understand the connection between the *spiritual, emotional, physical,* and *mental* elements we possess, perhaps applying these thoughts to your personal life may help.

- As a child, at what age in your life do you remember having an *awareness* of God?
- Do you remember your level of faith in Him at that point?
- If possible, think back to the *first* time you remember being emotionally scarred or devastated.
- If you have been affected by one negative emotional upset after another, how long did it take for your faith or spirit to be weakened or broken?
- How long did it take for negative thinking to set in?
- How long did it take before you began to question God's existence—i.e., "If there is a God, why is there so much evil in the world?"
- If you have done this, when did you begin to question God's love for you—i.e., "If God really loves me, why am I hurting? Why are all these bad things happening to me?"
- Through all of this, have you lost hope?
- Subsequently, do you find yourself becoming more cold and indifferent regarding what happens to you in life?

On the other hand,

* Do kind words spoken by others nourish you at an emotional, physical, mental, or spiritual level?
* Is it possible to gain or regain the desire to "press on" after receiving encouragement from another?
* Did it lead you to reading God's Word more?
* When your heart is at peace, do you have more energy in your body?
* Do you enjoy looking at smiling or downcast faces?
* Either way, how do these facial expressions affect your heart, mind, soul, and health?

These questions can only be answered by the individual. Perhaps you can honestly say that you have never questioned His existence or love for you. If this is true, *praise God!* This is the result of your parents, grandparents, or other positive mentors in your life, grounding you in the Word of God, which has resulted in a deep trust in Him.

However, if you did not receive this same type of guidance in life, ask yourself:

* Has my awareness of God been pushed aside?
* Has my faith in Him diminished only to be followed by my questioning His existence?

When we do not recognize the various emotions within ourselves, it is very difficult—if not impossible—to have a clear view of God's love for us. Without the proper emotional structure,

- * people, in general, will remain
    - * unable to recognize or identify with God's love; and
    - * spiritually starved.
- * Christians will not
    - * feel the love, joy, and peace that He intends;
    - * have the proper understanding of the Golden Rule;
    - * gain the proper understanding of the purpose for regaining, retaining, and maintaining the "fruit of the Spirit" within us;
    - * be capable of reflecting Christ's true likeness(love) to the world;
    - * live the full life that is available to those who choose to follow God.

Any form of negative thinking is from the devil and will be used to distort the thinking of mankind regardless of age. If allowed to grow, these deadly seeds can rapidly develop into a mind-set that says, "There is no God." In other words, our "spiritual attachment" to God becomes weaker and weaker as Satan's efforts to destroy us within become rampant and more successful.

Understanding My Frame

To offset the negative, every positive effort *must* be made to retain, maintain, and preserve the unseen Christ like attributes hidden within "my frame." When this becomes center focus, a solid foundation built upon truth will be easier to establish.

Keeping these various thoughts in mind, do we have better insight regarding how "fearfully and wonderfully" we are made and how tightly our spiritual, emotional, physical, and mental attributes are woven within? Truly, each of them is a *contributing component* to our spiritual motherboard (our soul) that greatly influences our willingness to interact with God.

As you read the Bible from this point forward, watch closely for other verses that indicate the intertwining of the four areas of man's inner being.

Even though all of this can be overwhelming, it is critically important that we gain a deeper understanding regarding the God-designed spiritual being within us. Accepting this truth and allowing God to help us grow spiritually will lead to the development of our full spiritual potential. This will make it possible to enjoy the full life available.

The multiple Father and child connections between God and His offspring are a few of the reasons why we, as individual people, are valuable in His sight. Indeed, we are precious to Him.

May these thoughts bring refreshment to your soul. Pray to God and ask him for healing in __*every*__ part of your life.

Onward

to

Higher Ground

⊛

References

(1) *Dandy Designs*, 2006, Volume 4, p. 29–30, "The Golden Orb Weaver Spider," John Clayton, Does God Exist? P.O. Box 2704, South Bend, IN 46680-2704

(2) biblehub.com, Greek #4100

(3) Ibid., Greek #1721

(4) Ibid., Greek #2513

(5) Ibid., Green #2588

(6) Ibid., Greek #4893

(7) Ibid., Greek #4102

(8) *Webster's* 1982, op. cit., 458

(9) *Hebrew-Greek Key Word Study Bible*, op.cit., p. 1712, item 639. Permission granted by AMG Publishers.

Chapter Three

Continuing On!
I Have an Even Greater Connection to My Father

As a reminder, let's think back to the characteristics of a *good, well-meaning, godly* Christian father in a healthy home:

* a good, kind, gentle communicator;
* spiritual leader for the purpose of protecting family members from any satanic attacks that may be lurking at their door;
* appreciates Mom's contribution to the home as together they establish the day-to-day guidelines for their Christian home;
* through love, guidelines for Christian living are conveyed to all family members;
* his "final authority"; and

* his motivation for accepting these responsibilities is to honor God through *love for his family*—not an attitude of *control*.

The very fact that *love is the foundation of the home* gives soul-anchoring strength, stability, and inner peace.

Have you ever asked yourself, "Why is this true?" Again, this is just one of many ways that a responsible father reflects the "image" and "likeness" of God.

If and when we do not have this type of love, guidance, and protection from our physical parents during our developmental years, spiritual problems can easily arise later in life. What type of problems?

Recently a young man who has experienced the lack of parental leadership expressed his thoughts.

> "I have the head knowledge of what a real father is and what a son is, but I can't figure out the heart knowledge. Until just recently, my Dad has deferred all decisions and responsibilities to my Mom. And she tries to tell me where to go and what to do. So I have basically ignored her and never relied on her at all. She won't help me with how to do things, which is what I ask for. So I essentially raised myself without much help from my parents, whom I don't trust. And now I'm having trouble trusting God as a result. Can you help me with this in some way?"

As so aptly stated, when a child's relationship with physical parents is not what God intends, it is very difficult for her or him *to relate to and trust* a Heavenly Father that *cannot* be seen. Nonetheless, God wants to be the best Father to us anyone has ever known.

How can help be extended to children who are having difficulty trusting God? The following suggestions are offered in an effort to offset any fear or negativity we may experience as we cross the bridge from lack of trust to complete trust in Him.

* First of all, realize our spiritual connection to Him is completely different than the connection we have with our physical parents.
* Pray to God and ask for guidance in your thinking processes.
* Look and listen for His response.
* Recognize all good things in life are from God.
* Start counting the blessings given to you on a daily basis.

Perhaps this will be easier to do as we focus upon His relationship with us. As we have already learned, God brought into existence a physical connection between earth and humanity. This was followed by an even greater spiritual connection between Him and mankind.

> [7] Then the LORD God formed a man from the dust of the ground and breathed into his nostrils the breath of life, and the man became a living being.
>
> Genesis 2:7 (NIV)

This is *not* true of animals. He did not breathe life into any animal. They were created with the ability to breathe.

Knowing that God cannot give something that is not in His possession, have you ever given thought to the fact that God and Jesus have souls? Scriptures confirm this truth.

In reference to God:

> [5] The Lord examines the righteous,
> but the wicked, those who love violence,
> he hates with a passion.
>
> Psalms 11:5 (NASB)

Jesus said to His disciples:

> [38] Then he said to them, "My soul is overwhelmed with sorrow to the point of death. Stay here and keep watch with me."
>
> Matthew 26:38 (NIV)

In addition to humanity being created in His "image" and "likeness," our spiritual commonality with God through our emotions is another reason God considers mankind to be His ultimate masterpiece. This truth cannot be said of any other part of creation.

Indeed, as the result, we have a priceless, irreplaceable bond or relationship with our Heavenly Father!

What is a bond? One definition,

> a uniting force; tie; link (the bonds of friendship).[1]

What is a relationship?

1. the quality or state of being related; connection
2. connection by blood or marriage; kinship
3. a particular instance of being related.[2]

Does this help us gain a clearer understanding that we are all *individually connected with Him through our souls? Indeed, we have a special bond with our Heavenly Father!* We have never had nor will we ever have a possession of greater value. There is absolutely nothing that can be given in exchange for this relationship. Truly, it is priceless and irreplaceable.

Jesus tries to impress upon us the value of our souls through these words:

> [26] It is worth nothing for a man to have the whole world if he loses his soul. He could never pay enough to buy back his soul.
>
> Matthew 16:26 (ICB)

To be properly nourished, my soul needs *spiritual food*. How does it differ from physical food?

> [4] Jesus answered, "It is written: 'Man shall not live on bread alone, but on every word that comes from the mouth of God.'"
>
> Matthew 4:4 (NIV)

Our spiritual needs are no different. The same words spoken thousands of years ago still apply to us today. These two facts will never change:

* the physical body requires physical food or it will die (no further interaction with loved ones on earth),
* the soul requires spiritual nourishment or it will experience spiritual death (no further interaction with God) through a never-ending eternity.

It certainly is possible for *spiritual death* to occur before physical death. If our souls are not properly fed on an ongoing basis, they will quickly become malnourished. As a result, we will continue to live a "cheated life." In fact, not only is it possible, it is *certain* to happen.

Our souls are what will stand before God at judgment. Our eternal destinies will be based upon the lives we have chosen to live here on earth. *Only those who have lived in keeping with the Bible guidelines, thereby properly nourishing their souls, will be allowed to enter heaven.*

At every turn, God extends an invitation to each of us to come to Him for guidance through life. No man can live the *full life* He intended without accepting the help He has to offer. His support staff—Wisdom, Jesus, and the Holy Spirit—is also available 24/7 to guide us.

Accepting this counsel is the only way we will be able to protect our souls for eternity. Remember, our Heavenly Father's dream is to have His children home with Him to live throughout eternity. Then, as the result of trusting Him, we will have a one-on-one relationship with Him, never to be separated again.

Please don't disappoint Jesus. Listen as He says, "Come Home, please Come Home."

Onward

to

Higher Ground

References

(1) *Webster's* 1982, op cit., p. 160
(2) Ibid., p. 1198

Section Four

Satan Runs Interference with God's Plan for Man

Prelude

Have you ever wondered why the world is in the condition it is today? We cannot hear a newscast or read a newspaper without learning about worldwide tragedies generated by deep-seated angers sprung forth from the hearts of mankind.

Have you ever wondered why it is getting worse as time goes on? Certainly all of this does not lend itself to the peace of mind that each one of us craves within—the same peace God desires for each one of us.

The purpose of section four is to provide greater insight into Bible answers to these troublesome questions.

Foundational to learning truth, it is important to understand that, from the beginning of time, there have been two factors in the world that affect our lives on a daily basis—good and evil. Let's take a moment to make this observation:

God = Good (simply spelled by adding another o to God)
All good comes from God.

"Lady Luck" is *not* responsible for any good that enters into our lives. The truth is, she does not exist.

Let's give God the credit for all "good."

Devil = Evil (the word "evil" is contained within the word "devil")

All evil comes from Satan.

With the same clarity that God's Word describes His Personality, it also exposes Satan for what he is. Listen as his true personality is clearly defined.

Words Jesus used to describe him:

* A murderer   John 8:44 (NIV)
* The father of lies   John 8:44 (NIV)

The Apostle John gives this insight:

* The devil has been sinning from the   I John 3:8 (NIV)
  beginning

Further terminology to describe Satan used within Scriptures:

* More crafty than any wild animal   Genesis 3:1 (NIV)
* Devil   Matthew 4:1 (NIV)

- * Tempter   Matthew 4:3 (NIV)
  I Thessalonians 3:5 (NIV)
- * The prince of this world   John 14:30 (NIV)
- * Schemer   II Corinthians 2:11 (NIV)
- * The god of this age   II Corinthians 4:4 (NIV)
- * Masquerader as angel of light   II Corinthians 11:14 (NIV)
- * The ruler of the kingdom of the air   Ephesians 2:2 (NIV)
- * The spirit now at work in the disobedient   Ephesians 2:2 (NIV)
- * Prowler   I Peter 5:8 (NIV)

It is very important for every person to always remember—never to be forgotten—God's goal is to protect you and me from spiritual, emotional, physical, and mental harm. He does not desire to interfere with the healthy Father and child relationship He so skillfully developed between Him and Adam in the Garden of Eden. We had the same relationship at birth.

Is Satan's goal the same? Although this verse has been shared before, it is a truth that we must never forget.

> ⁴ The god of this age has blinded the minds of unbelievers, so that they cannot see the light of the gospel that displays the glory of Christ, who is the image of God.
>
> II Corinthians 4:4 (NIV)

Because Satan's deception and trickery have been so successful, man does not realize he is suffering from spiritual blindness. Therefore, he stumbles around in the dark in search of peace of mind and purpose in life. He has been kept from the truth that a working knowledge of God's Word and obedience to His commandments are the elements needed to see the glory of Christ and receive the joy of living.

Then and only then will we receive the guidance and leadership needed to achieve the full life desired. Keeping this truth in the forefront of our thinking will become a safeguard against the devil's schemes as he tries to influence us on a daily basis. We must constantly be aware of how desperate he is to redirect our thinking away from God.

Why is this true? The devil knows the end of the world is coming; thus, his time to do his deceptive, dirty work is getting shorter and shorter. Therefore, his efforts are getting more intense.

Is it now becoming clearer why evil is so rampant in our world today?

In relationship to God's Word, Satan would have us believe "ignorance is bliss." He does not want us to become aware of the truth that our disobedience to God's commands will result

Prelude

in absolute horror when we stand before Him on judgment day. Instantly we will realize how much of a deceptive *liar* Satan truly is.

The two words "blissful" and "horrible" are not even comparable!

As part of His one-on-one parenting with Adam, God warned him not to eat of the tree of the knowledge of good and evil. The Bible gives no indication that God explained to Adam why he was asked not to do this. God's desire was that Adam would simply trust his Father's leadership.

Certainly God had a strong motivation for giving this guidance to Adam. His desire was for Adam to remain spiritually pure, never knowing evil. Thus, the Father and child relationship between them would be maintained.

God also knew that when the evils of sin were introduced into mankind's life, His relationship with them *must* be broken. Therefore, God warned Adam in an effort to avoid this tragedy. Regardless, Adam ate the food from the forbidden tree. The door was thereby opened for evil to enter into his heart and destroy the good God had planted within him.

Certainly, God did not want either of them to experience the spiritually and emotionally devastating heartbreak that would follow. How can this heartbreak be defined?

* God wanted the relationship to be restored.
* Adam wanted the same but felt it was not possible.

Satan Runs Interference with God's Plan for Man

- * Consequently both God and Adam suffered indescribable anguish as the result of Adam not listening to his Father.

Despite all the disappointment and heartache Adam and Eve caused God to suffer, <u>He did not turn His back on them.</u> They turned away from God! It is critically important for *all* of mankind to understand this truth!

<u>God was rejecting the sin, not the person guilty of sin!</u>

Sin has a way of changing man's whole personality. Thus, despite His love for His child, God had to turn away in pain because of this lost relationship. Adam was no longer His child. Rather, he became a follower (child) of Satan.

Are you wondering, "Why does God even allow Satan to exist?" Like He did with man, God gave the devil freedom of choice in all areas of his life. Without the gift of free choice, God would be a dictator or controller.

Satan chose evil over good. His thoughts were evil continuously. Through multiple tools of deception, he was successful in changing Adam and Eve's behavior simply by redirecting their thoughts from good to evil. He did not present himself as a "controller." Rather, he presented evil in ways that appeared attractive and beneficial to them. His plan proved to very successful. Incidentally, his goal has never changed!

Why did Satan want to break man's connection to God? Jesus provides great insight:

Prelude

[18] "I saw Satan fall like lightning from heaven.
                                                  Luke 10:18 (NIV)

Obviously, before falling, one had to be in the place from which he had fallen. Why was Satan not allowed to stay in heaven?

Although it may appear to be unrelated, this question is being asked to answer the previous one.

Have you ever given thought to these questions?

- *   Where was the first war fought?
- *   Who were the first combatants involved in this war?
- *   Who won?
- *   What was the purpose of the fight?

The Bible provides the answer to these questions.

- *   It was a spiritual war in heaven.
- *   The war was between God (good) and the devil (evil).
- *   God won, and Satan was kicked out of heaven.
- *   To protect the souls of men.

Another purpose of the war was to protect heaven from being contaminated by evil (sin). As the result of God reigning, peace and purity remained. Nonetheless, Satan will continue to work in the hearts of men in this world until the end of time. Ultimately, God will be victorious. His truth can never be destroyed.

Satan Runs Interference with God's Plan for Man

As the result of Satan being removed from heaven, enraging anger consumed him. His goal to work in the hearts of mankind for the purpose of pulling them away from God became even more intense!

Adam and Eve were the devil's first targets through which he would put his plan into action. No time could be wasted. Spiritual havoc and emotional anguish within the minds of men had to be achieved immediately—*before Adam and Eve had children!*

Why? It was important to Satan that they teach their offspring how to focus on things of the world rather than on God. Disrespect for God through Adam and Eve's lack of obedience would then be passed on to all generations that followed. Satan wanted all of mankind to experience a "tug of war" or a sense of "emptiness" within them as the result of sin remaining in their lives.

How does this war within affect us individually? We feel as though we are being totally pulled apart as the result of God quietly encouraging us to come back to Him, versus Satan deceitfully doing everything possible to keep us from accepting God's invitation. With this unsettled feeling, man remains restless and discontent with life, in need of spiritual and emotional fulfillment.

Is it now possible to understand why Satan is interested in US? He knows how important you and I are to God and that is exactly why he is trying to destroy us. Certainly it is not because

PRELUDE

he has a sincere personal interest in the well-being of humanity. In reality, he could not care less about us as individual people. *Truly, he does not care if he leads all of mankind into hell.* His primary interest is revenge against our Heavenly Father. It will never be satisfied.

Bluntly stated, Satan is trying to use us, use us, use us—you and me—in his efforts to achieve his never-ending goal of seeking revenge against God. This truth cannot be emphasized enough!

Yes, it is important that everyone feels needed. However, how many of us enjoy being used, to achieve the selfish desires of another?

The motivation to choose God over Satan may come by asking and answering this question: "How much longer am I going to continue feeding Satan's ego by allowing him to use me in his efforts to promote evil?"

The truth is God will accept us back. His love for man was shown by giving him a choice as to whom he would serve—God (good) or the devil (evil).

The battle between Satan and God belongs to God! Humanity does not have the power or wisdom to fight and win against the devil. Our power to win the daily battles of life *must* come from Jesus Christ. We must be on His team. Then and only then will we be connected to the *true* source of power to win spiritual battles against the devil. Only Jesus can give us the power to enter and win this battle as we put on the spiritual armor (Ephesians

6:10–13). This is God's will for daily living. It starts with a positive but truthful mind-set of placing our trust in God.

However, if following the devil continues to be our choice, the individual heart will remain in anguish because the spiritual connection to God has been broken. It is the consequence of choosing to remain blinded.

Only my loving spiritual Father deserves my honor and allegiance.

> [28] "Come to me all of you who are tired from the heavy burden you have been forced to carry. I will give you rest. [29] Accept my teaching. Learn from me. I am gentle and humble in spirit. And you will be able to get some rest. [30] Yes, the teaching that I ask you to accept is easy. The load I give you to carry is light."
>
> Matthew 11:28–30 (ERV)

Jesus is pleading with you—hear, listen, and obey. The choice is clearly left to each individual person. Please, make the right one!

Onward

to

Higher Ground

Chapter One

What Not to Believe

Remember the truth—Satan's goal is to make us captive in our thinking. Again, consider this warning:

> [8] See to it that no one takes you captive through hollow and deceptive philosophy, which depends on human tradition and the elemental spiritual forces of this world rather than on Christ.
>
> Colossians 2:8 (NIV)

Certainly, the advancement of deceptive philosophies presented by man is clearly the result of neglecting to learn and follow God's truth! Consequently, a close correlation between deceptive philosophies and rationalism clearly comes to light.

Remember, the definition of rationalism:

* "The principle or practice of accepting reason as the only authority in determining one's opinions or course of action."
* Pertaining to philosophy:
  The doctrine that knowledge comes wholly from pure reason without aid from the senses."
* Pertaining to theology:
  The doctrine that rejects revelation and the supernatural and makes reason the sole source for religious truth."

At the top of the list of what not to believe is, "Do not believe any false philosophies introduced through human rationalism." It is critically important that we learn to discern God's truth from Satan's lies.

The Bible is filled with multiple tools of *truth* exposing the various ways the devil is working in our world today. As our Bible knowledge increases, we will become more aware of how religious error springs forth as the result of spiritual blindness. Certainly the teaching we respond to, whether right or wrong, determines our spiritual, emotional, physical, and mental health throughout life.

One of the major religious errors promoted is that we are born with a sinful nature. Although it is taught, is it true? Certainly not!

Why? Believing that we are born with a sinful nature robs mankind of any hope for a better life. *It is definitely a form of negative thinking.* Only truth can lead us to a genuine hope for a brighter future. Therefore, let's press on with a more positive mind-set.

As the result of Adam turning away from God, the human mind may *assume* that his children were born with a sinful nature. The misapplication of this verse could result in believing a lie.

> ³ When Adam had lived one hundred and thirty years, he became the father of *a son* in his own likeness, according to his image, and named him Seth.
> Genesis 5:3 (NASB)

After closely examining these words, a better understanding based upon truth comes into view. When shared with others, the promotion of this false teaching can be stopped. Therefore, let's look closely into Scriptures to gain great insight.

Remember, we have already learned,

> ²⁶ Then God said, "Let us make mankind in our image, in our likeness."
> Genesis 1:26 (NIV)

Comparing the two thoughts, in whose image and likeness was all of mankind made? God's!

In whose likeness and image was Seth born? It was that of *one* man, his physical father. The two phrases "in his own" and "according to his" indicate singular possession.

Just as the words "own" and "his" indicate personal possession, "our" indicates plural possession. All people have been created as spiritual beings reflecting the purity and characteristics of our Heavenly Father, Jesus, and the Holy Spirit—all encompassed under one umbrella.

In fullness of thought, Seth was born *both* in the image and likeness of God—his Heavenly Father—and Adam, his physical father.

This is true of every person born since Cain, Adam and Eve's firstborn. Unlike God, all bear human flesh and, to some degree, reflect the physical appearance of their ancestors. At the same time, from a spiritual viewpoint, man bears the "image" and "likeness" of God in many ways.

Without this understanding, it would be easy to assume that because Adam had *become* a sinner, his children would be *born* with a sinful nature. Therefore, the erroneous conclusion would be that all babes to follow would be born similarly. This is definitely a *false assumption*—this teaching is not supported by God's Word!

Unknown are the number of parents who are mentally burdened with the thought that their deceased children are in eternal torment because they were not baptized before death. Believing the teaching of God's truth will bring you mental peace in this area of your life.

The following Bible story provides spiritual assurance that babies go to heaven when they die.

II Samuel chapters 11 and 12 relate the story of the adulterous relationship between David and Bathsheba. A child was conceived out of wedlock. This violation of God's teaching resulted in David experiencing severe consequences.

God said to David:

> [11] "This is what the LORD says: 'Out of your own household I am going to bring calamity on you.
> II Samuel 12:11 (NIV)

This came in many forms—one of which was the death of their infant son. Before his son's death, David refused to eat and spent nights lying on the ground. Despite the ongoing encouragement and support of others for him during his time of sorrow, he continually refused.

However, after the child's death, his attitude reversed. He got up, washed, put on lotions, changed his clothes, and went into the house of the Lord and worshipped. After worship, he ate food.

Why the change in behavior?

In David's own words,

> [22] He answered, "While the child was still alive, I fasted and wept. I thought, 'Who knows? The Lord may be gracious to me and let the child live.' [23] But now that he is dead, why

should I go on fasting? Can I bring him back again? I will go to him, but he will not return to me."
II Samuel 12:22–23 (NIV)

What truth is revealed here? David's confidence in his son's eternal salvation was expressed when he said, "I will go to him…" indicating that his son's soul had gone to heaven.

Like all newborns, at birth, David's son reflected the pure spiritual characteristics of God. He had not yet been taught to sin. Therefore, David's son could not have been born in the likeness of his *physical* parents—guilty of sin. Consequently, David was assured that the baby's eternal life would be spent in heaven.

Even though the child's salvation was assured, in light of his own sin, how could David be confident of his own salvation? He had developed a very close relationship with God. David knew God's fairness. He knew God would listen to his *repentant* prayer. It is recorded in Psalms 51.

God's attitude toward David reaffirms this truth:

[22] After removing Saul, he made David their king. God testified concerning him: 'I have found David son of Jesse, a man after my own heart; he will do everything I want him to do.'
Acts 13:22 (NIV)

Collectively this is ample evidence to help us understand the need to refocus our energies toward learning more about God and His love. It must begin by examining *my* life to discover how Satan is working within *me* through his countless schemes.

Years ago a minister asked the Sunday morning audience this question. Now it is being asked of you!

How long will it be before we become angry with Satan rather than God?

God is not to blame! It is very important to place the blame for the destruction of our mental peace and spiritual security in God where it belongs—on Satan.

Our personal battles within can be won through Christ alone! The power and strength to resist Satan can only be gained by allowing the Word that has been *planted* within us to grow. This, in turn, gives us great confidence as we claim ownership of the promises of God. As we do this, a deeper trust in God will become a reality.

As each individual person tries to absorb these beautiful truths, please allow them to bring *refreshment* to your aching heart—a ray of hope!

Onward,

to

Higher Ground

Chapter Two

Satan's Approach through Eve

Some might be inclined to think that Satan began his effort to sever man's spiritual relationship with God through Eve because of a weakness within her character. Rather than a negative view, simply consider the fact that he was using the close bond between husband and wife to his advantage. By using her powerful influence in Adam's life, the devil would be successful in destroying the Father and child relationship between God and Adam. Also weakened would be the emotional bond between the newlyweds.

Generally speaking, it is not man's nature to think about where various elements of life originate. However, if a better understanding of mankind is to be gained, there are times when this must be done. Let's begin by asking, "Where was the first seed of <u>doubt</u> planted?"

Obviously, for seeds to grow, soil is required. Eve's heart was the first soil chosen by Satan for planting. Even though she was created with a pure heart, Satan's first goal was to recondition the soil of her heart. By doing this, it would no longer be spiritually pure. How did he do it?

Read carefully—notice the devil's technique to develop an attitude of worldliness within her.

Eve told Satan:

> [16] And the Lord God commanded the man, "You are free to eat from any tree in the garden; [17] but you must not eat from the tree of the knowledge of good and evil, for when you eat from it you will certainly die."
>
> Genesis 2:16–17 (NIV)

Satan's response to her:

> [1] Now the serpent was more crafty than any of the wild animals the Lord God had made. He said to the woman, "Did God <u>really</u> say, 'You must not eat from any tree in the garden'?"
>
> Genesis 3:1 (NIV)

Placing these two verses together clearly demonstrates Satan's plan of attack. He is the first one to rewrite history by *tweaking* God's Word. Because the devil knows God's teachings, he knows how to cleverly *twist* them slightly in a way that is appealing to man, unnoticed by the spiritually untrained mind.

Planting doubt in Eve's mind through the use of the word "really" is a clear example of this truth.

Another example of him tweaking truth is seen when he made one slight change from God's Words ("the tree") to ("any tree"). Certainly this would add confusion to her thinking.

With doubt and confusion successfully planted in her mind, the door was thrown wide open for Eve to wonder if God could be trusted! With these three elements—doubt, confusion, and lack of trust—in place, the stage was set for Satan to move forward with his plan to destroy man's relationship with God.

Without complete trust in Him, it would be more difficult for Eve to believe what God said. Therefore, the devil, as a masquerader of truth, could manipulate her thinking into believing what he said. How did he do it? The comparison of these two verses explains:

> [2] The woman said to the serpent, "We may eat fruit from the trees in the garden, [3] but God did say, 'You must not eat fruit from the tree that is in the middle of the garden, and you must not touch it, or you will die.'"
>
> Genesis 3:2–3 (NIV)
>
> [4] "You will not certainly die," the serpent said to the woman. [5] "For God knows that when you eat from it your eyes

Satan's Approach through Eve

will be opened, and you will be like God, knowing good and evil."

Genesis 3:4–5 (NIV)

Another tweaking of truth is revealed here. Satan wanted Eve to *think* she would be like God. One of his major objectives was to lead her into believing she would have no need for Him in her life. After all, if she were like God, she would be able to think for herself, make her own decisions, and have a full life completely independent of Him. In other words, Satan was redirecting her to put more trust in herself than in God. What *she* wanted would become more important than what God wanted for her. As a result, selfishness would quickly take root deep within her heart.

Throughout the whole process, *Eve was completely blind to the fact that Satan had multiple goals. Two of them were to break her spiritual relationship with God and the tight marital bond she had with her husband, Adam.*

Satan was well aware of her lack of insight. Therefore, he quickly moved forward with his plan to separate *both* Adam and Eve from God. *He was delighted when she helped him to promote it.* She had blindly fallen into his trap!

> [6] When the woman saw that the fruit of the tree was good for food and pleasing to the eye, and also desirable for gaining wisdom, she took some and ate it.

<u>And Satan was *delighted* with her decision.</u>

> She also gave some to her husband, who was with her, and he ate it.
>
> Genesis 3:6 (NIV)

One of Satan's top priorities was to *use Eve* to turn Adam away from God. The devil wanted their relationship with God to be completely destroyed forever and always! By teaching them to disobey God, the same example would be passed on from generation to generation. His tactic remains the same today—work in the mind of one individual and then let his satanic influence be passed on to those around. Through the process, mankind's relationship with God will be destroyed—one person at a time.

Satan understood how quickly his plan would work. Therefore, it gave him tremendous motivation to plant seeds of doubt regarding God's love for man as quickly as possible. Why? When nurtured, doubt, lack of trust, and failure to believe God would quickly grow into many destructive characteristics within the minds of people. Anger, resentment, hate, and other disobedient attitudes are only a few of Satan's destructive tools that will throw open a wide door leading to a complete *faithlessness* in God. As a result of Satan's influence, this happens within a relatively short time.

This is *not* conjecture. A clear demonstration of this truth can be seen by recognizing the fact that Adam and Eve's son, Cain (the *third* person in the world), became a criminal. This certainly was not God's plan for Cain's life. However, as the result of learned behavior from his parents, this once spiritually pure child developed attitudes of resentment and rebellion as he grew into adulthood. Because he did not choose to use self-control, it resulted in the murder of his brother, Abel.

It is so very important that this discussion be left on a positive note. Therefore, a small tidbit of Abraham's life is being shared to help us understand the power within a strong faith and belief in God. Regardless of Abraham and Sarah's ages and how wild God's promise seemed to be, He made a promise to them that they would become parents of their very own son.

Nevertheless, Scripture teaches, Abraham *never* lost hope.

> [18] There was no hope that Abraham would have children, but Abraham believed God and continued to hope. And that is why he became the father of many nations. As God told him, "You will have many descendants." [19] Abraham was almost a hundred years old, so he was past the age for having children. Also, Sarah could not have children. Abraham was well aware of this, but his faith in God never became weak. [20] He never doubted that God would do what he promised. He never stopped believing. In fact, he grew stronger in his faith and just praised God. [21] Abraham felt sure that God was able to do what he promised. [22] So that's why "he was accepted as one who is right with God."

²³ These words ("he was accepted") were written not only for Abraham. ²⁴ They were also written for us. God will also accept us because we believe. We believe in the one who raised Jesus our Lord from death. ²⁵ Jesus was handed over to die for our sins, and he was raised from death to make us right with God.

Romans 4:18–25 (ERV)

Like Abraham, we can put our trust in God. Our Father will be just as faithful in keeping His promises to us as He was with Abraham. We must simply do our part by believing and trusting Him. There must be hand-in-hand cooperation between God and man. Without developing this bond, *Same Page Thinking with God will never become a reality.* We must simply continue to follow Him.

⁷ So it is just as the Holy Spirit says:
"If you hear God's voice today,
⁸ don't be stubborn as you were in the past,
when you turned against God.
  That was the day you tested God in the desert.
⁹ For 40 years in the desert, your people saw what I did.
  But they tested me and my patience.
¹⁰ So I was angry with them.
I said, 'Their thoughts are always wrong.
They have never understood my ways.'
¹¹ So I was angry and made a promise:
'They will never enter my place of rest.'"
¹² So, brothers and sisters, be careful that none of you has the evil thoughts that cause so much doubt that you stop following the living God. ¹³ But encourage each other every day, while you still have something called "today."

Help each other so that none of you will be fooled by sin and become too hard to change. [14] We have the honor of sharing in all that Christ has if we continue until the end to have the sure faith we had in the beginning. [15] That's why the Spirit said,
"If you hear God's voice today,
don't be stubborn as in the past
when you turned against God."

Hebrews 3:7–15 (ERV)

Through His graciousness we have been given the power of choice. The choice given is to put forth the effort to learn and obey His will or continue to be blinded by the devil. There is no other.

The choice is ours. What will yours be?

Onward

to

Higher Ground

Section Five

The Great Physician's Prescription

Prelude

Have you ever given thought to going to your primary care doctor asking him how to build a meaningful life? The only symptoms you could offer include, "My heart is hurting, my heart feels pain," "I have a feeling of emptiness deep within," or "My life is filled with worry." He may lead you into believing that a prescription for chemical drugs or a change in diet will lead to healing. Because of your lack of knowledge, you may believe him. However, after following all of the counsel given, the emptiness remains. It simply will not go away. Through the whole process you come to realize that believing he could help you regain your health was being more than naive. It is beyond his ability because his medical training did not include the development of the skills needed.

You realize it is time to change doctors. It is very important that you find a doctor that will be totally honest rather than mislead you. Equally important is locating one who has the skills and knowledge base to give an accurate diagnosis.

Chapter One

Choosing the Right Doctor

To build a meaningful life, spiritual guidance is absolutely necessary. A spiritually minded doctor must be consulted. God wants you to know how important you are to Him. He is the only One qualified to prescribe the right medicine needed to completely heal you at all levels—spiritual, emotional, physical, and mental. He is absolutely delighted that you have turned to Him for counsel, guidance, and healing. He speaks only truth.

Your contribution to His healing plan must be *positive thinking* and the realization that you cannot recover without His help. Anything short of this will prevent healing.

To begin, God refers you to His Son, Jesus, to guide you. He gives you a special invitation:

²⁸ "Come to me, all you who are weary and burdened, and I will give you rest."

Matthew 11:28 (NIV)

It is important to understand who Jesus is. He was God in flesh form sent to earth to show man how to live in a manner pleasing to our Heavenly Father. Without following Jesus, it will be impossible for you to find your own way through life. His instructions are clear. You will not become confused. He will help you gain understanding along the way.

Does all of this sound too good to be true? Through Jesus, all things are possible. Listening to God's reference to His Son, Jesus, will help us to learn more about Him.

¹ And a voice came from heaven: "You are my Son, whom I love; with you I am well pleased."

Mark 1:1 (NIV)

Jesus said:

¹² "I am the light of the world. Whoever follows me will never walk in darkness but will have the light of life."

John 8:12 (NIV)

⁶ "I am the way and the truth and the life. No one comes to the Father except through me.
> John 14:6 (NIV)

With these credentials before us, everyone can be absolutely certain that God, through Jesus Christ, is capable of leading us to complete spiritual healing.

Onward
to
Higher
Ground

Chapter Two

How to Build a Meaningful Life

Not only is it important that you *listen* to Him but *accept* His guidance. Therefore, it is time to take these steps.

Step One
TRUST IS A MUST!

If one is to have each day's needs,
trust in One outside of self is a must.

If one is to have peace of mind,
trust in One outside of self is a must.

If one is to enjoy life to the fullest,
trust in One outside of self is a must.

But, oh, where to find such a valuable thing?
It certainly does not come with gold and diamond rings!

It can only come from one true source.
That is God, of course.

Oh, don't turn your back on that thought.
Doing so only causes you to become more and more distraught.
Worry and anger you don't need in your life.
Peace and quiet you desire will remove lots of strife.
So please, my friend,
Put more effort into trusting God because

TRUST IS A MUST!

Without trust in God, misery results
At a very high cost—turmoil, frustration, and life without joy.

He is patiently waiting as you learn

TRUST IN GOD IS A MUST!

So begin today—reach for Him, without any more fuss.

STEP TWO
Recognize My Value in the Sight of God

ME
Who am I?
Have you ever really thought about it?
Yes, and His answers should set us aglow!
God's Word gives us reasons to feel this way.
…I am a creation of God;
…I have been made in His image;
…I have been made in His likeness.
The Bible tells me so!

Though, in man's terms, I may be considered "nothing,"
God wants me to both "know" and "feel" this is not true.
There is absolutely nothing good He will not do for me.

Not that I should have a big head,
Going around boasting day and night,
But He wants me, His creation, to have the confidence,
"You are worth My fight."

At birth, He looked at me and said,
"This creation of mine is VERY GOOD."
Many of my traits are within every person

—each one represents love!
Oh, the risk of putting my child into the world
—this beautiful one, My Creation, could become wild!
Is it any wonder the Bible tells us
God is a "jealous" God?

Wouldn't you be jealous too, if another tried to steal your child
away from you for selfish reasons of their own?
Just as any good parent works to protect his child,
God has my long-term, eternal protection in mind
each and every day in a much greater way.

From the very beginning,
He planted seeds within me for reasons of survival
—Hunger, need for love, need for Him, need for protection—
Just to name a few.
So you see it is very important that I cooperate with Him.
It is not His fight--it is our fight.
I cannot do it without Him--nor will He do it alone.
How badly does God want to protect me
from the wilderness of life—and hell?
With a loving smile, He says,
"My Son, Jesus Christ, died for you.
Please, take My hand, My child, and let Me lead you home."

Why all this interest in "little ol' me"?
God's answer:

[10] for every animal of the forest is mine,
and the cattle on a thousand hills.
[11] I know every bird in the mountains,
and the insects in the fields are mine.
[12] If I were hungry I would not tell you,
for the world is mine, and all that is in it.

Psalms 50:10–12 (NIV)

Because God owns me,
He is very concerned about my well-being here on earth.
Therefore, He wants me to take Jesus' hand
so He can lead me home to be with Him throughout eternity.
WOW!

With God's deep interest in my personal well-being,
He is more than willing to *listen* while I describe my symptoms.

He wants to know why I have come to see Him. He cannot help me if I do not give truthful answers. If I am honest, doing this will lead to sharing some deep pains buried within.

Nonetheless, it is critically important to take the next step.

STEP THREE
Admit the Truth
MY HEART IS HURTING, MY HEART FEELS PAIN

Oh, how true these statements are.

Something I do not want to admit.

Nonetheless, the pain hurts—it makes me blue.

True, true, yes, it is true.

But I certainly don't know what to do!

For whatever reason, I do not know if I even believe in God.

Or, if I do, I've stomped on Him, denied Him through my life.

Now it is a mix of turmoil, stress, and strife!

Lord, even if I don't believe in or trust You,

can You—will You—provide relief?

Lord, even though I've denied you all this time,

can I still come to You.

Will you accept me?"

His answer is very straightforward.

"If you do not believe in Me, I will not help you.

If you do not trust me, I cannot help you.

On the other hand, *if* you change your thinking,

I will be delighted to help you."

"How can this be done?" I ask.

"You must accept My diagnosis as the cause of your illness.
You must accept Me as Final Authority.
Also, without following My directions,
you will *never* recover from the deep pain within.
The cause of the 'emptiness' within you
is your separation from me.
The sin in your life is the cause of the separation.
If it is not removed, it will continue to eat away
at the core of your inner being—your spiritual soul.
Applying the spiritual medicine prescribed in the Bible
is the only way you will recover.
In the same way your physical body needs physical food
your soul must be nourished with spiritual food."

The Great Physician warns me:
"There is an urgency involved if you want to live.
Your diet must change immediately.
If this is not done, your condition will worsen through time.
You will never have peace of mind.
Therefore, you must make a personal choice—

follow My counsel or ignore it?
The choice is yours.
It is the most important one you will ever make.
If you choose to follow me,
I promise that I will walk with you throughout your lifetime."

To understand the impact spiritual allergies have on our lives, a comparison must be made between the meanings of allergy and energy, this knowledge will be gained.

Read carefully. The origination of both words is given to reveal a powerful truth.

* First, *allergy*:

  a hypersensitivity to a specific substance or condition.

  (1) a strong aversion.[1]

* Secondly, *energy*:

  (1) force of expression or utterance

  (2) potential forces; inherent power; capacity for vigorous action

  (3) strength or power efficiently exerted.[2]

Are you surprised to see the similarity between the definitions of these two words?

* Because *aversion* is part of the definition of allergy, it is important that we closely examine its meaning also.
  1. an intense or definite dislike, antipathy; repugnance
  2. the object arousing such dislike
  3. the act of turning away

  SYN.

  aversion and antipathy both imply an ingrained feeling against that which is disagreeable or offensive, aversion stressing avoidance or rejection, antipathy, active hostility;
  repugnance emphasizes the emotional resistance or opposition one offers to that which is incompatible with one's ideas, tastes, etc.;
  loathing suggests a feeling of extreme disgust or intolerance;
  revulsion suggests a drawing back or away from in disgust, horror, etc.;
  abhorrence implies a feeling of extreme aversion or repugnance.[3]

In my ignorance, I respond by saying,

"I have no idea of what you are talking about. I grew up in a home where there was no spiritual training. Would you please explain to me what sin is? Why do You hate it?"

The Great Physician (God) answered by revealing some of His personality traits.

* Does God have a hypersensitivity to sin?

    YES

* Does He have an intense or definite dislike, active hostility, or ingrained feeling against it?

    YES

* Is it disagreeable or offensive to Him?

    YES

* Does He have an extreme disgust or intolerance for it?

    YES

* Does He Himself turn away from it?

    YES

* Does He draw back away from it in disgust and horror?

    YES

* Does He emotionally resist or oppose sin because it is incompatible with His principles of integrity?

    YES

* Does He have an aversion against Satan, the one arousing sin within mankind?

    YES

* Does He stress to mankind the importance of rejecting or avoiding Satan and sin?

    YES

* Does He understand Satan has the capacity for using sin as a vigorous action against man?

    YES

* Through the Bible, does God explain to those He created that Satan will apply all of his energies to pull us away from Him?

    YES

* Does He understand Satan will efficiently exert his strength against mankind?

    YES

Notice, the answer to all twelve questions is YES. Obviously, sin, as it is described here, not only distorts but destroys the "image" and "likeness" of God reflected within us at birth.

When the combined effects of energy, allergy and aversion are considered from a spiritual viewpoint, the stage is set for a huge explosion of sin within man's soul.

⁂

*The Great Physician goes on to explain
that the development of sin within human life*

is very deceptive and misleading.
Too often, an abortion, a divorce, and addictions
are thought to be an everyday part of life.
Nonetheless, regardless of the opinions of men,
they are considered to be sin in My sight.
I cannot be in the presence of sin;
therefore, the spiritually pure relationship
man once had with Me has been broken.
Rather than facing the reality of sin being in your life,
you have chosen not to accept this truth.
Thus, you are experiencing the feeling of emptiness within your soul.
This is caused by spiritual starvation.
You have not been providing your soul
with the nourishment it needs for survival.

※

With these thoughts in mind, I asked,
"Doctor, would you please be kind enough to share
with me those things that You consider to be sins?
What is creeping into my life that I must guard against?
I want to be healed."

※

My Great Physician answered,
"The list is long.
Reading my Word will teach you many things.
Not only will it teach you
how to live a meaningful life pleasing to Me,
it will teach you the difference
between heaven where I live
and
hell where the disobedient will live with Satan
throughout eternity."

I asked,
"How can I be certain I will live in heaven
throughout eternity?"

My new, all-knowing, truth-telling Great Physician
gave me the prescription for spiritual healing:
*"Submit to my teachings, allow Me to lead you
—stop telling Me what you are going to do.*
When and if you decide to do this,
your life will be blessed—by Me, through Jesus.
This is My desire *for* you;
however, the choice remains with you.

Life in Me will not be problem or pain-free.
Nonetheless, Jesus will guide you along the only path
that will bring you to heaven
where you can live in peace throughout eternity!
A better offer does not exist.
Just remember,
for these promises to be yours,
you must stop being a "scoffer"
and
accept My offer.
Your life must follow My plan—not any plan defined by man!"

If heaven is to be my eternal home, I must be willing to pay the price by submitting to a lifestyle in keeping with my Father's teaching. As always, God leaves the choice up to each individual person. Be wise. Please don't allow Satan to separate you from God for eternity.

Onward
to
Higher Ground

References

(1) *Webster's* 1982, op cit., p. 36

(2) Ibid., p. 463

(3) Ibid., p. 96

Section Six

The Rampant Growth of Sin

Prelude

Although walking in a dense forest without a guide may appear to be fun, it is not wise. Nonetheless, some choose to do it.

The independent, adventure-seeking hiker decides to embark upon a journey that he hopes will reveal beauty yet unseen in his lifetime.

As evening falls, darkness sets in. There is a chill in the air. This individual decides to build a fire to provide light, heat and comfort. It was built to fulfill an immediate need. It was meant for good.

While by the fire, it is not long before fatigue overtakes him and sleep set in.

Soon he is awakened by excessive heat because the fire has gotten out of control. He soon realizes his vision is blurred because of the smoke.

All of a sudden he hears a loud explosion. The fire had come in contact with an unseen gasoline storage tank. Needless to say, the fire quickly spread and became out of control. Now the hiker's anticipation of excitement has developed into one of great fear because he realizes he is trapped.

Death is just around the corner. All joy is gone. Death is imminent. He has no way of escape. Not only does he *want* help, he needs it.

Now let's build an analogy to be applied to our personal lives:

* Some are in search of memorable, fun-filled adventure while living in this world.
* After months and years of seeking this lifestyle, cold, loneliness and the loss of adventure have set in. Although some beauty has been seen, it is now realized that what we thought would be exciting and fulfilling was not. Physical, mental, and emotional fatigue have become evident.
* We now realize that our vision has been clouded for many years. As a result, we feel trapped within because we do not see a way of escape. We have failed to understand our deep need for spiritual fulfillment. Though physically alive, we are spiritually dead.
* From our perspective, we feel doomed with no hope for recovery--death is just around the corner.

Yes, as the result of Satan's influence in our lives, life gets out of control.

Prelude

This section will help us understand what God considers to be sin. With these points of identification, He has provided us with the information that will guide us away from being trapped by spiritual explosions in the dark forest of sin.

Chapter One

It Exploded like Wildfire

Based upon what we see in our world today, little thought has been given to the rapid growth of sin. There are several reasons for this. The root cause of sin is not asking God for His guidance. Therefore, independent thinking prevails. Consequently, we do not understand what sin is in the sight of God. Ultimately, we do nothing to stop its growth; thus, it rages out of control.

These truths are illustrated throughout Scripture. The first one:

> [3] In the course of time Cain brought some of the fruits of the soil as an offering to the Lord.
> Genesis 4:3 (NIV)

> ⁴ And Abel also brought an offering—fat portions from some of the firstborn of his flock. The LORD looked with favor on Abel and his offering,
>
> Genesis 4:4 (NIV)

Obviously, Cain did not have the same generous attitude of heart. His offering consisted only of what *he* chose to give. Consequently, God was displeased.

- * Cain did not ask for guidance; he acted on his own.
- * God's desire was not part of Cain's thought process.
- * Cain chose to be angry.
- * God tried to counsel him by saying:

> ⁷ If you do well, will not *your countenance* be lifted up? And if you do not do well, sin is crouching at the door; and its desire is for you, but you must master it."
>
> Genesis 4:7 (NASB)

Despite the love God extended to him,

- * Cain ignored His guidance.
- * He refused God's chastisement;
- * He became angry;
- * Jealousy developed;

The Rampant Growth of Sin

* Resentment set in;
* Hatred grew--
* Cain became a murderer—he killed Abel!

Consequences suffered by Cain:

> [13] Cain said to the Lord, "My punishment is more than I can bear. [14] Today you are driving me from the land, and I will be hidden from your presence; I will be a restless wanderer on the earth, and whoever finds me will kill me."
>
> Genesis 4:13-14 (NIV)

In other words, Cain wanted God's blessings without submitting to His will. However, God let him know, "It doesn't work that way."

The information revealed within the following three verses helps us to calculate how long people sinned before they began to turn back to God—

* Adam was 130 years old when Seth was born
Genesis 5:3 (NIV)

* Then, when Seth was 105, his son, Enosh, was born
Genesis 5:6 (NIV)

* At that time people began to call on the name of the Lord."
Genesis 4:26 (NIV)

Based upon this information a total of 235 years had passed before people began to turn back to God.

Despite the fact that *some* people began to turn to God, *eight generations after Adam*, sin continued to advance through Cain's great, great, great, great grandson, Lamech.

* He married two wives; as a result, he was guilty of polygamy
* He also was guilty of killing another human

Genesis 4:23 (NIV)

Scriptures indicate a definite contrast in character between Lamech, the father, and his son, Noah.

How was Noah different?

> [9] This is the history of Noah's family. He was a good man all his life, and he always followed God.
>
> Genesis 6:9 (ERV)

How did God respond to the explosion of sin throughout mankind?

> [5] The LORD saw that the people on the earth were very evil. He saw that they thought only about evil things all the time. [6] The LORD was sorry that he had made people on the earth. It made him very sad in his heart. [7] So the LORD said, "I will destroy all the people I created on the earth. I will destroy every person and every animal and everything that

crawls on the earth. And I will destroy all the birds in the air, because I am sorry that I have made them."
Genesis 6:5–7 (ERV)

After reading these verses, there can be no doubt how angry God became as the result of most men not reaching out to Him and accepting His leadership.

Why were Noah and his family saved?

[22] Noah did everything just as God commanded him.
Genesis 6:22 (NIV)

Therefore, Noah was chosen to build the ark. Why?

This would provide protection from destruction by the forthcoming flood for him, his family, and a pair of each of the animals God had created.

[20] In it only a few people, eight in all, were saved through water.
I Peter 3:20b (NIV)

Think about it! Out of the thousands, if not millions living at that time, only eight people were saved from destruction!

Genesis chapters 7 and 8 explain that after the ark was completed and Noah's family--along with all the chosen animals--were safe inside, rain fell for forty days and nights. Everything on the earth was destroyed and then renewed.

Both the Old and New Testaments provide great insight regarding some of the reasons sin has continuously advanced so quickly throughout time—descriptive of society since the beginning.

First, it is important to remember

> [15] You were blameless in your ways
> from the day you were created
> till wickedness was found in you.
>
> Ezekiel 28:15 (NIV)

༺ঊ༻

> [12] Because of the increase of wickedness, the love of most will grow cold.
>
> Matthew 24:12 (NIV)

What causes mankind to be filled with violence? What causes the human heart to grow cold? Sin! Without knowing how to identify sin, we will be blindly led into everlasting darkness—hell.

Therefore, it is one of our Great Physician's top priorities to warn us regarding those things that will result in spiritual death—what will break my relationship with Him, what He considers to be sin.

Yes, it would be nice if every person living could say, "I have no sin in my life." We can only dream of how our world would be today if that were true. How different it would be! But it is not.

Therefore, if we truly want to be pleasing in God's sight, it is *critically* important that we understand how He defines sin. It is quite possible that we accept some of these characteristics within our lives without realizing their presence breaks His heart and separates us from our Creator.

Defining Sin through the Eyes of God

The following Scriptures clearly identify what God says is sin in His sight. They are not presented for the purpose of making anyone angry. Rather, it is meant to help us understand what will separate us from our Creator throughout eternity.

These words were spoken to the Israelites, God's chosen people. If they were to be pleasing in His sight, they were commanded to follow His instructions.

> [2] "I am the Lord your God. I am the one who freed you from the land of Egypt, where you were slaves.
> [3] "You must not worship any other gods except me.
> [4] "You must not make any idols. Don't make any statues or pictures of anything up in the sky or of anything on the earth or of anything down in the water. [5] Don't worship or

serve idols of any kind, because I, the Lord, am your God. I hate my people worshiping other gods. People who sin against me become my enemies, and I will punish them. And I will punish their children, their grandchildren, and even their great-grandchildren. ⁶ But I will be very kind to people who love me and obey my commands. I will be kind to their families for thousands of generations.
⁷ "You must not use the name of the Lord your God to make empty promises. If you do, the Lord will not let you go unpunished.

Exodus 20:2-7 (ERV)

⁂

¹⁸ "You must not allow any woman to do evil magic. If she does magic, you must not let her live.
¹⁹ "You must not allow anyone to have sexual relations with an animal. If this happens, that person must be killed.
²⁰ "Whoever makes a sacrifice to a false god should be destroyed. The Lord is the only one you should make sacrifices to.
²¹ "Remember, in the past you were foreigners in the land of Egypt. So you should not cheat or hurt anyone who is a foreigner in your land.
²² "You must never do anything bad to women whose husbands are dead or to orphans. ²³ If you do anything wrong to these widows or orphans, I will know it. I will hear about their suffering. ²⁴ And I will be very angry. I will kill you with a sword. Then your wives will become widows, and your children will become orphans.

Exodus 22:18-24 (ERV)

¹ "You might be called as a witness and take an oath to tell the truth. If you saw something or knew something but did not tell it, you are guilty of doing wrong and must bear the responsibility for your guilt.
                              Leviticus 5:1 (ERV)

༄

²⁶ "You must not eat any meat with blood still in it.
                              Leviticus 19:26 (ERV)

༄

²² You shall not set up for yourself a *sacred* pillar which the LORD your God hates.
                              Deuteronomy 16:22 (NASB)

༄

¹⁰ Don't sacrifice your sons or daughters in the fires on your altars. Don't try to learn what will happen in the future by talking to a fortuneteller or by going to a magician, a witch, or a sorcerer. ¹¹ Don't let anyone try to put magic spells on other people. Don't let any of your people become a medium or a wizard. And no one should try to talk with someone who has died. ¹² The LORD hates anyone who does these things. And because these other nations do these terrible things, the LORD your God will force them

out of the land as you enter it. ¹³ You must be faithful to the Lord your God, never doing anything he considers wrong.

Deuteronomy 18:10-13 (ERV)

---

²³ And as for me, I would never stop praying for you. If I stopped praying for you, I would be sinning against the Lord. I will continue to teach you the right way to live a good life.

I Samuel 12:23 (ERV)

---

²³ Refusing to obey is as bad as the sin of sorcery. Being stubborn and doing what you want is like the sin of worshiping idols.

I Samuel 15:23 (ERV)

<u>Words spoken by Solomon:</u>

¹⁶ The Lord hates these seven things:
¹⁷ eyes that show pride,
    tongues that tell lies,
    hands that kill innocent people,
¹⁸ hearts that plan evil things to do,
    feet that run to do evil,
¹⁹ witnesses in court who tell lies,

and anyone who causes family members to fight.
Proverbs 6:16-19 (ERV)

◦◦◦

¹ Wine and beer make people lose control; they get loud and stumble around. And that is foolish.
Proverbs 20:1 (ERV)

◦◦◦

⁹ Leaders of Jacob and rulers of Israel, listen to me!
   You hate the right way of living!
If something is straight,
   then you make it crooked!
¹⁰ You build Zion by murdering people.
   You build Jerusalem by cheating people!
¹¹ The judges in Jerusalem accept bribes
   to help them decide who wins in court.
The priests in Jerusalem must be paid
   before they will teach the people.
People must pay the prophets
   before they will look into the future.
Then those leaders expect the Lord to help them.
   They say, "The Lord lives here with us,
   so nothing bad will happen to us."
¹² Leaders, because of you, Zion will be destroyed.
   It will become a plowed field.
Jerusalem will become a pile of rocks.
   Temple Mount will be an empty hill overgrown with bushes.
Micah 3:9-12 (ERV)

Words spoken by Jesus:

³¹ "So I tell you, people can be forgiven for every sinful thing they do and for every bad thing they say against God. But anyone who speaks against the Holy Spirit will not be forgiven. ³² You can even speak against the Son of Man and be forgiven. But anyone who speaks against the Holy Spirit will never be forgiven—not now or in the future.
Matthew 12:31-32 (ERV)

※

¹ About that time the followers came to Jesus and asked, "Who is the greatest in God's kingdom?"
² Jesus called a little child to come to him. He stood the child in front of the followers. ³ Then he said, "The truth is, you must change your thinking and become like little children. If you don't do this, you will never enter God's kingdom. ⁴ The greatest person in God's kingdom is the one who makes himself humble like this child.
⁵ "Whoever accepts a little child like this in my name is accepting me.
Jesus Warns About Causes of Sin
⁶ "If one of these little children believes in me, and someone causes that child to sin, it will be very bad for that person. It would be better for them to have a millstone tied around their neck and be drowned in the deep sea.
⁷ I feel sorry for the people in the world because of the things that make people sin. These things must happen, but it will be very bad for anyone who causes them to happen.
Matthew 18:1–7 (ERV)

The Rampant Growth of Sin

²⁰ And Jesus said, "The things that make people wrong are the things that come from the inside. ²¹ All these bad things begin inside a person, in the mind: bad thoughts, sexual sins, stealing, murder, ²² adultery, greed, doing bad things to people, lying, doing things that are morally wrong, jealousy, insulting people, proud talking, and foolish living. ²³ These evil things come from inside a person. And these are the things that make people unacceptable to God."

Mark 7:20-23 (ERV)

<u>Words written to Christians by various writers:</u>

¹⁸ God shows his anger from heaven against all the evil and wrong things that people do. Their evil lives hide the truth they have. ¹⁹ This makes God angry because they have been shown what he is like. Yes, God has made it clear to them. ²⁰ There are things about God that people cannot see—his eternal power and all that makes him God. But since the beginning of the world, those things have been easy for people to understand. They are made clear in what God has made. So people have no excuse for the evil they do. ²¹ People knew God, but they did not honor him as God, and they did not thank him. Their ideas were all useless. There was not one good thought left in their foolish minds. ²² They said they were wise, but they became fools. ²³ Instead of honoring the divine greatness of God, who lives forever, they traded it for the worship of idols—things made to look like humans, who get sick and die, or like birds, animals, and snakes.

[24] People wanted only to do evil. So God left them and let them go their sinful way. And so they became completely immoral and used their bodies in shameful ways with each other. [25] They traded the truth of God for a lie. They bowed down and worshiped the things God made instead of worshiping the God who made those things. He is the one who should be praised forever. Amen.

[26] Because people did those things, God left them and let them do the shameful things they wanted to do. Women stopped having natural sex with men and started having sex with other women. [27] In the same way, men stopped having natural sex with women and began wanting each other all the time. Men did shameful things with other men, and in their bodies they received the punishment for those wrongs.

[28] People did not think it was important to have a true knowledge of God. So God left them and allowed them to have their own worthless thinking. And so they do what they should not do. [29] They are filled with every kind of sin, evil, greed, and hatred. They are full of jealousy, murder, fighting, lying, and thinking the worst things about each other. They gossip [30] and say evil things about each other. They hate God. They are rude, proud, and brag about themselves. They invent ways of doing evil. They don't obey their parents, [31] they are foolish, they don't keep their promises, and they show no kindness or mercy to others. [32] They know God's law says that anyone who lives like that should die. But they not only continue to do these things themselves, but they also encourage others who do them.

Romans 1:18–32 (ERV)

The Rampant Growth of Sin

¹⁰ As the Scriptures say,
"There is no one doing what is right,
  not even one.
¹¹ There is no one who understands.
   There is no one who is trying to be with God.
¹² They have all turned away from him,
  and now they are of no use to anyone.
There is no one who does good,
  not even one."
¹³ "Their words come from mouths that are like open graves.
   They use their lying tongues to deceive others."
"Their words are like the poison of snakes."
¹⁴ "Their mouths are full of cursing and angry words."
¹⁵ "They are always ready to kill someone.
¹⁶ Everywhere they go they cause trouble and ruin.
¹⁷ They don't know how to live in peace."
¹⁸ "They have no fear or respect for God."

Romans 3:10-18 (ERV)

---

¹ I want you to know what happened to our ancestors who were with Moses. They were all under the cloud, and they all walked through the sea. ² They were all baptized into Moses in the cloud and in the sea. ³ They all ate the same spiritual food, ⁴ and they all drank the same spiritual drink. They drank from that spiritual rock that was with them, and that rock was Christ. ⁵ But God was not pleased with most of those people, so they were killed in the desert.
⁶ And these things that happened are examples for us. These examples should stop us from wanting evil things like those people did. ⁷ Don't worship idols as some of them did. As the Scriptures say, "The people sat down to

eat and drink and then got up to have a wild party." ⁸ We should not commit sexual sins as some of them did. In one day 23,000 of them died because of their sin. ⁹ We should not test Christ as some of them did. Because of that, they were killed by snakes. ¹⁰ And don't complain as some of them did. Because they complained, they were killed by the angel that destroys.

I Corinthians 10:1–10 (ERV)

⁓⊙⊝⁓

¹⁹ The wrong things the sinful self does are clear: committing sexual sin, being morally bad, doing all kinds of shameful things, ²⁰ worshiping false gods, taking part in witchcraft, hating people, causing trouble, being jealous, angry or selfish, causing people to argue and divide into separate groups, ²¹ being filled with envy, getting drunk, having wild parties, and doing other things like this. I warn you now as I warned you before: The people who do these things will not have a part in God's kingdom.

Galatians 5:19–21 (ERV)

⁓⊙⊝⁓

¹⁷ I have something from the Lord to tell you. I warn you: Don't continue living like those who don't believe. Their thoughts are worth nothing. ¹⁸ They have no understanding, and they know nothing because they refuse to listen. So they cannot have the life that God gives. ¹⁹ They have lost their feeling of shame and use their lives to do what is

morally wrong. More and more they want to do all kinds of evil. [20] But that way of life is nothing like what you learned when you came to know Christ. [21] I know that you heard about him, and in him you were taught the truth. Yes, the truth is in Jesus. [22] You were taught to leave your old self. This means that you must stop living the evil way you lived before. That old self gets worse and worse, because people are fooled by the evil they want to do. [23] You must be made new in your hearts and in your thinking. [24] Be that new person who was made to be like God, truly good and pleasing to him.
[25] So you must stop telling lies. "You must always speak the truth to each other," because we all belong to each other in the same body. [26] "When you are angry, don't let that anger make you sin," and don't stay angry all day. [27] Don't give the devil a way to defeat you. [28] Whoever has been stealing must stop it and start working. They must use their hands for doing something good. Then they will have something to share with those who are poor.

Ephesians 4:17–28 (ERV)

[4] Also, there must be no evil talk among you. Don't say things that are foolish or filthy. These are not for you. But you should be giving thanks to God.

Ephesians 5:4 (ERV)

¹ Remember this: There are some terrible times coming in the last days. ² People will love only themselves and money. They will be proud and boast about themselves. They will abuse others with insults. They will not obey their parents. They will be ungrateful and against all that is pleasing to God. ³ They will have no love for others and will refuse to forgive anyone. They will talk about others to hurt them and will have no self-control. They will be cruel and hate what is good. ⁴ People will turn against their friends. They will do foolish things without thinking and will be so proud of themselves. Instead of loving God, they will love pleasure. ⁵ They will go on pretending to be devoted to God, but they will refuse to let that "devotion" change the way they live. Stay away from these people!

II Timothy 3:1-5 (ERV)

²⁵ We must not quit meeting together, as some are doing. No, we need to keep on encouraging each other. This becomes more and more important as you see the Day getting closer.

Hebrews 10:25 (ERV)

¹ So then, stop doing anything to hurt others. Don't lie anymore, and stop trying to fool people. Don't be jealous or say bad things about others. ² Like newborn babies hungry for milk, you should want the pure teaching that feeds your

spirit. With it you can grow up and be saved. ³ You have already tasted the goodness of the Lord.

I Peter 2:1–3 (ERV)

The Scriptures above illustrate only a small demonstration of this truth:

²⁹ This only have I found:
 God created mankind upright,
 but they have gone in search of many schemes."

Ecclesiastes 7:29 (NIV)

Like allergies, the development of sin within our lives through the schemes of Satan is very deceptive, misleading, and never-ending. It is a camouflage covering up the trap he has cleverly set for us. The cause of all sin pours forth from his heart of evil. He knows his multiple tools of destruction have the power to destroy us spiritually. Not all of them are known to man. He will use whatever will be most effective in destroying an individual's relationship with God.

There are basically two ways a child can be trained. God's directive is:

⁶ Start children off on the way they should go,
 and even when they are old they will not turn from it.

Proverbs 22:6 (NIV)

There are Christian mothers who begin this training by reading the Bible or Bible stories to the unborn child. Certainly doing this gives the child a head start in his or her spiritual training.

Remember the strong warning Jesus gives regarding how we are to train children:

> [6] "If anyone causes one of these little ones—those who believe in me—to stumble, it would be better for them to have a large millstone hung around their neck and to be drowned in the depths of the sea.
>
> Matthew 18:6 (NIV)

Have you ever seen a millstone? My opportunity came while visiting Windmill Island Gardens in Holland, Michigan. It is home to the 251-year-old windmill De Zwaan[1] which was actually transported from the country of Holland and reconstructed in Holland, Michigan.

Tours are offered during which time pictures can be taken. This one is of an actual *large millstone*. Immediately, my thoughts went back to Matthew 18. It is a clear visual aid used by Jesus to clearly impress upon our minds *the degree of anger He feels toward those who teach people—young or old—to sin*. Keeping it in the forefront of our thinking will help us to be more aware of every word, action, and thought we share with people whom we come in daily contact.

As a result of Satan's never-ending efforts to destroy humanity, most people remain emotionally devastated as the result of not *living* in the *light of Jesus* but merely *existing* in the darkness of sin.

This truth places great emphasis upon the importance of fighting back and not allowing the devil to win! We do not want to fall into God's condemnation as the result of being unaware of the devil's work.

The only way we can fight the battle against Satan is to identify the sins within each of us and then allow Jesus to help us overcome them. The Apostle John left these words of encouragement for us:

> [8] If we say that we have no sin, we are fooling ourselves, and the truth is not in us. [9] But if we confess our sins, God will forgive us. We can trust God to do this. He always does what is right. He will make us clean from all the wrong things we have done. [10] If we say that we have not sinned, we are saying that God is a liar and that we don't accept his true teaching.
>
> I John 1:8–10 (ERV)

Yes, God has a plan whereby He will make us clean through Jesus Christ. If we are to gain spiritual peace of mind while living on earth, we must actively engage in God's war against Satan by following Christ!.

Therefore, it is important that we allow the Great Physician to heal us from our spiritual allergies. Are you ready? The power of choice lies within each of us. What do you choose?

Do you feel too weak to change paths?

Please continue to be assured Jesus will guide. He will provide everything needed to achieve the goal.

To experience success, learn His ways, and follow Him. We will grow together.

Onward

to

Higher Ground

References

[1] Permission granted for use of picture by City of Holland, Michigan

Chapter Two

Spiritual Killers

❦

Independence
Negative Thinking
Being a Workaholic
Materialism
Competition

❦

Satan has been very effective interjecting various types of distractions into life, taking us away from God and His plan for our salvation.

The spiritual killers listed above are in the order shown for a reason. Each of them had a beginning somewhere. For example:

* Independence came into being as the result of Satan redirecting Eve's thinking from a spiritual mindset to one of selfishness. He led her to believe that she could live without God.
* As the result of Satan's interaction with Adam, he did not believe that God would accept him back. This was the beginning of man's negative mindset that he could not have a restored relationship with his Father. Consequently, Adam believed that he would have to do everything on his own without God's help.
* After leaving the Garden of Eden, Adam toiled among the thorns, thistles, and plants of the ground. As a result, it is quite possible that he became the first workaholic as the result of his efforts to regain God's acceptance through performance.
* Many times, becoming a workaholic in today's society results from man's efforts to gain material possessions rather than merely providing family needs.
* This can easily lead to a competitive attitude which can take our eyes off of our spiritual goal to live in accordance with God's will.

Notice the progression from one attitude to another. To help us gain deeper insight into these truths, this section elaborates upon some of the most destructive tools Satan uses in his daily efforts to redirect our thinking away from God.

Remember, these are but a few. Each of us simply must examine our own lives to identify the destructive tools he is trying to use within each of us.

It is so very important that each individual does this. Otherwise, the devil wins!

Chapter Three

INDEPENDENCE

It is important that we learn to be *responsible*, not *independent* from others!

THERE ARE TIMES WHEN WE ALL NEED HELP!

Independence is an attitude of mind
With which we have been instilled.
We struggle and strive to reach it,
Because, to us, it means we are all grown up, fulfilled.

But, then, there comes a time in life
When it becomes "too much."
Then, I have conflicts within because I realize the pain
Of trying to live life "untouched."

The Rampant Growth of Sin

Untouched by the love, comfort, and joy
That comes only from letting God and others share their lives
with me.
Therefore, unknowingly, angers and fears have set in.
From these, please Lord, set me free.

Life is teaching me that *freedom* does not mean
Doing my own thing,
as I thought.
Rather, I'm learning that freedom to love, give, and serve
Others, not self, holds the happiness I've sought.

God and others are willing to help me to begin this change.
Though hard it may be,
I must all remember, life is not meant to be lived alone,
But to be shared with others continually.

For only in this way,
can I learn to believe in, follow,
depend upon, trust, love
and obey my Creator,

If I will but follow
Your leader,
Jesus Christ, the Son of God.

Independence

Every parent knows that raising children is *more* than challenging. There are many bumps in the road as we work toward the goal of developing our children into mature adults. Many times our parental approach follows that of our parents, the misconceptions we have gained by watching others, or the idealistic views promoted by child psychologists. Frequently, parenting is pursued without asking God's counsel.

In relation to training children, a common thinking of parents is to teach them how to become *independent* before leaving home and moving into society.

However, do we *really* mean that we want our children to be independent after leaving home? Understanding the true definition of the word will help to answer this question:

(1) Not dependent, not subject to the control of others; not subordinate. God is the only being who is perfectly *independent*.

(2) Not holding or enjoying possessions at the will of another, not relying on others; not dependent. We all wish to be *independent* in property; yet few men are wholly *independent* even in property, and none *independent* for the supply of their wants.

(3) Affording the means of independence; as an *independent* estate

(4) Not subject to bias or influence; not obsequious; self-directing; as a man of an *independent* mind.

(5) Not connected with. It is believed the soul may exist *independent* of matter.

(6) Free; easy; self-commanding; bold; unconstrained; as an *independent* air or manner.

(7) Separate from; exclusive.[1]

There are times in children's lives when they should be allowed to practice their efforts to be independent for the purpose of building reassurance.

> For example, one of our children required eye surgery at the age of seventeen months. She came out with bandages hairline to hairline. Mom wanted to hold her hand as we walked the hospital corridors. She jerked her hand away as she very clearly made her statement, "I do it meself!" She was allowed to do it because she was trying to overcome her fear by building confidence that she could meet the immediate challenge at hand.

On the other hand, there are times when reinforcing the word "no" is critically important in developing character. When a child stomps his or her foot or cries loudly in the grocery store until the box of cereal or toy desired is purchased, this is clearly an example of the child's efforts to exert an *unhealthy* independence.

All too often this type of attitude carries over into the way we think regarding our spiritual needs. For example, "Oh, I don't need God! I can handle life's problems on my own." Indeed, this mind-set represents false security and pride.

To retain and maintain the concept of *freedom* throughout life—no longer needing guidance, thinking for ourselves without the influence of others, is *extremely* unhealthy. A warped view of "free thinking" might lead to an able-bodied eighteen to thirty-year-old child's decision to live at home without getting a job to help pay for expenses. Equally dangerous is the attitude of expecting others to give me what I need without assisting them with their needs.

Again, is this view of independence *truly* realistic? No! We cannot go to the grocery store without previous help from others! Surely someone had to display the groceries on the shelves, making them available for purchase. Another example: fuel for our vehicles has to be put in the underground storage tanks before it can be pumped into the gas tank.

What about surviving life from day to day? Whether we want to admit it or not, if we have any quality of life at all, we need healthy interaction with other people.

After a few weeks, months, or even years of this type of false rationalization, we become utterly miserable. The empty void continually grows deeper.

So what is the answer? Listen carefully. There is only one—teach and encourage people at all levels to become *responsible.* How does this differ from independence? It is very important that we have the correct understanding. *Webster's* definition, in part:

1. expected or obliged to account (for something, to someone); answerable; accountable
2. involving accountability, obligation, or duties (a responsible position)
3. ...
4. able to distinguish between right and wrong and to think and act rationally, and hence accountable for one's behavior.[2]

The first definition certainly has spiritual applications—we will be held accountable and answerable to God at judgment after death. It will be difficult to answer why we chose to live *independent* of Him on earth. A very dangerous position, indeed!

The fourth definition is the ideal goal for training children. People who have been trained to distinguish right from wrong and pursue life from a *realistic* viewpoint while being accountable to others are *much* more content with day-to-day living.

One term God uses to define independence is *rebellion*. One of the many purposes of Scripture is to help us clearly understand that man *cannot* live an independent life based upon rebellion and still be pleasing to Him.

If independence or rebellion dominates your life, <u>do not lose hope regarding your salvation.</u> King David made this request to God. The same will lead us to the changes needed.

> ⁴ Lord, help me learn your ways.
> Show me how you want me to live.
> ⁵ Guide me and teach me your truths.
> You are my God, my Savior.
> You are the one I have been waiting for.
> ⁶ Remember to be kind to me, Lord.
> Show me the tender love that you have always had.
> ⁷ Don't remember the sinful things I did when I was young.
> Because you are good, Lord, remember me with your faithful love.
> ⁸ The Lord is good and does what is right.
> He shows sinners the right way to live.
> ⁹ He teaches his ways to humble people.
> He leads them with fairness.
> ¹⁰ The Lord is kind and true to those
> who obey what he said in his agreement.
> ¹¹ Lord, I have done many wrong things.
> But I ask you to forgive them all to show your goodness.
>
> Psalms 25:4–11 (ERV)

Certainly it is true that the importance of becoming independent is an attitude of mind with which we have been instilled.

However, personal examination must be done to determine if becoming "responsible" is our true focus or if Satan is being allowed to lead us away from God through an attitude of "independence."

It is very important that we give serious thought and consideration to our views of independence. Ask God for guidance while making this effort!

Onward

to

Higher Ground

References

[1]   *Webster's* 1828, op. cit., Vol. 1: A-M
[2]   *Webster's* 1982, op. cit., p. 1211

CHAPTER FOUR

NEGATIVE THINKING

SATAN'S COCKTAIL

This attractive, crystal-like container contains nothing but deadly poison.
Why? It is grounded in negative, dead soil. Some recognize it as "stinkin' thinkin'."
Do your conversations and thought patterns follow these lines?

The Rampant Growth of Sin

Someone else can do it better than I can.
I don't want to embarrass anyone else.
Nobody can help. Leave me alone.
There is nothing I can do to help.
I don't want to be embarrassed.
God does not care about me.
I don't need anyone else.
Nobody will listen to me.
I don't have any talent
I can't trust anyone.
I'm not good enough.
They are hypocrites.
They don't need me.
I don't have time.
It is not my job.
It is too hard.
It won't work.
God is dead.
Impossible.
"Poor Me."
No.
I

J
U
S
T

C
A
N
'
T.
All of this grew
from a single basic
thought—"I just can't."
Although these thoughts may form
what appears to be an attractive container,
something desirable, they will poison our mind.

Remember

<u>Satan would have you deceived every day in every way!</u>

It is true—not all negative thinking is self-inflicted. Many times, its roots develop as the result of circumstances of life or the behavior of others. However, whether or not those roots are allowed to grow deep within me becomes *my* choice.

If allowed to grow, negative thinking becomes deadly! Undoubtedly, it *will* kill! This is why it is one of Satan's favorite tools to *blindly* lead mankind into desperation and brokenness. Yes, we can become broken emotionally, spiritually, mentally, and physically—broken in any and every way imaginable. Then, if I allow him to destroy me, Satan will be pleased because I have fallen into his trap.

Certainly negative thinking is a major contributor to harmful emotions like jealousy, low self-image, anger, and resentments. These are but a few of the heartfelt, gut-wrenching consequences of allowing negative thinking to become a part of my life.

If more effort were directed toward learning the effects of negative thinking upon our physical health, only the foolish would refuse to make *great effort* in overcoming it. *Clearly, it is a choice!* Hold on to negative thinking and we will quickly become our own worst enemy!

Not only does negative thinking rob us of positive energy needed to heal the mind, body, and soul, it is more than capable of robbing us of hope and joy in daily living. Certainly we do not recognize the beauty and benefits of God's creation around us when we are drowning in negative thinking. It has a way of *closing our eyes* to many opportunities in life.

In her book, *You Can Heal Your Life,* Louise Hay states, "Ingrained negative thoughts and negative feelings that are not released can cause cancer! Likewise, it can be dissolved through positive thinking."[1]

From a spiritual viewpoint, any negative attitude toward God lays the foundation for sin that prevents us from moving forward. Negative thinking plunges us into the depths of darkness at every level. No Scripture illustrates that truth better than these verses.

Sin's effect on us at a spiritual level:

> [21] People knew God, but they did not honor him as God, and they did not thank him. Their ideas were all useless. There was not one good thought left in their foolish minds. [22] They said they were wise, but they became fools. [23] Instead of honoring the divine greatness of God, who lives forever, they traded it for the worship of idols—things made to look like humans, who get sick and die, or like birds, animals, and snakes.
> Romans 1:21-23 (ERV)

At a physical level:

> [24] People wanted only to do evil. So God left them and let them go their sinful way. And so they became completely

immoral and used their bodies in shameful ways with each other. ²⁵ They traded the truth of God for a lie. They bowed down and worshiped the things God made instead of worshiping the God who made those things. He is the one who should be praised forever. Amen.

²⁶ Because people did those things, God left them and let them do the shameful things they wanted to do. Women stopped having natural sex with men and started having sex with other women. ²⁷ In the same way, men stopped having natural sex with women and began wanting each other all the time. Men did shameful things with other men, and in their bodies they received the punishment for those wrongs.

Romans 1:24-27 (ERV)

At a mental level:

²⁸ People did not think it was important to have a true knowledge of God. So God left them and allowed them to have their own worthless thinking. And so they do what they should not do. ²⁹ They are filled with every kind of sin, evil, greed, and hatred. They are full of jealousy, murder, fighting, lying, and thinking the worst things about each other. They gossip ³⁰ and say evil things about each other. They hate God. They are rude, proud, and brag about themselves. They invent ways of doing evil. They don't obey their parents, ³¹ they are foolish, they don't keep their promises, and they show no kindness or mercy to others. ³² They know God's law says that anyone who lives like that should die. But they not only continue to do these things themselves, but they also encourage others who do them.

Romans 1:28–32 (ERV)

Undoubtedly, these verses show the progression of sin through negative thinking toward God. Let's not be stubborn, foolish, and stiff-necked by choosing to walk the same path. To do so is a form of self-hatred, which ultimately leads to self-destruction.

If these words describe you, *please,* Think, Turn, Trust, and Obey God.

Onward

to

Higher Ground

∽∾

References

[1] Hay, Louise, *You Can Heal Your Life*; http://www.the-benefits-of-positive-thinking.com/effects-of-negative-thinking.html

Chapter Five

Being A Workaholic

THE QUESTION TO BE PONDERED

Why are you working so hard?
    Is it to use some training from the past or
Have a better life in the future?
Has someone fed you a line of baloney?
        It goes something like this:
"Only money will bring you the happiness you want and need!"
Have you ever considered—or perhaps you've learned—
This is one of many lies Satan has told you as you walk the path of life?
The truth is
Following the devil's guidance leads only to mega problems and
        strife.
Could it be there are more important goals to be achieved?
The answer is yes, and in pursuing them,
Peace of mind, happiness, and contentment will be received.

Can't do it your way though.
It must be God's way, for no other will bring you what He wants for you.
So,
    Slow down,
        Take a deep breath,
            Decide to read and obey God's Word each day,
                Oh, yes, don't forget to pray along the way
                    Follow the guidance He gives to you as you travel life's road.

Then, you will experience the
peace of mind, happiness, and contentment
as you walk the path He lays before you.

Being a workaholic has become a way of life within the American culture. Far too often, a large percentage of our income is used to pay the bills incurred by our materialistic, competitive attitudes. Debt has piled up so high that we must work to keep our creditors at bay. This becomes overpowering and leads to tremendous mental stress.

Another downfall is the fact that many times we are so busy that we do not *take* the time to care for ourselves. Consequently, our health suffers. Neither of these scenarios is good.

On the other hand, work, as God intended, is meant to be a good thing—an important component in a balanced life.

Throughout the New Testament we are given teachings regarding work. It is necessary to provide for family needs as well as those of the Lord's church.

These principles are established by the Apostle Paul. He clearly describes himself and those with him (Silas and Timothy) as being workaholics while, at the same time, promoting the teachings of Christ. But notice their reasons for working so hard:

> [8] We never accepted food from anyone without paying for it. We worked and worked so that we would not be a burden to any of you. We worked night and day. [9] We had the right to ask you to help us. But we worked to take care of ourselves so that we would be an example for you to follow. [10] When we were with you, we gave you this rule: "Whoever will not work should not be allowed to eat."
> [11] We hear that some people in your group refuse to work. They are doing nothing except being busy in the lives of others. [12] Our instruction to them is to stop bothering others, to start working and earn their own food. It is by the authority of the Lord Jesus Christ that we are urging them to do this. [13] Brothers and sisters, never get tired of doing good.
> II Thessalonians 3:8–13 (ERV)

Obviously, despite their hard work, they had *balance* in their lives. It came from their continual prayer to God for strength and direction.

In contrast to them, as the result of becoming independent in our thinking, we try to do things our way (no time for God;

too busy working) with our wisdom (work harder, get ahead). However, it produces nothing but worry because our focus is not on the strength God provides. Thus, we miss many of the joys of living!

These thoughts are being presented simply to help us understand how the attitude of becoming a workaholic can hinder our spiritual growth. We are the only ones that can make a change on a personal level.

Foolishly, we (the ones needing guidance) try to put the cart before the horse (the power) and get absolutely nowhere. Nothing happens except the horse gets frustrated and the cart cannot be used for the purpose intended.

Another analogy: a monkey chasing his tail around a flagpole gets nowhere.

And this is exactly what happens when we follow the world's philosophy that hard work and money are the way to success. It is not long before they develop into false gods in life.

After creating the earth, the Lord rested on the seventh day. He knows man's need for rest. He knows our need to have a day set aside—the first day of the week—to come together and worship him. However, in the name of independence, competition and materialism, His will has been pushed aside—"I just don't have time to rest or worship God!"

What are the results?

Confusion, anger, headaches, loss of hope, no peace, deeper emotional emptiness within—you name it!

Consider this—*if we do not have time for God this side of eternity, will He allow us to live with Him in heaven?*

Another important point,
> [28] Anyone who has been stealing must steal no longer, but must work, doing something useful with their own hands, that they may have something to share with those in need.
> Ephesians 4:28 (NIV)

This verse brings us to the thought of gift giving. Notice the reason we are to work—that we have something to share with those *in need.*

So what do people need? We all share this same commonality—food, clothing, shelter!

Yes, we should be using our hands to work and our mouths to speak for the purpose of providing multiple needs for ourselves and others. Looking beyond the physical, let's ask how our hands can be used to fill the spiritual and emotional needs of others. What are some of the ways this can be achieved? Some suggestions as door openers or icebreakers:

* tell people you meet how much you appreciate them as individuals;
* give warm, meaningful hugs to others;

- take time to visit others—the lonely, the sick, people in general;
- call people who are basically isolated in their homes—they pay the phone bill, but their phone seldom rings;
- provide transportation for others to buy groceries, go to the doctor—whatever helps to meet their needs;
- visit those confined in care centers, group homes, hospitals;
- just simply listen to others;
- speak only things that build up the hearers;
- consider the *needs* of others more important than your own; and
- repair homes of those who cannot do it for themselves.

Simply let people know that you care about them. In the process, their hearts and souls will be strengthened and encouraged in ways that a million dollars or any prescription drug could not accomplish.

Let people know that they are important. The only cost is time, patience, and the giving of the greatest gift—love.

When we really put our hearts and souls into this, the list of ways we can build others up is endless. Doing this is far more important than focusing on an overabundance of material possessions.

Benefits? There will be no financial debt to be paid, and an emotional void will be filled.

Be assured—God will Guide if you choose to pursue.

Onward
to
Higher Ground

Chapter Six

Materialism

LESS IS BEST!
Put it to the test.

When I have less,
   I have a greater appreciation for what God has already given me.
When I have less,
   My creative juices have greater opportunity to be utilized in meeting family needs.
When I have less,
   It is easier for others to buy gifts because I don't have everything.
When I have less,
   Many rich memories will linger from times when I "Waited on the Lord."

Materialism

When I have less,
    I develop greater empathy for the poor.
When I have less,
    I do not overindulge in food or expenditures, which result in problems sore.
When I have less,
    It helps me to look to Christ and depend upon Him more and more.

Do not allow the problems of society to be repeated in your life because you have not learned "Less is Best" thus creating problems o'er and o'er.

    "Lord, please teach me to be content and stop wanting more and more."
    This only leads to greed, expensive storage places, too
    Expenditures exceed my income—frustration and depression run high.
    You want me out of debt, not deeper in—
    free from "stuff" that kills within.
    Oh, if I would only listen to the wise counsel You have given,
    Then financial peace of mind would be mine.

    As you travel life's road, wherever it may lead,

> May you take the time to help others, this important message to heed.

Certainly there are basic *needs* to be fulfilled when the first child is born into a family. However, if great caution is not exercised, gifts purchased can *far exceed the need.* Buying simply because something is cute, pretty, or "he or she would look good in this," are not justifiable reasons.

If this pattern is allowed to continue, as youths grow older, they will *want* something else because a style has changed and they want to keep up with the modern-day fashion. Many purchases are made simply because the item is on sale—not to fulfill a *need.*

Where do these thought patterns begin? They certainly did not come from the minds of Paul, Silas, or Timothy!

Consider this when you choose gifts for children as they grow. When the standards of the world described above are used, the result is the child ends up with far more toys and clothing than *needed* during growth spurts. Thus, in reality, what is purchased based upon a false standard of "being cute" is actually a waste of money.

Have you ever found yourself in the dilemma of what to buy for someone who has everything? To know that the gift you chose for your loved one was taken back simply because they did not *like* it is indeed heartbreaking and discouraging to the giver. Whatever happened to the idea of accepting the gift, even though you may not like it, and learning to use and appreciate the gift out of respect for the giver?

The often chosen answer to the dilemma is a gift card. If the money is just spent with no memory of connecting the giver with the item purchased, what is gained? Is true appreciation developed or expressed?

And then, over a period of time, excessive gifts given by parents, grandparents, extended family members, or friends can easily add to one's selfishness. All of this can contribute to enabling, where the individual—though grown in body—never matures at meaningful levels. It is quite easy and not uncommon for the recipient to get to a point of expecting gifts—bigger, better, and more expensive.

This is another factor for serious thought! If purchased on a credit card but not paid in full each month, the cost of the purchase increases as the result of the accumulation of interest. What was once a minor purchase made while on sale becomes a monumental debt to pay. From the giver's viewpoint, the burden of excessive spending or debt incurred must be considered.

Even more dangerous is the fact that many people evaluate themselves based upon what they give to others, their performance, or their possessions. The gift purchased is given basically for the purpose of impressing the receiver. Can any of these motivations be pleasing to God?

The Rampant Growth of Sin

As we have rightfully said over and over, our value comes from having been created in the "image" and "likeness" of God. No greater value can be placed upon man. Truly man has a badly distorted view of value in today's world that throws us into a swirl.

What is a swirl?

It "twists" and "turns" us as we dash through life—

                                        it leads to a lot of strife.

Being attracted by meaningless distractions along the way

              will certainly rob us of the many joys in life each day.

They can come in many forms.

WORRY

Food, Clothing, Shelter

During His Sermon on the Mount, Jesus gave this admonition. Notice the caption! Does it say to avoid worry by putting work first?

<u>Put God's Kingdom First</u>

[25] "So I tell you, don't worry about the things you need to live—what you will eat, drink, or wear. Life is more important than food, and the body is more important than what you put on it. [26] Look at the birds. They don't plant, harvest, or save food in barns, but your heavenly Father feeds them. Don't you know you are worth much more than they are? [27] You cannot add any time to your life by worrying about it.

[28] "And why do you worry about clothes? Look at the wildflowers in the field. See how they grow. They don't work or make clothes for themselves. [29] But I tell you that even Solomon, the great and rich king, was not dressed as beautifully as one of these flowers. [30] If God makes what grows in the field so beautiful, what do you think he will do for you? It's just grass—one day it's alive, and the next day someone throws it into a fire. But God cares enough to make it beautiful. Surely he will do much more for you. Your faith is so small!

[31] "Don't worry and say, 'What will we eat?' or 'What will we drink?' or 'What will we wear?' [32] That's what those people who don't know God are always thinking about. Don't worry, because your Father in heaven knows that you need all these things. [33] What you should want most is God's kingdom and doing what he wants you to do. Then he will give you all these other things you need. [34] So don't worry about tomorrow. Each day has enough trouble of its own. Tomorrow will have its own worries.

Matthew 6:25–34 (ERV)

God says to seek Him first and He will take care of the rest.

A plaque bearing the following message is part of my home decor.

"Good Morning, this is God.

Today I will be handling all of your problems.

I won't be needing your help.

Have a nice day."

In keeping with this truth, several short verses have been published in various forms regarding worry. The authors are unknown, but the messages need to be added to our memory bank!

"Worry is a form of atheism.
It is like saying there is no God to help me."
Author Unknown

"Worry does not empty tomorrow of its troubles.
It empties today of its strength[1]
Corrie Ten Book

Wealth

The Bible contains this message from Jesus, the Son of God:

> [13] No servant can serve two masters; for either he will hate the one and love the other, or else he will be devoted to one and despise the other. You cannot serve God and wealth."
>
> Luke 16:13 (NASB)

Wisdom, God's craftsman at His side, said:
¹⁰ Take my instruction instead of silver,
and knowledge rather than choice gold,

Proverbs 8:10 (ERV)

OUR LOVING GOD GIVES STRONG WARNINGS REGARDING MATERIAL POSSESSIONS.

¹⁶ And behold, a man came up to him, saying, "Teacher, what good deed must I do to have eternal life?" ¹⁷ And he said to him, "Why do you ask me about what is good? There is only one who is good. If you would enter life, keep the commandments." ¹⁸ He said to him, "Which ones?" And Jesus said, "You shall not murder, You shall not commit adultery, You shall not steal, You shall not bear false witness, ¹⁹ Honor your father and mother, and, You shall love your neighbor as yourself." ²⁰ The young man said to him, "All these I have kept. What do I still lack?" ²¹ Jesus said to him, "If you would be perfect, go, sell what you possess and give to the poor, and you will have treasure in heaven; and come, follow me." ²² When the young man heard this he went away sorrowful, for he had great possessions.
²³ And Jesus said to his disciples, "Truly, I say to you, only with difficulty will a rich person enter the kingdom of heaven. ²⁴ Again I tell you, it is easier for a camel to go through

the eye of a needle than for a rich person to enter the kingdom of God."

Matthew 19:16–24 (ERV)

The Rampant Growth of Sin

⁷ God, I ask you to do two things for me before I die. ⁸ Don't let me tell lies. And don't make me too rich or too poor—give me only enough food for each day. ⁹ If I have too much, I might deny that I need you, Lord. But if I am too poor, I might steal and bring shame to the name of my God.

Proverbs 30:7–9 (ERV)

How often do we stop to think how absolutely burdensome it is to try to hold onto things to no avail, only for "My Camel" to lead us in the wrong direction?

MY CAMEL

I loaded up my camel rich and high
And marched him up to the needle's eye.
He was laden with riches many fold,
With bales of silk, and sacks of gold.
    I urged my camel with angry din,
    I pressed my camel to enter in.
    But far too large was his loading high,
    He could not pass through the needle's eye.
        I rode the camel a night and day,
        And sought to enter some other way.
        But though I traveled a wearisome round,

Materialism

Only the needle's eye way I found.
    I groaned because I did not have enough,
    So I took from the camel the bulkier stuff.
    And with gold and gems I would fain get by,
    Still the camel stuck at the needle's eye.
                  So I left the camel alone outside,
                And all by myself the entrance I tried.
                But with my pockets stuffed—alas—
                The needle still would not let me pass.
So, at length, I threw all my wealth away,
And sank upon lowly knees to pray.
I begged the Lord to forgive my sin,
And let a poor traveler enter in.
                Lo, the marvelous needle's eye,
                Grew to an entrance wide and high.
              And proud and glad, in a beggar's dress
              I passed through the portals of happiness.
            But, where the camel decided to go,
              I did not care and I do not know.
              (Author Unknown)

It is extremely important that individual people focus upon the truth that our spiritual connection to God is what gives us our value in His sight. It does not come from any prestige placed upon us by man, possessions gained, or performances achieved during our lives on earth. Nothing we <u>do</u> in this life defines our value in the sight of God!

Oh, how easy it is to become our own worst enemy as the result of not knowing or listening to God's counsel!

Onward

to

Higher Ground

References

(1)   Taken from http://www.brainyquotes.com/

Chapter Seven

Competition, Man's Distorted View

For someone to win, others have to lose.
The players are chosen by a process of "pick and choose."
        If you are good enough, you are "picked."
            If not, you lose.
Many competitions on the playing field of life
Result in example after example of man's strife.
        We are told "Winning is everything.
          It is all that matters in this life."
But, in the eyes of God, this is absolutely not true.
Cause after winning trophies on earth, you die.
    Perhaps, because you have performed so well on earth,
   Surely, you think, God will treat you as a winner in like kind.
He will accept you into heaven based upon your performance on earth.

The Rampant Growth of Sin

Oh, the disappointment when you learn competition's real worth.
God is not impressed with our big accomplishments in life.
    In reality, they offer no meaningful fulfillment—only stress and strife.
Competing to be part of the best in first place
Just takes our eyes off the goal as we run with haste.
        Competition in this life is sin.
    Because it takes our focus off Jesus and promotes men.
The real goal of life is not to win as you push others aside.
The true prize to win, most important of all,
    to live life to the full, according to His plan.
    Then Jesus will escort you to the Promised Land.
Any other endeavor one may seek
Leads only to endings that are empty and bleak.
        So, before it is too late,
    Let's live the purpose of life each day.
Jesus says, "Come, just as you are, as I show you the way."
Then God will allow us to enter heaven on that day.

The idea that winning is the most important thing in life is often promoted through sports, schools, corporate America, or many other avenues. It is clearly the world's view and another of Satan's lies. It is the exact opposite of *truth* and needs to be recognized for what it is—a poisonous seed planted in the minds of people.

What happens when one doesn't win? The feelings that remain are those of disappointment, pain, and inadequacy. These result in overall disturbances to the structure of our emotional inner beings. All of them can become spiritually, physically, mentally, and emotionally degenerating! Yes, it is possible for these thoughts to lead to suicide.

The truth is that negative thinking, independence, the deliberate quest for material gain, and competition contribute nothing positive to our physical or spiritual life. They serve no good purpose *within the body of Christ*. As Christians, if we allow ourselves to embrace these worldly goals, it is very easy for us to feel cheated or less than, as the result of mentally comparing ourselves to others.

It is also important to remember that these attributes are in *direct opposition* to cooperating with God. If pursued, *Same Page Thinking* with Him will never become a reality in our lives. When we choose to fight against Jesus' desire to develop His plan within us, we place ourselves in great danger spiritually. Moreover, these negative forces will become a source of major depression in a Christian's life because we will remain stuck in the "Me, Myself, and I" mind-set of the world.

On the other hand, from a positive point of view, by God's design, everyone has been given talents to be used in His service. By allowing those talents to be developed within us, we will be better prepared to help others experience a deeper appreciation for God as we reach out to them. When we allow God to use us in this way, our Heavenly Father will provide us countless blessings which will redirect our thinking. As a result we will not be focusing upon our own problems; rather, we will be giving a positive response to this teaching:

> ² Carry each other's burdens, and in this way you will fulfill the law of Christ.
>
> Galatians 6:2 (NIV)

This is reason to feel *privileged*—not egotistical or discouraged. Why? We have been led in areas of service that differ from those of others.

As a result, the giver and receiver both *know* and *feel*

* a sense of belonging,
* they are needed, and
* their faith is increasing.

The positive truth is everyone becomes a winner when we follow the guidance of Jesus, the Son of God, and allow God's plan to work within our lives!

And may God be glorified as we live an *exciting* life in Him using our God-given talents.

Onward

to

Higher Ground

Chapter Eight

How Effective Have Satan's Schemes Been?

This is a question we all need to answer with regard to our personal lives.

It is absolutely impossible to realize the total impact that negative thinking, materialism, independence, competition, and overworking has had on society.

The following article written by Batsell Barrett Baxter gives insight as to how Satan continues to use the characteristics of man to pull us away from Our Father.

SATAN'S DESIGN FOR DESTRUCTION

Some may want to read the "Conclusion" of this message first, in order to understand its source.

The Rampant Growth of Sin

In the closing days of the nineteenth century there went out an urgent call from Satan's headquarters in hell for all his generals and their key subordinate officers to assemble for a meeting of unprecedented importance. Accordingly, from all corners of the earth, Satan's most experienced and most influential leaders gathered in the Throne Room of Hell. The meeting began at ten o'clock in the final night of the last year of the nineteenth century. It continued on past midnight and into the dawning of the twentieth century. It was obvious that Satan had chosen an especially strategic hour for this unique meeting.

The assembled leaders sat in absolute silence as they awaited the arrival of their Master. At precisely the appointed hour the door opened and His Satanic Majesty entered the dark, smoke-filled room and took his seat on his ebony throne. Immediately he began to speak: "I have called you here for this special meeting because we stand on the threshold of this the greatest century in the history of mankind. All that has happened before is prologue. The entire population of the world, after all of the centuries of man's existence, has only now reached the billion mark. Yet in the century about to be born, the population of the world will reach five billion or even more. Man's greatest inventions are about to be discovered. The world will change more in this century than in the previous millennium. The stakes are exceedingly high and we must not be found unprepared."

Then, Satan distributed copies of an unusual document to his henchmen. It was printed in black ink on black paper and was visible only to those with special Satanic insight. This manifesto was titled, "DESIGN FOR DESTRUCTION."

After a few preliminary remarks, in which Satan made it very clear that the Satanic orders which he was about to give constituted his master plan for conquering mankind, especially those who live in the United States, he came to his first charge.

I

Suddenly there was the sound of a loud gong and as its vibrations died away Satan's voice, amplified to the loudness of thunder, declared: "I CHARGE YOU TO DESTROY MAN'S RELIGIOUS FAITH. In the moments that followed he explained that he wanted his servants to go forth throughout the earth to destroy man's faith in God, in the divinity of Christ, and in the inspiration and authority of the Bible.

"Raise doubts about the very existence of a personal God," he said. "Make much of the fact that they cannot see God, that they cannot touch him, and that they cannot hear his voice. Chide them with believing in a superstition. Call them ignorant and unenlightened. Start a 'God is dead' movement. Overwhelm their minds with arguments that arouse their feelings. Entice them by showing them how free they can be: free from moral responsibility, free to use their money and their time as they wish, free to enthrone themselves as gods. Appeal to their vanity and pride.

"Destroy their faith in the divinity of Christ. Let him be merely a man, perhaps a great teacher, or a great leader, but not divine. Encourage them to write plays and to compose music that picture Jesus in his humanity, leaving out his divinity. Cause confusion, make his message unmeaningful.

"As you destroy their faith in God and the divinity of Christ, make very sure that you also destroy the Bible, else your work will be in vain. Make fun of the Bible, speak of its contradictions, its primitive 'world view,' and its old-fashioned requirements that do not fit the modern twentieth century. Encourage people not to read it nor to try to understand it. Make them feel that it is too big, too abstruse, too impractical for modern man. Have it translated into many versions, some of which are inaccurate and misleading.

"As you carry out this most basic of my commands, use every device and trick at your command. Plant atheistic professors in all the universities. Subsidize atheistic books and magazines. Raise up someone, perhaps a woman, to challenge the right of the public schools to read the Bible and to have prayer. Try to separate religion from politics, from business, from education, from everything. Isolate it to a single day of the week and to a single hour on that day. Spend lavishly, reward those who serve our cause richly, leave no stone unturned for this is the foundation of our entire campaign. If we can destroy their Christian faith, we have won the victory.

"With their religion destroyed we can tell men that they were not created, but that they have evolved through long eons of time and that they are only graduate animals. Tell them that there is no such thing as spirit or soul. Tell them that there are no guidelines on how to live. Everyone may do his own thing. There is no judgment to fear and no life beyond. It is eat, drink, and be merry, for there is nothing more to come.

"But if you should fail in destroying their faith completely, do not be discouraged. Try another trick. Sow error in their hearts. Pervert and distort the doctrines of the Bible. And by all means encourage hypocrisy among the Christians."

THE RAMPANT GROWTH OF SIN

BUT GOD SAYS:

"In the beginning God created the heavens and the earth...And God said, let us make man in our image, after our likeness:...And God created man in his own image, in the image of God created he him; male and female created he them...And Jehovah God formed man of the dust of the ground, and breathed into his nostrils the breath of life; and man became a living soul"
Genesis 1:1, 26, 27; 2:7

"This is the end of the matter, all hath been heard: Fear God, and keep his commandments; for this is the whole duty of man. For God will bring every work into judgment, with every hidden thing, whether it be good, or whether it be evil."
Ecclesiastes 12:13–14

"And inasmuch as it is appointed unto men once to die, and after this cometh judgment; so Christ also, having been once offered to bear the sins of many, shall appear a second time, apart from sin, to them that wait for him, unto salvation."
Hebrews 9:27–28

II

Again, there is the sounding of the gong and the voice of Satan saying, "I CHARGE YOU TO UPSET MAN'S SYSTEM OF VALUES. Deny that there is any system of ultimate, absolute truth. There is nothing absolutely good or absolutely evil. Everything is relative. Values change; values are never the same.

Introduce the idea of situation ethics, emphasizing that what may be right at one time is wrong at another and what may be right for one person is wrong for another. Encourage everyone to go by his own feelings. Tell everyone that honesty and integrity are out, while lying and deception are in. Tell them that everybody is doing it. Encourage every kind of crime, until the nation is inundated, unable to supply enough police, enough courts, enough prisons. Make fun of virtue and chastity. Encourage free sex. Leave the people in a state of utter confusion."

BUT GOD SAYS:

"Ye shall know the truth, and the truth shall make you free."
John 8:32

"Jesus saith unto him, I am the way, and the truth, and the life: no one cometh unto the Father, but by me."
John 14:6

"Sanctify them in the truth: thy word is truth."
John 17:17

III

Again, there is the sounding of the gong followed by the voice of Satan saying, "I CHARGE YOU TO PROMOTE MATERIALISM EVERYWHERE. Encourage a higher standard of living. Emphasize luxury, leisure, and ease. Advertise things from morning till night. Bombard everyone with advertisements about things in the magazines, the newspapers, and on television. Emphasize materialistic rather than spiritual goals. Cause men to spend their lives in acquiring more and more and more things. Tell them that things are more important than people. Things are more important than principles. Fill every waking moment with the thought of money and the things that money can buy."

BUT GOD SAYS:

"Lay not up for yourselves treasures upon the earth, where moth and rust consume, and where thieves break through and steal; but lay up for yourselves treasures in heaven, where neither moth nor rust doth consume, and where thieves do not break through nor steal: for where thy treasure is, there will thy heart be also...Be not anxious for your life, what ye shall eat, or what ye shall drink; not yet for your body, what ye shall put on. Is not the life more than the food, and the body than the raiment?...But seek ye first his kingdom, and his righteousness; and all these things shall be added unto you."
Matthew 6:19–21, 25, 33

IV

Again, the gong, followed by the voice of Satan saying, "I CHARGE YOU TO ENCOURAGE SENSUALISM IN EVERYONE. Tell the people that every human urge or desire is natural and therefore should be satisfied freely.

Urge them to avoid repression as they would avoid the plague. Promote sensualism by scanty dress, even nudity. When you have ultimately eroded the nation's sense of values, they will accept it. Spread pornography everywhere. Use the movies, books, and magazines. Start a magazine and call it 'Playboy,' and open clubs around the world. Call men to be free from Puritanical hang-ups. Urge them to throw off the old inhibitions. Increase the impact through more and more sensual music. Gradually become more and more explicit. Have someone write a song about "Strangers in the Night." Have someone else compose a song with the lyrics, "I don't care what's wrong or right, just help me make it through the night." You will be pleased to see the cumulative destructive effect of sensual music, accompanied by alcoholic beverages and lustful scenes, upon the moral behavior of a nation."

BUT GOD SAYS:

"Blessed are they that hunger and thirst after righteousness: for they shall be filled...Blessed are the pure in heart: for they shall see God...Ye have heard that it was said, Thou shalt not commit adultery: but I say to you, that everyone that looketh on a woman to lust after her hath committed adultery with her already in his heart."

Matthew 5:6, 8, 27–28

"Finally, brethren, whatsoever things are true, whatsoever things are honorable, whatsoever things are just, whatsoever things are pure, whatsoever things are lovely, whatsoever things are of good report; if there be any virtue, and if there be any praise, think on these things. The things which ye both learned and received and heard and saw in me, these things do: and the God of peace will be with you."

Philippians 4:8–9

"Keep thyself pure."

I Timothy 5:22

V

Once again the sound of the gong brought forth the voice of Satan: "I CHARGE YOU TO CAUSE DIVISION AND STRIFE IN EVERY SITUATION OF LIFE. Drive a wedge between parents and children; speak of the generation gap. Set capital and labor at each other's throats. You will be surprised how labor strife can bring a nation to its knees. Set the rich against the poor; the whites against the blacks; nation against nation, until war reddens the earth. But be especially sensitive to your opportunities of sowing division among Christians. Divide churches. Inflame good people against each other. This is the kind of division and strife that is most satisfying to your master."

BUT GOD SAYS:

"A new commandment I give unto you, that ye love one another; even as I have loved you, that ye also love one another. By this shall all men know that ye are my disciples, if ye have love one to another."

John 13:34–35

"Neither for these only do I pray, but for them also that believe on me through their word; that they may all be one; even as thou, Father, art in me, and I in thee, that they also may be in us: that the world may believe that thou didst send me."

John 17:20–21

"Now I beseech you, brethren, through the name of our Lord Jesus Christ, that ye all speak the same thing, that there be no divisions among you; but that ye be perfected together in the same mind and in the same judgment."

I Corinthians 1:10

"But now abideth faith, hope, love, these three; and the greatest of these is love."

I Corinthians 13:13

VI

If possible, the gong sounded even louder than before as Satan spoke: "I CHARGE YOU TO BREAK UP THEIR HOMES

AND FAMILIES. "Encourage divorce. Let the statistics rise year by year, generation by generation. Advertise the fact that still more families are unhappy. Encourage premarital sex so that families will be doomed even before they start. Encourage extra-marital sex so that homes may be divided with ugly, lurid quarrels before the children. Let the pace of life increase until busyness crowds out all spiritual values from the home. Ultimately, when you have prepared the people well, deny even the value of the institution of marriage. Tell them that marriage is outmoded and obsolete. Let the people be free of all the responsibilities of the home and marriage, but carefully prevent them from seeing that they will also be free of strength and support, of companionship and love."

BUT GOD SAYS:

"This is now bone of my bones, and flesh of my flesh: she shall be called Woman, because she was taken out of Man. Therefore shall a man leave his father and his mother, and shall cleave unto his wife: and they shall be one flesh."
Genesis 2:23–24

"Whosoever shall put away his wife, except for fornication, and shall marry another, committeth adultery: and he that marrieth her when she is put away committeth adultery."
Matthew 19:9

"Children, obey your parents in the Lord: for this is right. Honor thy father and mother (which is the first commandment with promise), that it may be well with thee, and thou mayest live long on the earth. And ye fathers, provoke not your children to wrath: but nurture them in the chastening and admonition of the Lord."

Ephesians 6:1–4

VII

Introduced by the sound of the gong, once again Satan spoke: "I CHARGE YOU TO USE MAN'S EDUCATIONAL SYSTEM TO DESTROY HIS OWN SOCIETY. "Raise up an educator who will advocate permissiveness. Let him teach teachers 'never to say no, lest you scar the child's spirit.' Later, for this is best done on the college and university level, lead the students to be critical of past institutions and traditions. Call for rebellion. Teach the methods of rebellion. It is helpful if you can supply methods for making Molotov cocktails and time bombs. Teach against the free enterprise system. Advocate Communism when the climate permits. By all means remove the reading of the Bible and prayer from the public schools. Call for the separation of church and state, but carefully camouflage the fact that when you remove religion from the schools you automatically are turning the youth toward secularism."

BUT GOD SAYS:

"...Abraham shall surely become a great and mighty nation, and all the nations of the earth shall be blessed in him. For I have known him, to the end that he may command his children in his household after him, that they may keep the way of Jehovah, to do righteousness and justice."

Genesis 18:18–19

"Train up a child in the way he should go, and even when he is old he will not depart from it."

Proverbs 22:6

VIII

Once again the gong introduced the voice of Satan: "I CHARGE YOU TO UNDERMINE THE WORK ETHIC. "Cause the people to look down on work. Encourage them to be half-hearted in their work. Let them demand more pay for less work. Let them experience boredom in their work. Let them seek shorter hours, more holidays and longer vacations. Ultimately let them expect something for nothing. You can encourage this by establishing lotteries and sweepstakes and other gambling devices. Encourage get-rich schemes. Whatever you do, destroy pride and satisfaction in work well done."

BUT GOD SAYS:

"Six days shalt thou labor, and do all thy work."

Exodus 20:9

"But if any provideth not for his own, and specially his own household, he hath denied the faith, and is worse than an unbeliever."

I Timothy 5:8

"If any will not work, neither let him eat. For we hear of some that walk among you disorderly, that work not at all, but are busybodies. Now them that are such we command and exhort in the Lord Jesus Christ, that with quietness they work, and eat their own bread."

2 Thessalonians 3:10–12

IX

Once again, with the clanging of the gong Satan's voice boomed: "I CHARGE YOU TO OVERCOME MAN'S SELF-CONTROL. "Lead them to overindulging in food, drink, work, and even exercise. Let him develop the drug habit. Encourage him to smoke regularly and often to the destruction of his body. Let the people become so self-indulgent that they demand entertainment day and night. Cause them to feel deprived if there is not a movie to see, a ball game to watch, a game to play, somewhere to go, or music to hear. Let the twentieth century be a century of license and indulgence."

BUT GOD SAYS:

"But know this, that in the last days grievous times shall come. For men will be lovers of self, lovers of money, boastful, haughty, railers, disobedient to parents, unthankful, unholy, without natural affection, implacable, slanderers, without self-control, fierce, no lovers of good, traitors, headstrong, puffed up, lovers of pleasure than lovers of God; holding a form of godliness, but having denied the power thereof: from these also turn away."
2 Timothy 3:1–5

X

Finally, the gong sounded once more and the voice of Satan entoned, "I CHARGE YOU TO USE MAN'S MODERN INVENTIONS TO DESTROY HIM. Let the press be devoted to the printing of salacious and destructive literature. Use the movies to disillusion and to destroy man's morals. Let radio and television be used to advertise the ugly and the bad. From the four corners of the earth let them bring news of violence and evil of every kind into every home in the land. Do it repeatedly; morning, noon and night. And thus spread evil from community to community, city to city, and nation to nation. Use the latest means of transportation to help man run away from responsibility. Help him to lose himself in the nameless, irresponsible throngs to the cities. Let industry foul the air, besmirch the countryside, and contaminate the streams. Let him exhaust his natural resources and wallow in the filth of his own refuse."

BUT GOD SAYS:

"But God saw everything that he had made, and, behold, it was very good."
Genesis 1:31

"Every good gift and every perfect gift is from above, coming down from the Father of lights, with whom can be no variation, neither shadow that is cast by turning.
James 1:17

Conclusion

If you are wondering why this message has been presented in this form, the answer is to be found in a sentence from the Apostle Peter in his short letter near the end of the Bible. In I Peter 5:8 we read, "Be sober, be watchful: your adversary the devil, as a roaring lion, walketh about, seeking whom he may devour: whom withstand steadfast in your faith, knowing that the same sufferings are accomplished in your brethren who are in the world. And the God of all grace, who called you unto his eternal glory in Christ, after that ye have suffered a little while, shall himself perfect, establish, and strengthen you. To him be the dominion forever and ever. Amen" This message is an effort to warn those of us who are under the constant bombardment of Satan's warfare. To know something of the enemy's schemes and plans of action is the first long stride toward self-protection.

If there is a curious soul who wonders just how it is that we can know exactly what Satan said at that crucially important evening when he gave his marching orders for the twentieth century to his chief generals, we would answer that we know the battle plan by a careful observation of the day-to-day combat of Satan's army. After all, we stand at the three-quarter mark of the century with the war well along toward completion. The hindsight of history tells us what his commands must have been.

Actually, it was the memory of reading C. S. Lewis's famous book, *The Screwtape Letters,* that encouraged this venture. You may remember that Lewis purported to be publishing a series of letters from *Screwtape,* a chief devil in hell, to Wormwood, one of Satan's lieutenants on earth. The value of the book has its unique way of focusing attention on the schemes and methods by which Satan seeks to conquer mankind. Taking a leaf from *The Screwtape Letters,* we have imagined, with the hindsight of history, what Satan's master plan, "THE DESIGN FOR DESTRUCTION" must have been.

Finally, from a letter from a long-time friend, Clark Hanna, a member of the Lord's church, who by profession is a Captain or pilot of a Pan American 707 on the Pacific Run, came the suggestion:

> "For several weeks I have been 'mulling over' in my mind the results, both good and bad, if a tract was printed which would have as its subject a thought such as: If I were determined to bring mankind to ruin, and civilization to chaos, these would be the methods I would use…"

I, too, mulled the idea over in my mind. With the encouragement of *The Screwtape Letters* and even more especially I Peter 5:8, I send forth this message with the hope that it will help to warn thoughtful men and women of the wiles of Satan and thereby help to save us from destruction[1]

Used by Permission

Perhaps you, like I, find his sermon interesting. Keep in mind it was given forty years ago. Despite that, to our country's shame, the words spoken are just as truthful today as they were in 1974. Perhaps, if the truth were known, they may be more applicable!

Before the words of this message are lost in our memory banks, two important points must be made.

You, the reader, may be familiar with a similar article that has been widely circulated through the Internet and private distribution. It concludes with this thought. Busy means

Buried Under Satan's Yoke

Clearly when our lives become so cluttered with countless meaningless activities, life can become a heavy yoke because it is out of balance.

Not only is Satan's goal to destroy our relationship with Jesus but our relationships with *people* also. When our schedules are full with the busyness of life, little (if any) time is left to care for family, friends, loved ones, or people in general. It is our responsibility to examine our personal lives to see where areas of change are needed. Growth in Christ is *so very rewarding*—be aware lest our eyes are taken off of Him.

As individual people, we simply must answer this question for ourselves:

<u>How effective has Satan been in destroying *my* relationship with Jesus?</u>

The only cure for the dilemma we find ourselves in is to engage in BTST. What does that mean?

Balance **T**hrough **S**piritual **T**eaching

Making it a daily habit to feed our spiritual souls through the Word of God *and* putting into practice what we have learned will ensure balance in life. Gaining this balance is well worth the time required!

Onward

to

Higher Ground

❦

References

[1] Satan's Design for Destruction, sermon delivered by Batsell Barrett Baxter, November 10, 1974. Used by permission.

SECTION SEVEN

IT WAS BECAUSE OF THIS

Prelude

Have you ever been struck by something while standing in an area that was *assumed* to *be* safe.

Perhaps this assumption was the result of following the guidance of another. Perhaps it was the result of making your own conclusion based upon what *seemed* to be reasonable.

Notice both of these thought processes originate in the minds of men.

Nonetheless, the object literally came out of nowhere! As a result, you may have sustained serious injury.

When we are seeking a close relationship with God, it is *not* wise to *assume* that what we offer to Him as worship is acceptable to Him.

This Scripture confirms this truth:

[8] "For My thoughts are not your thoughts,
Nor are your ways My ways," declares the Lord.
[9] "For *as* the heavens are higher than the earth,
So are My ways higher than your ways
And My thoughts than your thoughts.

Isaiah 55:8-9 (NASB)

This section will help us to understand God's viewpoints.

We can be assured that *not* following His ways will result in long-term, emotionally devastating injury!

Chapter One

Assuming Is Dangerous

Are you wondering why a *loving God* would create a miserable hell? Before learning the difference between heaven and hell, it is important to understand why they *must* exist!

One of the most dangerous assumptions common among mankind is thinking that because an individual is a "good" person and lives a "clean" life, he or she will be allowed to enter heaven.

The Bible does not uphold this teaching. Why? Every person who has developed to the point of accountable age (who has learned right from wrong) must be cleansed of his or her sins through the blood of Christ. This is accomplished through immersion in water (Scriptural baptism). This cleansing is the only way we can be reconciled back to God. Without it, God considers us to be rebellious to His teaching.

Therefore, hell exists for two basic reasons.

Hell is God's expression of raging anger toward Satan for working throughout the ages to break the relationship once enjoyed between Father and child.

Hell is also God's response to *His offspring* who choose to be rebellious to His teaching. They choose to reject it rather than obeying. God cannot tolerate being in the presence of sin; therefore, He will separate Himself from these people for eternity!

It is very dangerous to assume that, because we reflect His "image" and "likeness" at birth, everyone will spend eternity in heaven with Him. To better understand the error of this thinking, let's evaluate whether or not it is even logical. Enough importance cannot be placed upon the need to stop and think rather than blindly accepting the assumptions and teachings of man.

Would it be fair for two students to both receive an "A" when one properly prepared for the exam while the other did nothing? One student chose to be irresponsible by ignoring the need to prepare; the other was diligent in preparation. Nonetheless, they both receive the same commendable grade. Why? Because the teacher chooses to enable the poor student by accepting his or her excuses for lack of preparation rather than holding him or her accountable for making the wrong decision.

It is impossible for God to give a follower of Jesus (the prepared) and a follower of Satan (the blinded, unprepared) the same reward. Certainly that would be *totally* unfair.

God does *nothing* to enable man. Rather He holds each person accountable for the choices made in life.

> [10] You, then, why do you judge your brother or sister? Or why do you treat them with contempt? For we will all stand before God's judgment seat. [11] It is written:
> "'As surely as I live,' says the Lord,
> 'every knee will bow before me;
> every tongue will acknowledge God.'"
>
> Romans 14:10–11 (NIV)

It is very important to understand that at whatever point we choose to follow the devil, we will no longer be "a child of God." Rather, we become a follower of the devil, whose leadership will lead us directly into the pits of hell.

There is no doubt that Satan will spend eternity in hell. The devil is well aware of this truth. His time to pursue his revenge against God is growing shorter with each passing day. Therefore, the devil continues to work daily, diligently, to push as many people as possible toward spiritual death. In the process, God is continually being robbed of the joy of having relationships with those He created. This will continue to happen until the final day of the earth's existence. Our Father's day of revenge will be clearly demonstrated at the end of time.

It is important to understand that the goal of our Heavenly Father is to protect His children from the everlasting pain and suffering caused by the never-ending fire in hell.

With these thoughts in mind, let's listen closely to this true story.

Several years ago, a father of three young children was interviewed on TV after rescuing one of them from a burning building.

The interviewer referred to the father as a "hero." Never will I forget his response.

The perturbed father said, "I am *not* a hero—I am their father!"

Indeed he was doing the right thing. As a result, the child was brought to safety. This father wanted to experience the joy of, once again, being reunited with his child.

Now let's consider this from two different viewpoints:

* What if the child in danger of death saw his father walk away, ignoring the child's cry for help?
* How would this make the child feel at an emotional level? If not rescued, not only would he perish from physical pain, but he would die both knowing and feeling his father's rejection.
* Another thought. What if the father did everything possible to rescue his child only to have him or her say, "That's OK, Daddy, I will be just fine. Just leave me here!"
* What would the love of the father *compel* him to do? Would he listen to his child? Of course not! The father's knowledge of his child's immaturity and immediate

danger would not allow Dad to give his child freedom of choice.

Physical fathers reflect the "image" and "likeness" of God when they make every effort possible to save their children from danger.

Now let's make a spiritual application.

Why is it we call a human father a hero because of his efforts to save the life of his child, but we consider God to be "too demanding and strict" when He is trying to save us from experiencing fire for eternity?

Because our Father is *fair*, He provides us with a complete description of the agonies of hell this side of eternity. This is a demonstration of His love for mankind.

HELL

How does the Bible describe hell?

> [41] The Son of Man will send out his angels, and they will weed out of his kingdom everything that causes sin and all who do evil. [42] They will throw them into the blazing furnace, where there will be weeping and gnashing of teeth.
> Matthew 8:12 (NIV)
> Matthew 13:41–42 (NIV)
> Matthew 24:51 INIV)

It Was Because of This

Listen carefully to Jesus' own words as He tells us what will happen at the end of time. This describes the final judgment.

> [31] "The Son of Man will come again with divine greatness, and all his angels will come with him. He will sit as king on his great and glorious throne. [32] All the people of the world will be gathered before him. Then he will separate everyone into two groups. It will be like a shepherd separating his sheep from his goats. [33] He will put the sheep on his right and the goats on his left.
> [34] "Then the king will say to the godly people on his right, 'Come, my Father has great blessings for you. The kingdom he promised is now yours. It has been prepared for you since the world was made. [35] It is yours because when I was hungry, you gave me food to eat. When I was thirsty, you gave me something to drink. When I had no place to stay, you welcomed me into your home. [36] When I was without clothes, you gave me something to wear. When I was sick, you cared for me. When I was in prison, you came to visit me.'
> [37] "Then the godly people will answer, 'Lord, when did we see you hungry and give you food? When did we see you thirsty and give you something to drink? [38] When did we see you with no place to stay and welcome you into our home? When did we see you without clothes and give you something to wear? [39] When did we see you sick or in prison and care for you?'
> [40] "Then the king will answer, 'The truth is, anything you did for any of my people here, you also did for me.'
> [41] "Then the king will say to the evil people on his left, 'Get away from me. God has already decided that you will be punished. Go into the fire that burns forever—the fire that

was prepared for the devil and his angels. [42] You must go away because when I was hungry, you gave me nothing to eat. When I was thirsty, you gave me nothing to drink. [43] When I had no place to stay, you did not welcome me into your home. When I was without clothes, you gave me nothing to wear. When I was sick and in prison, you did not care for me.'

[44] "Then those people will answer, 'Lord, when did we see you hungry or thirsty? When did we see you without a place to stay? Or when did we see you without clothes or sick or in prison? When did we see any of this and not help you?'

[45] "The king will answer, 'The truth is, anything you refused to do for any of my people here, you refused to do for me.'

[46] "Then these evil people will go away to be punished forever. But the godly people will go and enjoy eternal life."

Matthew 25:31–46 (ERV)

Other Scriptures describing hell:

*	fire that never goes out	Mark 9:43, 48 (NIV)
*	the worms that eat them do not die	Mark 9:48 (NIV)
*	being able to see from hell those who are in heaven	Luke 16:23 (NIV)
*	no water to cool the tongue while in the fire	Luke 16:24 (NIV)
*	hell is unparalleled agony; those in heaven will not be able to comfort those in hell	Luke 16:25 (NIV)

This teaching reveals more truth:

It was Because of This

> ⁹ The Lord is not slow in keeping his promise, as some understand slowness. Instead he is patient with you, not wanting anyone to perish, but everyone to come to repentance.
>
> II Peter 3:9 (NIV)

Learning the meaning of perish will help us to understand why He does not want anyone to experience this fate. In this verse, the Greek meaning of "perish" is:

> "away from," "to destroy"—properly, *fully* destroy, cutting off *entirely;* implies permanent (absolute) destruction, i.e., to cancel out (remove): "to die, with the implication of ruin and destruction"; cause to be *lost* (utterly perish) by experiencing a miserable end.[1]

This definition is in relationship to *eternity.* Those who choose not to live in accordance with God's teaching will be completely cut off from Him. God does not want us to be eternally lost! Indeed this is a miserable end for both Father and child. This is a very important message to remember:

> ²³ Do I take any pleasure in the death of the wicked? declares the Sovereign LORD. Rather, am I not pleased when they turn from their ways and live?
>
> Ezekiel 18:23 (NIV)

Regardless of our past lifestyles, our Heavenly Father will never reject us if we are willing to repent of our sins and return to the lifestyle He requires of us. He is waiting for that moment! Indeed, God wants to protect us from the eternal fires of hell.

There is no need for us to stand before the Lord afraid that we will not be allowed to enter heaven if we believe, accept, and follow His guidance. Trust in the Lord and follow His teachings. Therein is our security.

Onward

to

Higher Ground

References

[1] biblehub.com, Greek #622

SECTION EIGHT

UNDERSTANDING THE TRINITY

Prelude

Trying to understand the Trinity can be confusing. Although we may never completely understand how the three blend together, there is knowledge to be gained as growth takes place while walking along the spiritual path laid before us.

Because the word "Trinity" is not found in the Bible, we must gain an understanding of its meaning from *Webster*:

3a the union of the three divine persons (Father, Son, and Holy Spirit, or Holy Ghost) in one Godhead[1]

There are several examples in everyday life that can help us understand this principle in a non-spiritual setting.

* A man can be an employee or employer, a husband, a father to his children, and eventually even a father-in-law. Yet he is one person. Even though he is one person, this same man relates to his job, his wife, children, and extended family members in different ways. His roles to each vary based upon the need.

* In the same manner, a girl is a daughter, becomes a student, perhaps a wife and mother. Again, different areas of responsibility apply.
* As a newborn, the same baby can be referred to as a son or daughter, brother or sister, or grandchild. All terms are representative of the same family.

Likewise, God, Jesus Christ, and the Holy Spirit represent the same spiritual family. Several verses illustrate this truth:

> [16] So Jesus was baptized. As soon as he came up out of the water, the sky opened, and he saw God's Spirit coming down on him like a dove. [17] A voice from heaven said, "This is my Son, the one I love. I am very pleased with him."
> Matthew 3:16–17 (ERV)

"God's Spirit" refers to the Holy Spirit, "a voice from heaven" refers to God, and "Son" refers to Jesus.

> [28] But I use the power of God's Spirit to force out demons, and this shows that God's kingdom has come to you.
> Matthew 12:28 (ERV)

"I" refers to Jesus, "God's Spirit" refers to the Holy Spirit, and "God" refers to the Father.

Prelude

❦

Jesus' message to his disciples before His death on the cross:

> [16] I will ask the Father, and he will give you another Helper to be with you forever. [17] The Helper is the Spirit of truth. The people of the world cannot accept him, because they don't see him or know him. But you know him. He lives with you, and he will be in you.
>
> John 14:16–17 (ERV)

"I" refers to Jesus, "Father" refers to God, and "another Helper" refers to the Holy Spirit. Notice the Holy Spirit is also referred to as "the Spirit of truth."

❦

> [4] But then the kindness and love of God our Savior was made known. [5] He saved us because of his mercy, not because of any good things we did. He saved us through the washing that made us new people. He saved us by making us new through the Holy Spirit. [6] God poured out to us that Holy Spirit fully through Jesus Christ our Savior. [7] We were made right with God by his grace. God saved us so that we could be his children and look forward to receiving life that never ends.
>
> Titus 3:4–7 (ERV)

All three members of the Trinity are clearly identified within these four verses.

Just as each member of a family household has different responsibilities, the same is true for each member of the Trinity.

Onward

to

Higher Ground

References

(1) *Webster's* 1982, op cit., p. 1520

Chapter One

God, The Father

Isaiah 40 provides us with a portrait of God!
>GOD IS TENDERHEARTED IN HIS ATTITUDE
>HE SPEAKS WORDS OF COMFORT
>(Verse 1)
>Comfort, comfort my people, says your God.

>HE SPEAKS KINDLY
>(Verse 2)

Speak tenderly to Jerusalem and proclaim to her that her hard service has been completed, that her sin has been paid for, that she has received the Lord's hand double for all her sins.

GOD IS INFINITELY STRONG: OMNIPOTENT[1]
HIS POWER IS GREAT
(Verse 10)

See, the Sovereign Lord comes with power and his arm rules for him. See, his reward is with him, and his recompense accompanies him.

HE IS CARING AND TENDER LIKE A SHEPHERD
(Verse 11)

He tends his flock like a shepherd: He gathers the lambs in his arms and carries them close to his heart; he gently leads those that have young.

HE DEALS WITH THE OCEANS AS BUT A DROP
(Verse 12)

Who has measured the waters in the hollow of his hand, or with the breadth of his hand marked off the heavens? Who has held the dust of the earth in a basket, or weighed the mountains on the scales and the hills in a balance?

GOD IS ALL KNOWING: OMNISCIENT[2]
HE HAS NO ADVISERS OR CONSULTANTS
(Verses 13–14)

Who has understood the mind of the Lord, or instructed him as his counselor? Whom did the Lord consult to enlighten him, and who taught him the right way? Who was it that taught him knowledge or showed him the path of understanding?

GOD IS SOVEREIGN
THE MOST POWERFUL NATIONS ARE BUT A SPECK OF DUST
HE CAN LIFT UP THE ISLANDS AS FINE DUST

(Verse 15)

Surely the nations are like a drop in a bucket; they are regarded as dust on the scales; he weighs the islands as though they were fine dust.

(Verse 17)

Before him all the nations are as nothing; they are regarded by him as worthless and less than nothing.

(Verses 23–24)

He brings princes to naught and reduces the rulers of this world to nothing.

No sooner are they planted, no sooner are they sown, no sooner do they take root in the ground, than he blows on them and they wither, and a whirlwind sweeps them away like chaff.

HIS KNOWLEDGE AND WISDOM ARE UNLIMITED
GOD IS INCOMPARABLE
"TO WHOM THEN WILL YOU LIKEN GOD!"

(Verse 18)

To whom, then, will you compare God? What image will you compare him to?

(Verse 25)

"To whom will you compare me? Or who is my equal?" says the Holy One.

NEITHER MAN NOR MATTER
CAN EVER EXPRESS THE MAJESTY OF GOD
(Verses 19–20)

As for an idol, a craftsman casts it, and a goldsmith overlays it with gold and fashions silver chains for it. A man too poor to present such an offering selects wood that will not rot. He looks for a skilled craftsman to set up an idol that will not topple.

GOD IS TRANSCENDENT[3]
HE SITS ENTHRONED ABOVE THE CIRCLE OF THE EARTH
HE STRETCHES OUT THE HEAVENS
LIKE A CURTAIN, LIKE A TENT
(Verse 22)

He sits enthroned above the circle of the earth, and its people are like grasshoppers. He stretches out the heavens like a canopy, and spreads them out like a tent to live in.

GOD IS ETERNAL
HE MOVES THROUGH ETERNITY WITH UNHURRIED STEP
(Verses 26–27)

Lift your eyes and look to the heavens: Who created all these? He who brings out the starry host one by one, and calls them each by name. Because of his great power and mighty strength, not one of them is missing.

Why do you say, O Jacob, and complain, O Israel, "My way is hidden from the Lord; my cause is disregarded by my God"?

"THE HIGH AND EXALTED ONE LIVES FOREVER"
(Isaiah 57:15)

For this is what the high and lofty One says—he who lives forever, whose name is holy: "I live in a high and holy place, but also with him who is contrite and lowly in spirit, to revive the spirit of the lowly and to revive the heart of the contrite…"

GOD IS IMMUTABLE
THE EVERLASTING GOD
--DOES NOT BECOME WEARY OR TIRED--
HE CHANGES NOT.
HIS JUDGMENT IS SURE
and
SO IS HIS MERCY AND GRACE

Understanding the Trinity

>   (Verse 28)
> Do you not know? Have you not heard? The Lord is the everlasting God, the Creator of the ends of the earth. He will not grow tired or weary, and his understanding no one can fathom. He gives strength to the weary and increases the power of the weak.
>
>   Summarized by Ron Bryant
>   (Used by permission)

The following definitions are provided to help us gain a better understanding:
- (1) "Omnipotent" having unlimited power or authority; all-powerful
- (2) "Omniscient" having infinite knowledge, knowing all things
- (3) "Transcendent" surpassing, excelling, extraordinary

God's love for mankind made it necessary for Him to put a plan in place whereby man can be forgiven of his sin. As a result of this cleansing, we can live with Him in eternity.

May we move forward with the confidence that our Father will never mislead us. Certainly, He is worthy of our praise.

Onward
to
Higher Ground

References

(1) *Webster's* 1982, p. 993
(2) Ibid., p. 993
(3) Ibid., p. 1509

Chapter Two

Jesus Christ, The Son Of God

In the earlier chapters of this book, many references to and quotations from Jesus have been given. However, up to this point, we have not really answered the question of who Jesus is.

WHO IS JESUS?

Ask this of those you know. Quite likely, a wide range of answers will be given. Some say He was no more than a mere man. Others deny His existence. Still others say He is the One they put their trust in.

You may be thinking, "The Bible was written *long* before I was born! What does it have to do with me?" The answer lies within this passage:

> [1] In the past God spoke to our ancestors through the prophets at many times and in various ways, [2] but in these last days he has spoken to us by his Son, whom he appointed heir of all things, and through whom also he made the universe.
>
> Hebrews 1:1–2 (NIV)

The Apostle John gives this insight:

> [1] In the beginning was the Word, and the Word was with God, and the Word was God. [2] He was in the beginning with God. [3] All things were made through Him, and without Him nothing was made that was made. [4] In Him was life, and the life was the light of men.
>
> John 1:1–4 (NKJV)

Does this help us to understand why it is important for us to learn more about Jesus? Listening to Him is critically important because *Jesus is the only one who is capable of guiding us along the path of life leading to heaven.*

> [7] So Jesus said again, "I assure you, I am the gate for the sheep. [8] All those who came before me were thieves and robbers. The sheep did not listen to them. [9] I am the gate. Whoever enters through me will be saved. They will be able to come in and go out. They will find everything they need. [10] A thief comes to steal, kill, and destroy. But I came to give life—life that is full and good.
>
> John 10:7–10 (ERV)

How did the people living in His hometown, Bethlehem, react to Him?

¹ Jesus left and went back to his hometown. His followers went with him. ² On the Sabbath day Jesus taught in the synagogue, and many people heard him. They were amazed and said, "Where did this man get this teaching? How did he get such wisdom? Who gave it to him? And where did he get the power to do miracles? ³ Isn't he just the carpenter we know—Mary's son, the brother of James, Joses, Judas, and Simon? And don't his sisters still live here in town?" So they had a problem accepting him.
⁴ Then Jesus said to them, "People everywhere give honor to a prophet, except in his own town, with his own people, or in his home." ⁵ Jesus was not able to do any miracles there except the healing of some sick people by laying his hands on them. ⁶ He was surprised that the people there had no faith. Then he went to other villages in that area and taught.

Mark 6:1–6 (ERV)

¹⁰ The Word was already in the world. The world was made through him, but the world did not know him. ¹¹ He came to the world that was his own. And his own people did not accept him.

John 1:10–11 (ERV)

The fact that the world did not understand who Jesus was did not take away from the fact that He was the representative figure of God on earth. *Truth is truth*!

This is Jesus' résumé:

The Son of God is the Same as God

¹⁵ No one can see God,
  but the Son is exactly like God.
  He rules over everything that has been made.
¹⁶ Through his power all things were made:
  things in heaven and on earth, seen and not seen—
all spiritual rulers, lords, powers, and authorities.
  Everything was made through him and for him.
¹⁷ The Son was there before anything was made.
  And all things continue because of him.
¹⁸ He is the head of the body, which is the church.
  He is the beginning of everything else.
And he is the first among all who will be raised from death.
  So in everything he is most important.
¹⁹ God was pleased for all of himself to live in the Son.
²⁰ And through him, God was happy to bring all things back to himself again—
  things on earth and things in heaven.
God made peace by using the blood sacrifice of his Son on the cross.

Colossians 1:15–20 (ERV)

The author of Hebrews uses the words "God" and "Lord" interchangeably.

* In 1:8, God refers to Jesus: "...about the Son he says, 'Your throne, O God...'"
* In 1:10, "He also said, 'In the beginning, O Lord, you laid the foundations of the earth...'"

Collectively, in verse 3a,
"The son is the radiance of God's glory and the exact representation of his being, sustaining all things by his powerful word."

In contrast, Jesus' view of who He was:

⁵ Let this mind be in you which was also in Christ Jesus, ⁶ who, being in the form of God, did not consider it robbery to be equal with God, ⁷ but made Himself of no reputation, taking the form of a bondservant, *and* coming in the likeness of men. ⁸ And being found in appearance as a man, He humbled Himself and became obedient to *the point of death*, even the death of the cross. ⁹ Therefore God also has highly exalted Him and given Him the name which is above every name, ¹⁰ that at the name of Jesus every knee should bow, of those in heaven, and of those on earth, and of those under the earth, ¹¹ and *that* every tongue should confess that Jesus Christ *is* Lord, to the glory of God the Father.
Philippians 2:5-11 (NKJV)

This group of Scriptures helps us to understand why God replaced animal sacrifice for sin with the cleansing blood of Jesus.

⁶ He was like God in every way,
   but he did not think that his being equal with God was something to use for his own benefit.
⁷ Instead, he gave up everything, even his place with God.
   He accepted the role of a servant, appearing in human form. During his life as a man,
⁸ he humbled himself by being fully obedient to God,
   even when that caused his death—death on a cross.
⁹ So God raised him up to the most important place
   and gave him the name that is greater than any other name.
¹⁰ God did this so that every person will bow down to honor the name of Jesus.
   Everyone in heaven, on earth, and under the earth will bow.
¹¹ They will all confess, "Jesus Christ is Lord,"
   and this will bring glory to God the Father.

Hebrews 10:6-11 (ERV)

---

¹⁸ For Christ also suffered once for sins, the righteous for the unrighteous, to bring you to God. He was put to death in the body but made alive in the Spirit.

I Peter 3:18 (NIV)

---

⁶ Christ died for us when we were unable to help ourselves. We were living against God, but at just the right time

Christ died for us. ⁷ Very few people will die to save the life of someone else, even if it is for a good person. Someone might be willing to die for an especially good person. ⁸ But Christ died for us while we were still sinners, and by this God showed how much he loves us.

⁹ We have been made right with God by the blood sacrifice of Christ. So through Christ we will surely be saved from God's anger. ¹⁰ I mean that while we were God's enemies, he made friends with us through his Son's death. And the fact that we are now God's friends makes it even more certain that he will save us through his Son's life. ¹¹ And not only will we be saved, but we also rejoice right now in what God has done for us through our Lord Jesus Christ. It is because of Jesus that we are now God's friends.

Romans 5:6–11 (ERV)

---

¹⁰ We want all of you and all the people of Israel to know that this man was made well by the power of Jesus Christ from Nazareth. You nailed Jesus to a cross, but God raised him from death. This man was crippled, but he is now well. He is able to stand here before you because of the power of Jesus! ¹¹ Jesus is

    'the stone that you builders thought was not important.
    But this stone has become the cornerstone.'

¹² Jesus is the only one who can save people. His name is the only power in the world that has been given to save anyone. We must be saved through him!"

Acts 4:10-12 (ERV)

> [3] The Son is the radiance of God's glory and the exact representation of his being, sustaining all things by his powerful word. After he had provided purification for sins, he sat down at the right hand of the Majesty in heaven. [4] So he became as much superior to the angels as the name he has inherited is superior to theirs.
>
> Hebrews 1:3–4 (NIV)

No human has the power or ability to cleanse another of sins. Jesus is the only one who has the God-given authority to do this.

> [10] But I want you to know that the Son of Man has authority on earth to forgive sins."
>
> (Mark 2:10).

All of these Scriptures provide a much broader view, a much clearer understanding of who Jesus is!

Additionally, He is the foundation upon which His church is built.

> [15] Then Jesus said to his followers, "And who do you say I am?"
> [16] Simon Peter answered, "You are the Messiah, the Son of the living God."
> [17] Jesus answered, "You are blessed, Simon son of Jonah. No one taught you that. My Father in heaven showed you

who I am. ¹⁸ So I tell you, you are Peter. And I will build my church on this rock. The power of death will not be able to defeat my church.
Matthew 16:15–18 (ERV)

What is the meaning of the word "rock" as it is used in this verse?

>metaphorically, a man like a rock, by reason of his firmness and strength of soul:[1]

To help us better understand that Jesus, not Peter, is the head of the church, please consider these thoughts:

>²³ Jesus turned and said to Peter, "Get behind me, Satan! You are a stumbling block to me; you do not have in mind the concerns of God, but merely human concerns."
> Matthew 16:23 (NIV)

Questions:

* Would God choose a *fallible* man to be the head of an *eternal, spiritual* domain?
* Would God allow Peter—<u>*the man*</u> Jesus referred to as a "stumbling block" and "Satan"—to be the head of His church?

Colossians 1:18 teaches that Jesus is the head of the church. By learning who Jesus is, we learn who Peter was not! With regard to Peter, it is important to understand he is simply acknowledging the fact that Jesus is the Son of God—the one with the firmness and strength of soul needed upon which to build His church.

In like manner, Jesus was acknowledging Peter to be Peter. He was a man just like any other. Peter was *not* being identified as the rock upon which the church would be built.

So what *is* Jesus saying to Peter?

My Church will be built upon this foundation, this "rock truth."

I am the Christ, the Son of God.

Referring to the Israelites, the Apostle Paul provides more insight:

> ³ They all ate the same spiritual food ⁴ and drank the same spiritual drink; for they drank from the spiritual rock that accompanied them, and that rock was Christ.
> I Corinthians 10:3-4 (NIV)

Additionally, we are not to elevate religious leaders by giving them special titles lest we be led away from the path leading to heaven.

> ⁸ "But you are not to be called 'Rabbi,' for you have one Teacher, and you are all brothers. ⁹ And do not call anyone on earth 'father,' for you have one Father, and he is in heaven.
> Matthew 23:8-9 (NIV)

Reading the four gospels—Matthew, Mark, Luke, and John—will provide even greater insight in your search for the answer to the important question, "Who is Jesus?"

Always keep in mind the importance of accepting Him as our shepherd.

Onward

to

Higher Ground

References

[1] biblehub.com, Greek #4073

Chapter Three

The Holy Spirit

The first Bible reference to the Holy Spirit is made in relationship to creation.

> [1] In the beginning God created the heavens and the earth. [2] Now the earth was formless and empty, darkness was over the surface of the deep, and the Spirit of God was hovering over the waters.
>
> Genesis 1:1–2 (NIV)

Fast-forwarding to the New Testament, Jesus' goal was to return to God in heaven; however, He could not leave His disciples without providing the most valuable "ensurance" protection available.

Notice the word "ensurance" is used rather than "insurance." Why? There is a distinct difference between the two.

Insurance:

(1) an insuring or being insured against loss; a system of protection against loss in which a number of individuals agree to pay certain sums (premiums) periodically for a guarantee that they will be compensated under stipulated conditions for any specified loss by fire, accident, death, etc.

(2) a contract guaranteeing such protection, usually called an insurance policy.[1]

Ensurance:

(1) to make sure or certain; guarantee; secure [measures to *ensure* accuracy]

(2) to make safe; protect workers against accidents[2]

Speaking of the Holy Spirit, Jesus told His disciples,

> [16] And I will ask the Father, and he will give you another advocate to help you and be with you forever— [17] the Spirit of truth. The world cannot accept him, because it neither sees him nor knows him. But you know him, for he lives with you and will be in you. [18] I will not leave you as orphans; I will come to you.
>
> John 14:16–18 (NIV)

Jesus was certainly *ensuring* His disciples that they would never be left without His spiritual guidance and protection. He would always be with His followers *through the Holy Spirit.*

Before going to the cross, Jesus spoke these words to His disciples:

The Holy Spirit

²³ Jesus replied, "Anyone who loves me will obey my teaching. My Father will love them, and we will come to them and make our home with them. ²⁴ Anyone who does not love me will not obey my teaching. These words you hear are not my own; they belong to the Father who sent me. ²⁵ "All this I have spoken while still with you. ²⁶ But the Advocate, the Holy Spirit, whom the Father will send in my name, will teach you all things and will remind you of everything I have said to you. ²⁷ Peace I leave with you; my peace I give you. I do not give to you as the world gives. Do not let your hearts be troubled and do not be afraid.

John 14:23-27 (NIV)

¹³ But when he, the Spirit of truth, comes, he will guide you into all the truth. He will not speak on his own; he will speak only what he hears, and he will tell you what is yet to come. ¹⁴ He will glorify me because it is from me that he will receive what he will make known to you. ¹⁵ All that belongs to the Father is mine. That is why I said the Spirit will receive from me what he will make known to you."

John 16:13–15 (NIV)

Like Jesus, the Holy Spirit is another teacher sharing *Same Page Thinking* with God. No conflicts of interest. No confusion regarding their message, their goal, or their purpose. Unity in providing man with the strength, encouragement, and directives needed is required if the original spiritual purity placed within us is to be protected.

Recognizing the fact that Jesus left God's obedient children a "Counselor" to guide us 24/7 in our daily living is critically important to our spiritual survival. It will be available to God's children *forever* throughout our entire lifetime. His office is never closed. No insurance premiums are to be paid before benefits can be received from this professional counselor. There's no cash layout for services rendered. No person is turned away because of his or her inability to pay cash up front. God's "ensurance" plan is available to every ethnic group—regardless of race, creed, or color. Racial discrimination and favoritism are not part of the Trinity's vocabulary.

Yes, He will silently guide us through every day in every way. A personal experience illustrates this truth.

> In February 2013, the Spirit clearly told me, "Sell your house." It was in dire need of repair. Despite this, the home was sold within ten days without the assistance of a realtor or a sign in the yard. Two thirds of the money was in the bank.

This would have never happened through my own efforts.

To allow God to work within our lives through Jesus and the Holy Spirit is *truly* the only passageway from living the cheated lifestyle Satan offers to a "full life" in Christ.

As Jesus promised, His followers will never be left alone without guidance. This is His guarantee—you can take it to the bank.

Onward

to

Higher Ground

References

[1] *Webster's* 1982, op. cit., p. 731
[2] Ibid., p. 466

Section Nine

How to Build a Spiritual Life

Prelude

Is there anything more frustrating than being expected to do something without being told how to do it?

If a sewing machine, along with all of the necessary supplies for making a dress, was left at the door of a man, quite likely he would become very frustrated if he was expected to do it without instruction.

The same would be true if a car engine was placed outside of the average woman's home with expectation of repair without direction or training.

This absurd thinking is not characteristic of God. The love of our Heavenly Father will not allow Him to leave us meandering through life trying to get to heaven without day-to-day guidance.

Therefore, He has left many directives. They are offered as instructions to ensure continual spiritual growth.

His guidance is based upon *solid* truth. It is not based upon man's opinion. There will be *no* spiritual lies. Submission to His teachings will bring peace of mind.

Chapter One

Fear

One of the most misunderstood subjects in relationship to our spiritual well-being is *fear*. Because of this, our human response ranges from fear nothing, having reverence for God, to being petrified of Him.

This Scripture illustrates a contrast:

> [8] Let all the earth fear the Lord;
> Let all the inhabitants of the world stand in awe of Him.
> Psalms 33:8 (NASB)

The Hebrew word for fear is *yare'*. It means "to be afraid, to fear, to revere, to be feared, to be dreadful, to be reverenced, to terrify, to make afraid. There are two main types of fear described by *yare'*.

(a) the emotion and intellectual anticipation of harm, what one feels may go wrong for him.
(b) a very positive feeling of awe or reverence for God, which may be expressed in piety or formal worship."[1]

An example for the first definition: humanity's inherent desire to live will prompt those in immediate danger to escape from a burning building, fearing death or injury.

So how do we develop a *very positive feeling of awe or respect* for God—the type of fear that ensures our spiritual security throughout eternity?

Foundational truth

> [13] Now all has been heard;
> here is the conclusion of the matter:
> Fear God and keep his commandments,
> for this is the duty of all mankind.
> Ecclesiastes 12:13 (NIV)

Reminders

> [10] The fear of the Lord is the beginning of wisdom,
> and knowledge of the Holy One is understanding.
> Proverbs 9:10 (NIV)

[10] The fear of the LORD is the beginning of wisdom;
all who follow his precepts have good understanding.
To him belongs eternal praise.

Psalms 111:10 (NIV)

Encouragement

[12] Who, then, are those who fear the LORD?
   He will instruct them in the ways they should choose.
[13] They will spend their days in prosperity,
   and their descendants will inherit the land.
[14] The LORD confides in those who fear him;
   he makes his covenant known to them.

Psalms 25:12–14 (NIV)

---

[1] Praise the LORD.
Blessed are those who fear the LORD,
   who find great delight in his commands.

Psalms 112:1 (NIV)

The avenue to learning

[11] Teach me your way, LORD,
   that I may rely on your faithfulness;
give me an undivided heart,
   that I may fear your name.

Psalms 86:11 (NIV)

Special shelter for those who fear God

¹⁸ But the eyes of the Lord are on those who fear him,
  on those whose hope is in his unfailing love.

Psalms 33:18 (NIV)

───

¹¹ You who fear him, trust in the Lord—
  he is their help and shield.

Psalms 115:11 (NIV)

Rewards for those who honor God through sincere obedience

¹⁹ How abundant are the good things
  that you have stored up for those who fear you,
that you bestow in the sight of all,
  on those who take refuge in you.

Psalms 31:19 (NIV)

───

⁵ Those who look to him are radiant;
  their faces are never covered with shame.
⁶ This poor man called, and the Lord heard him;
  he saved him out of all his troubles.

⁷ The angel of the Lord encamps around those who fear him,
   and he delivers them.
⁸ Taste and see that the Lord is good;
   blessed is the one who takes refuge in him.
⁹ Fear the Lord, you his holy people,
   for those who fear him lack nothing.
¹⁰ The lions may grow weak and hungry,
   but those who seek the Lord lack no good thing.
                              Psalms 34:5–10 (NIV)

---

¹¹ For as high as the heavens are above the earth,
   so great is his love for those who fear him;
¹² as far as the east is from the west,
   so far has he removed our transgressions from us.
¹³ As a father has compassion on his children,
   so the Lord has compassion on those who fear him;
¹⁴ for he knows how we are formed,
   he remembers that we are dust.
¹⁵ The life of mortals is like grass,
   they flourish like a flower of the field;
¹⁶ the wind blows over it and it is gone,
   and its place remembers it no more.

¹⁷ But from everlasting to everlasting
   the Lord's love is with those who fear him,
   and his righteousness with their children's children—
                              Psalms 103:11–17 (NIV)

With the proper understanding of healthy fear for the Lord and submission to His directives, there is no reason to fear what is to come at our final judgment.

> [20] Moses said to the people, "Do not be afraid. God has come to test you, so that the fear of God will be with you to keep you from sinning."
>
> Exodus 20:20 (NIV)

Think about it. Is anything more important than developing a healthy fear of Him?

Onward

to

Higher Ground

〰️

References

[1] *Hebrew-Greek Key Word Study Bible,* op.cit., p. 1733, item 3372

Chapter Two

Trust In God

The word "trust" is easier spoken than identified in life. However, our skepticism regarding trust is closely linked to memories of times past when people have proven they could not be trusted.

When this happens, our automatic defense within leaps forward and quickly pulls us inward with the message, "I will never trust again. I have been burned too many times."

Unfortunately, this same attitude can be (and often times is) carried over into our relationship with our Heavenly Father. Consequently, being unable or refusing to trust either man or God, we conclude that the only person to be trusted is self. In time, this leads to being locked into a very dark box with no knowledge of how to escape.

Think for a moment. Do people become spiritually disobedient as the result of their continued blindness from truth, or have they learned the truth but chosen to live rebellious lives? Either way, they are being cheated from the *fulfillment of soul* that is available when they completely trust God.

In an effort to help us work through any negative thoughts we may have regarding God, ask yourself, "When has He shown that He cannot be trusted?"

Perhaps there has been a time when He did not give you what you asked for, but does that mean that He cannot be trusted? Because we want an instant response but do not receive it, does that mean God cannot be trusted? Or does it mean that it may not be best for us to have what we ask for when we ask? God's answer could be "Later."

May David's statements of truth from God's Word bring a ray of light into your life! As indicated in these verses, the beginning point is to "cry out."

⁶ Praise be to the Lord,
   for he has heard my cry for mercy.
⁷ The Lord is my strength and my shield;
   my heart trusts in him, and he helps me.
My heart leaps for joy,
   and with my song I praise him.
⁸ The Lord is the strength of his people,
   a fortress of salvation for his anointed one.

⁹ Save your people and bless your inheritance;
  be their shepherd and carry them forever.

                              Psalms 28:6–9 (NIV)

❧

David knew the importance of being patient:
  ¹⁵ Lord, I wait for you;
    you will answer, Lord my God.

                              Psalms 38:15 (NIV)

❧

¹ I called to the Lord, and he heard me.
  He heard my cries.
² He lifted me out of the grave.
  He lifted me from that muddy place.
He picked me up, put me on solid ground,
  and kept my feet from slipping.
³ He put a new song in my mouth,
  a song of praise to our God.
Many will see what he did and worship him.
  They will put their trust in the Lord.
⁴ Great blessings belong to those who trust in the Lord,
  for those who do not turn to demons and false gods for help.
⁵ Lord my God, you have done many amazing things!
  You have made great plans for us—too many to list.
I could talk on and on about them,
  because there are too many to count.

                              Psalms 40:1–5 (ERV)

Trust In God

¹ I must calm down and turn to God;
  only he can rescue me.
² He is my Rock, the only one who can save me.
  He is my high place of safety, where no army can defeat me.
³ How long will you people attack me?
  Do you all want to kill me?
I am like a leaning wall,
  like a fence ready to fall.
⁴ You want only to destroy me,
  to bring me down from my important position.
It makes you happy to tell lies about me.
  In public, you say nice things,
  but in private, you curse me. Selah
⁵ I must calm down and turn to God;
  he is my only hope.
⁶ He is my Rock, the only one who can save me.
  He is my high place of safety, where no army can defeat me.
⁷ My victory and honor come from God.
  He is the mighty Rock, where I am safe.
⁸ People, always put your trust in God!
  Tell him all your problems.
  God is our place of safety. Selah

Psalms 62:1–8 (ERV)

Because of David's steadfast belief, he invited God to give him hope! He turned to God alone for his *hope*, his *rock*, and his *salvation*. After being at the receiving end of man's acts of mistrust,

David knew God was his only *refuge* to whom he could run for protection.

Notice David's invitation to "people"—it includes you and me. He left these words of comfort and encouragement for us—*"always put your trust in God, tell him all your problems…God is our place of safety."*

༄

[12] Lord Almighty,
 blessed is the one who trusts in you.
Psalms 84:12 (NIV)

This is an undying truth.

Onward

to

Higher Ground

Chapter Three

Faith

Are you asking yourself, "What is faith?" Certainly this is an excellent question! The Bible offers a clear definition:

> [1] Now faith is confidence in what we hope for and assurance about what we do not see.
> Hebrews 11:1 (NIV)

Perhaps you are wondering, "How does one build faith in God when he or she has had little or no exposure to Bible teaching throughout his or her lifetime?"

Another excellent question worthy of a truthful answer based upon Scripture.

¹⁷ Faith comes from hearing the message, and the message is heard through the word about Christ.
Romans 10:17 (NIV)

How important is it to develop a spiritually based faith?

⁶ And without faith it is impossible to please God.
Hebrews 11:6 (NIV)

※

⁸ Be alert and of sober mind. Your enemy the devil prowls around like a roaring lion looking for someone to devour. ⁹ Resist him, standing firm in the faith, because you know that the family of believers throughout the world is undergoing the same kind of sufferings.
I Peter 5:8–9 (NIV)

※

⁷ Submit yourselves, then, to God. Resist the devil, and he will flee from you. ⁸ Come near to God and he will come near to you. Wash your hands, you sinners, and purify your hearts, you double-minded.
James 4:7–8 (NIV)

(Without submitting to God's teaching, this cannot happen!)

There are two Scriptures that connect fear with faith within the same passage; however, as always, it is important to keep them within the context in which they were written.

> [17] But if some of the branches were broken off, and you, being a wild olive, were grafted in among them and became partaker with them of the rich root of the olive tree, [18] do not be arrogant toward the branches; but if you are arrogant, *remember that* it is not you who supports the root, but the root *supports* you. [19] You will say then, "Branches were broken off so that I might be grafted in." [20] Quite right, they were broken off for their unbelief, but you stand by your faith. Do not be conceited, but fear; [21] for if God did not spare the natural branches, He will not spare you, either. [22] Behold then the kindness and severity of God; to those who fell, severity, but to you, God's kindness, if you continue in His kindness; otherwise you also will be cut off.
> Romans 11:17-22 (NASB)

◈

The second verse linking fear with faith expresses Paul's concern for the Christians in Thessalonica.

> [5] For this reason, when I could endure *it* no longer, I also sent to find out about your faith, for fear that the tempter might have tempted you, and our labor would be in vain.
> I Thessalonians 3:5 (NASB)

However, there is no teaching in the Bible indicating that those who are not Christians but recognize their desire and need for a restored relationship with God are to be afraid to pray to Him for fear that He will not hear them.

Lack of faith leads to fear. To remove fear, one must increase his or her faith in God. This is accomplished by *putting into practice* Bible teachings. Without faith we will remain captive *within our minds* with no hope of escape. Trusting God and following Jesus will enable us to develop stronger faith.

Both a growing faith and a living hope in Jesus are key elements to regaining and maintaining righteous living in the sight of God.

> [21] But God has a way to make people right, and it has nothing to do with the law. He has now shown us that new way, which the law and the prophets told us about. [22] God makes people right through their faith in Jesus Christ. He does this for all who believe in Christ. Everyone is the same. [23] All have sinned and are not good enough to share God's divine greatness. [24] They are made right with God by his grace. This is a free gift. They are made right with God by being made free from sin through Jesus Christ. [25-26] God gave Jesus as a way to forgive people's sins through their faith in him. God can forgive them because the blood sacrifice of Jesus pays for their sins. God gave Jesus to show that he always does what is right and fair. He was right in the past when he was patient and did not punish people for their sins. And in our own time he still does what is right. God worked all this out in a way that allows him to judge people fairly and still make right any person who has faith in Jesus.
>
> Romans 3:21–26 (ERV)

Faith

~~~~~

And when my soul is properly nourished through continuous feeding of spiritual food, my faith and hope in Jesus will flourish, beyond what anyone ever thought possible. The following is a very clear illustration of this truth!

> [3] Jesus has the power of God. And his power has given us everything we need to live a life devoted to God. We have these things because we know him. Jesus chose us by his glory and goodness, [4] through which he also gave us the very great and rich gifts that he promised us. With these gifts you can share in being like God. And so you will escape the ruin that comes to people in the world because of the evil things they want.
> [5] Because you have these blessings, do all you can to add to your life these things: to your faith add goodness; to your goodness add knowledge; [6] to your knowledge add self-control; to your self-control add patience; to your patience add devotion to God; [7] to your devotion add kindness toward your brothers and sisters in Christ, and to this kindness add love. [8] If all these things are in you and growing, you will never fail to be useful to God. You will produce the kind of fruit that should come from your knowledge of our Lord Jesus Christ. [9] But those who don't grow in these blessings are blind. They cannot see clearly what they have. They have forgotten that they were cleansed from their past sins.
>
> [10] My brothers and sisters, God called you and chose you to be his. Do your best to live in a way that shows you really are God's called and chosen people. If you do all this, you will never fall.

[11] And you will be given a very great welcome into the kingdom of our Lord and Savior Jesus Christ, a kingdom that never ends.

II Peter 1:3–11 (ERV)

And the final goal of our faith:
[3] Praise be to the God and Father of our Lord Jesus Christ! In his great mercy he has given us new birth into a living hope through the resurrection of Jesus Christ from the dead, [4] and into an inheritance that can never perish, spoil or fade. This inheritance is kept in heaven for you, [5] who through faith are shielded by God's power until the coming of the salvation that is ready to be revealed in the last time. [6] In all this you greatly rejoice, though now for a little while you may have had to suffer grief in all kinds of trials. [7] These have come so that the proven genuineness of your faith—of greater worth than gold, which perishes even though refined by fire—may result in praise, glory and honor when Jesus Christ is revealed. [8] Though you have not seen him, you love him; and even though you do not see him now, you believe in him and are filled with an inexpressible and glorious joy, [9] for you are receiving the end result of your faith, the salvation of your souls.

I Peter 1:3–9 (NIV)

---

[1] And let us run with perseverance the race marked out for us, [2] fixing our eyes on Jesus, the pioneer and perfecter of faith. For the joy set before him he endured the cross,

scorning its shame, and sat down at the right hand of the throne of God. ³ Consider him who endured such opposition from sinners, so that you will not grow weary and lose heart.

Hebrews 12:1–3 (NIV)

Any discouraging thoughts regarding prayer or the development of our faith in God are from Satan. The devil does not want us to benefit from strong spiritual relationships with our Heavenly Father through prayer!

These thoughts are being shared for one purpose—to help us to understand that *our desire to pray to God should be pursued through faith,* with the knowledge and reassurance that because of His love for us and our faith in Him, He *will* respond.

True trust and belief in God cannot float in the same boat with fear of rejection by Him. True belief and faith in Jesus can conquer the insurmountable because faith removes fear. Through our faith in Jesus, God's power will be passed on to us, the true followers of God, to do what we never thought possible!

> ¹ Therefore, since we have been justified through faith, we have peace with God through our Lord Jesus Christ, ² through whom we have gained access by faith into this grace in which we now stand. And we boast in the hope of the glory of God. ³ Not only so, but we also glory in our sufferings, because we know that suffering produces perseverance; ⁴ perseverance, character; and character, hope. ⁵ And hope does not put us to shame, because God's love

has been poured out into our hearts through the Holy Spirit, who has been given to us.
Romans 5:1–5 (NIV)

The testing of a Christian's faith is a part of the growth process that is critical to the development and survival of our spiritual well-being.

² Consider it pure joy, my brothers and sisters, whenever you face trials of many kinds, ³ because you know that the testing of your faith produces perseverance. ⁴ Let perseverance finish its work so that you may be mature and complete, not lacking anything.
James 1:2–4 (NIV)

---

³⁵ So do not throw away your confidence; it will be richly rewarded.
³⁶ You need to persevere so that when you have done the will of God, you will receive what he has promised. ³⁷ For,
"In just a little while,
he who is coming will come
and will not delay."
³⁸ And,
"But my righteous one will live by faith.
And I take no pleasure
in the one who shrinks back."

Hebrews 10:35–38 (NIV)

May these words of comfort and reassurance be kept in your mind for the purpose of increasing your faith and trust in your Heavenly Father.

Onward

to

Higher Ground

Chapter Four

Prayer

For some people, prayer is very difficult. Where does our reluctance to pray come from? Without a doubt, Satan does not want us praying to God asking for guidance throughout life. The devil wants us to continuously hold on to the thought that we are so bad God will never listen to us.

However, the truth is that when we pray with a sincere heart, God will answer. Therefore, teaching people how to pray was an important part of His Sermon on the Mount. These were His instructions:

> [6] But when you pray, go into your room, close the door and pray to your Father, who is unseen. Then your Father, who sees what is done in secret, will reward you. [7] And when you pray, do not keep on babbling like pagans, for they think they will be heard because of their many words. [8] Do

not be like them, for your Father knows what you need before you ask him.

⁹ "This, then, is how you should pray:

"'Our Father in heaven,
hallowed be your name,
¹⁰ your kingdom come,
your will be done,
on earth as it is in heaven.
¹¹ Give us today our daily bread.
¹² And forgive us our debts,
as we also have forgiven our debtors.
¹³ And lead us not into temptation,
but deliver us from the evil one.'

¹⁴ For if you forgive other people when they sin against you, your heavenly Father will also forgive you. ¹⁵ But if you do not forgive others their sins, your Father will not forgive your sins.

Matthew 6:6–15 (NIV)

Frequently it is taught that we should not pray the Lord's Prayer because His "kingdom" has already come. The Greek meaning of this word is kingship, sovereignty, authority, rule, especially of God, both in the world, and in the hearts of men; hence: kingdom, in the concrete sense.[1]

With this understanding, we can clearly see that we should make the Lord's prayer a regular part of our daily prayers in recognition of who He is.

The four gospels give us several examples of Jesus praying. This is a tremendously powerful legacy for His followers. He prayed

- During times of extremely high stress;   Matthew 14:1-12, 23 (NIV)
- Expressing expressed thankfulness   Matthew 14:19 (NIV)
- For little children   Matthew 19:13 (NIV)
- While suffering pain and anguish while on the cross   Matthew 26:42 (NIV)
- Before making a decision   Luke 6:12–16 (NIV)
- At the time of His transfiguration   Luke 9:29 (NIV)
- Prayed more earnestly   Luke 22:44 (NIV)
- For those who were killing him   Luke 23:34 (NIV)

Before His death on the cross, Jesus prayed a three-part prayer.

Part One: As He looked toward heaven, Jesus prayed for Himself!

Recognizing the end of His physical life on earth was imminent,

> [1] Jesus spoke these things; and lifting up His eyes to heaven, He said, "Father, the hour has come; glorify Your Son, that the Son may glorify You, [2] even as You gave Him authority over all flesh, that to all whom You have given Him, He may give eternal life. [3] This is eternal life, that they may know You, the only true God, and Jesus Christ whom You have sent. [4] I glorified You on the earth, having accomplished the work which You have given Me to do. [5] Now, Father, glorify Me together with Yourself, with the glory which I had with You before the world was.
>
> John 17:1–5 (NASB)

Part Two: Praying for Himself was followed by praying for current followers.

> ⁶ "I have manifested Your name to the men whom You gave Me out of the world; they were Yours and You gave them to Me, and they have kept Your word. ⁷ Now they have come to know that everything You have given Me is from You; ⁸ for the words which You gave Me I have given to them; and they received *them* and truly understood that I came forth from You, and they believed that You sent Me. ⁹ I ask on their behalf; I do not ask on behalf of the world, but of those whom You have given Me; for they are Yours; ¹⁰ and all things that are Mine are Yours, and Yours are Mine; and I have been glorified in them. ¹¹ I am no longer in the world; and *yet* they themselves are in the world, and I come to You. Holy Father, keep them in Your name, *the name* which You have given Me, that they may be one even as We *are*. ¹² While I was with them, I was keeping them in Your name which You have given Me; and I guarded them and not one of them perished but the son of perdition, so that the Scripture would be fulfilled.
>
> John 17:6–12 (NASB)

Part Three: Oh the strength to be gained through the knowledge that Jesus is praying that Christians have no division among us.

20 "I do not ask on behalf of these alone, but for those also who believe in Me through their word; 21 that they may all be one; even as You, Father, *are* in Me and I in You, that they also may be in Us, so that the world may believe that You sent Me.
Their Future Glory
22 The glory which You have given Me I have given to them, that they may be one, just as We are one; 23 I in them and You in Me, that they may be perfected in unity, so that the world may know that You sent Me, and loved them, even as You have loved Me. 24 Father, I desire that they also, whom You have given Me, be with Me where I am, so that they may see My glory which You have given Me, for You loved Me before the foundation of the world.
25 "O righteous Father, although the world has not known You, yet I have known You; and these have known that You sent Me; 26 and I have made Your name known to them, and will make it known, so that the love with which You loved Me may be in them, and I in them."

John 17:20–26 (NASB)

Indeed, Jesus was a man of prayer. He prayed

* Before going to the cross John 18:1 (NIV)

Strength and guidance are received when we focus upon the impact of Jesus' prayers. He was going to die an ugly death. Nonetheless, His focus was upon glorifying God through His death and asking God to protect those being left on earth to serve Him and all future believers.

Why was God responsive to Jesus' prayers?

> ⁷ During the days of Jesus' life on earth, he offered up prayers and petitions with fervent cries and tears to the one who could save him from death, and he was heard because of his reverent submission. ⁸ Son though he was, he learned obedience from what he suffered
>
> Hebrews 5:7–8 (NIV)

In contrast to this, there is a teaching that God does not hear a sinner's prayer. However to accept this without further study kills any hope within those seeking a relationship with God, their Heavenly Father.

Therefore, it is time to examine this teaching very closely. First, this statement of truth must be considered:

> ² But your iniquities have separated
>   you from your God;
> your sins have hidden his face from you,
>   so that he will not hear.
>
> Isaiah 59:2 (NIV)

It is very important that we understand these words were spoken to the Israelites (God's chosen people) who were continuously turning away from Him. They were a very rebellious people—continuously ignoring God's warnings, complaining and expressing discontent in many areas of their lives.

Now, let's turn our attention to Jesus' teaching regarding prayer during His Sermon on the Mount. It is important to keep in mind that He was speaking to the *masses*, which included many who were not obedient followers.

Although it is not always wise, let's use logic as we answer the question of whether or not Jesus hears the prayers of one who is not a Christian. These questions need to be asked:

* If the prayers of the lost will not be heard, why would Jesus instruct a massive crowd (including sinners) how to do it?
* What other avenue of approach does mankind have to come to Jesus?

It is impossible for us to come to Him physically. The only way humanity can respond to and accept His invitation is through prayer.

With these thoughts in mind, let's examine the Scripture used to say He does not hear the prayers of a non-Christian sincerely seeking God's guidance.

Jesus had restored the eyesight of a man who had been blind since birth. The Jewish leaders had considered the man to be "born in sin." They were not willing to accept the fact that Jesus had healed him. Therefore, they were basically calling the healed man a liar. And the man's reply was:

> ³¹ We all know that God does not listen to sinners, but he will listen to anyone who worships and obeys him. ³² This is the first time we have ever heard of anyone healing the eyes of someone born blind. ³³ This man must be from God. If he were not from God, he could not do anything like this."
>
> John 9:31–33 (ERV)

The truth is clearly illustrated that this false teaching began as the result of lifting a *partial* sentence from the context without asking, "Who said it to whom?" When read in context, it becomes very clear that this conclusion was made by a human--the one who had received his sight)—*not* Jesus.

Therefore, the leaders considered the healed man's response to be an insult. Thus, their answer was:

> ³⁴ The Jewish leaders answered, "You were born full of sin! Are you trying to teach us?" And they told the man to get out of the synagogue and to stay out.
>
> John 9:34 (ERV)

It is important to see that Jesus' compassion did not allow Him to leave this man emotionally battered. Rather, Jesus went looking for him.

> ³⁵ When Jesus heard that they had forced the man to leave, he found him and asked him, "Do you believe in the Son of Man?"

> ³⁶ The man said, "Tell me who he is, sir, so I can believe in him."
> ³⁷ Jesus said to him, "You have already seen him. The Son of Man is the one talking with you now."
>
> ³⁸ The man answered, "Yes, I believe, Lord!" Then he bowed and worshiped Jesus.
>
> John 9:35–38 (ERV)

After the verbal abuse the healed man had suffered from the Pharisees, Jesus calmed his shattered nerves. How did He do it? He simply identified Himself to the man who had been healed. As a result, the healed man knew his faith was placed in the right person.

Notice the difference in attitudes—the Pharisees had one of "we know everything" versus the blind man's attitude of being humble, open-minded, and receptive to truth.

Cornelius prayed to God *before* he became a Christian (Acts 10:4).
True hope is gained when the two teachings--God does not hear the prayers of sinners vs He listens to those who are earnestly seeking Him and desire spiritual healing--are laid side by side. Bible truth shines forth as this filter process is used.

Further, consider this truth. Before the Apostle Paul became a follower of God, his name was Saul. He was a sinner in the sight of God. Paul referred to himself as "the worst of sinners." Why?

> ¹ Meanwhile, Saul was still breathing out murderous threats against the Lord's disciples. He went to the high priest ² and asked him for letters to the synagogues in Damascus, so that if he found any there who belonged to the Way, whether men or women, he might take them as prisoners to Jerusalem.
>
> Acts 9:1–2 (NIV)

Despite having "been there, done that," did God hear Saul's prayer? This message will bring new hope!

> ¹⁰ In Damascus there was a disciple named Ananias. The Lord called to him in a vision, "Ananias!"
> "Yes, Lord," he answered.
> ¹¹ The Lord told him, "Go to the house of Judas on Straight Street and ask for a man from Tarsus named Saul, for he is praying.
>
> Acts 9:10–11(NIV)

Saul was doing *what*? Yes, he was *praying to God.* How could God allow such a sinful man to pray to Him? Paul's message:

> ¹² I thank Christ Jesus our Lord, who has strengthened me, because He considered me faithful, putting me into service, ¹³ even though I was formerly a blasphemer and a persecutor and a violent aggressor. Yet I was shown mercy because I acted ignorantly in unbelief; ¹⁴ and the grace of our Lord was more than abundant, with the faith and love which are *found* in Christ Jesus.
>
> I Timothy 1:12-14 (NASB)

Although Paul had been a strict Pharisee steeped in manmade laws, *after* his submission to God, he was transformed into a very powerful tool of service to Him. Paul became an apostle (Romans 1:1), proclaiming the truth regarding Jesus' power and message of salvation. Additionally, and through the guidance of the Holy Spirit, he authored thirteen books in the New Testament!

Indeed, God's purpose was then and still is today to help those blinded to the truth of the Gospel to see the real truth therein. When mankind responds to this, they will grow to know the reality of God's love for them through personal experience.

David was another person guilty of major sin. His story is recorded in I and II Samuel. Psalms 51 records his penitent prayer asking God for a clean and contrite heart.

Failing to share the following verses would not be sharing the *whole* truth. It is important to understand there are times when God will *not* hear or answer our prayers!

> [9] If anyone turns a deaf ear to my instruction,
> even their prayers are detestable.
> Proverbs 28:9 (NIV)

In other words, if we are not willing to listen to Him, He will not listen to us.

Also, God will not answer selfish prayers.

> [1] Do you know where your fights and arguments come from? They come from the selfish desires that make war inside you. [2] You want things, but you don't get them. So

you kill and are jealous of others. But you still cannot get what you want. So you argue and fight. You don't get what you want because you don't ask God. ³ Or when you ask, you don't receive anything, because the reason you ask is wrong. You only want to use it for your own pleasure.

⁴ You people are not faithful to God! You should know that loving what the world has is the same as hating God. So anyone who wants to be friends with this evil world becomes God's enemy. ⁵ Do you think the Scriptures mean nothing? The Scriptures say, "The Spirit God made to live in us wants us only for himself." ⁶ But the kindness God shows is greater. As the Scripture says, "God is against the proud, but he is kind to the humble."

James 4:1–6 (ERV)

These teachings may be very challenging for humanity. However, when the Christian life is pursued and accepted according to God's Word, Jesus brings peace to the heart and soul as we continually claim God's power to overcome. He *always* listens to prayers from a submissive heart.

These thoughts have been shared in an effort to provide hope and comfort to your spiritual future. May every person sincerely searching for God be assured with confidence that *Jesus will hear your prayers when approached with the same attitude as those of Paul and David!*

God, through Jesus, wants everyone to experience spiritual healing—no exclusions!

Certainly prayer before entering into Bible study is a must if we are to glean from it the understandings God intends. This goal cannot be attained without prayer:

¹⁵ Do your best to present yourself to God as one approved, a worker who does not need to be ashamed and who correctly handles the word of truth.

II Timothy 2:15 (NIV)

Onward

to

Higher Ground

⸙

References

[1] biblehub.com, Greek #932

This prose uniquely and eloquently expresses the connection between prayer and Bible study. Anyone wanting to grow in his or her faith has learned through time that the two are inseparable.

BIBLE STUDY and PRAYER

Bible Study points us to God.
Prayer acquaints us with God.

Bible Study gives evidence as to what God is like.
Prayer draws us to that likeness.

Bible Study reveals what God expects.
Prayer conforms us to those expectations.

Bible Study indicates what God's promises are.
Prayer claims those promises for us.

Bible Study declares God in past history.
Prayer incorporates Him into present reality.

Bible Study exhibits the involvement of the Father
the Son and the Holy Spirit.
Prayer integrates the one who prays into that involvement.

Bible Study convicts us of sin.

Prayer turns us from sin.

Anna M. Griffith
21st Century Christian
February 1992
(Used by Permission)

༄༅

Fear, trust in God, faith, prayer, and Bible study are all very important components to building a spiritual life. However, we will still experience spiritual emptiness if we do not *put into practice* God's commandments.

A healthy fear of God will encourage us to do this.

SECTION TEN

God's Desire for Man

PRELUDE

Throughout this book, many references have been made to the phrase "*Same Page Thinking*" with God. Now let's focus upon the primary reason why this attitude of mind must become part of our mindset.

God's Plan for Man is for us to spend eternity with Him in heaven. However, many people question whether they will be allowed to enter into that peaceful abode.

Nonetheless, through Jesus, we have ensurance that heaven will be our home when we allow *Same Page Thinking* with God to become our lifestyle.

Despite how hard we may try, it is impossible for the human mind to fully comprehend how to travel the road leading to heaven. Therefore, it is vitally important that we become "like-minded" and fix our eyes on Jesus. Remember, He is the only One who can lead us home.

Do you realize that our individual lives—yes, *yours and mine*—will influence when the end of the world will come? It is true!

> [10] But the day of the Lord will come like a thief. The heavens will disappear with a roar; the elements will be destroyed by fire, and the earth and everything done in it will be laid bare.
> [11] Since everything will be destroyed in this way, what kind of people ought you to be? You ought to live holy and godly lives [12] as you look forward to the day of God and speed its coming.
>
> II Peter 3:10–12 (NIV)

Did you grab hold of the words "as…you speed its coming"? Four very important points are very clear:

* This is a strong indication that God knows what quality of life we are living from day to day?
* He is encouraging us to live as closely to Jesus as possible.
* As a result, the evil world we know today will end sooner.
* This clearly demonstrates God's extreme patience and love for mankind.

Come along as we learn more about the lifestyle that will speed the end of this wicked world and how to enter into it.

Chapter One

Understanding The Need For Baptism By Immersion

For the purpose of providing a *truth-filled* concept of God's plan of salvation for man, it is necessary for us to have complete understanding of the knowledge base and mind-set needed before submitting to baptism. Without this foundation being laid, we are *not* true children of God in His sight!

As these Scriptures indicate, our spiritual salvation is *not* based upon any one factor alone. However, *faith* is absolutely foundational to our salvation.

> [6] And without faith it is impossible to please God, because anyone who comes to him must believe that he exists and that he rewards those who earnestly seek him.
> Hebrews 11:6 (NIV)

Remember,
> [17] Faith comes from hearing the message, and the message is heard through the word about Christ.
>
> Romans 10:17 (NIV)

༺ঔ༻

Then we must believe the words of Christ:

> *[16] Whoever believes and is baptized will be saved, but whoever does not believe will be condemned.*
>
> Mark 16:16 (NIV)

༺ঔ༻

Repent:

> [38] Peter replied, "Repent and be baptized, every one of you, in the name of Jesus Christ for the forgiveness of your sins.
>
> Acts 2:38 (NIV)

༺ঔ༻

> [8] Even if I caused you sorrow by my letter, I do not regret it. Though I did regret it—I see that my letter hurt you, but only for a little while— [9] yet now I am happy, not because you were made sorry, but because your sorrow led you to repentance. For you became sorrowful as God intended

and so were not harmed in any way by us. ¹⁰ Godly sorrow brings repentance that leads to salvation and leaves no regret, but worldly sorrow brings death. ¹¹ See what this godly sorrow has produced in you: what earnestness, what eagerness to clear yourselves, what indignation, what alarm, what longing, what concern, what readiness to see justice done.

II Corinthians 7:8–11 (NIV)

Confess our sins:

⁹ If you declare with your mouth, "Jesus is Lord," and believe in your heart that God raised him from the dead, you will be saved. ¹⁰ For it is with your heart that you believe and are justified, and it is with your mouth that you profess your faith and are saved.

Romans 10:9–10 (NIV)

These teachings are both preliminary and foundational to our salvation. They must be understood before submitting to baptism. Without a complete understanding of the purpose of baptism, any baptism submitted to earlier may not be valid in the sight of God.

When we are trying to decide whether or not we should do something, understanding the need, purpose, or goal for doing it makes the decision-making process much easier.

The same principle can be applied to deciding whether or not one should be baptized. In searching all forty-five Bible translations included in www.biblegateway.com, only two—the *Common English Bible* and *God's Word Translation*—contain the phrase "must be baptized."

Therefore, it would be easy to conclude that one does *not* have to be baptized. However, as we examine Scriptures more closely, a clearer understanding of the *need*, *purpose*, and *goal* of baptism shines forth.

First of all it is important to remember that at the time of our birth we were born spiritually pure. Sin had not yet been introduced into our lives; therefore, we had a direct spiritual connection with our Heavenly Father. To live a sin-free life was God's plan for man from the very beginning.

However, as the result of Satan's interaction with Eve in the Garden of Eden, sin was introduced to mankind. As a result, man's direct spiritual connection to God was broken. Therefore, the <u>need</u> for being reconnected exists.

Referring to Jesus:

[25] He was delivered over to death for our sins and was raised to life for our justification.
                                            Romans 4:25 (NIV)

> [8] God demonstrates his own love for us in this: While we were still sinners, Christ died for us.
>
> Romans 5:8 (NIV)

These verses clearly indicate how we are to be reunited with God—be "born of water" and "the Spirit." Why is this important? Listen carefully as the Bible explains:

> [1] Now there was a Pharisee, a man named Nicodemus who was a member of the Jewish ruling council. [2] He came to Jesus at night and said, "Rabbi, we know that you are a teacher who has come from God. For no one could perform the signs you are doing if God were not with him."
> [3] Jesus replied, "Very truly I tell you, no one can see the kingdom of God unless they are born again."
> [4] "How can someone be born when they are old?" Nicodemus asked. "Surely they cannot enter a second time into their mother's womb to be born!"
> [5] Jesus answered, "Very truly I tell you, no one can enter the kingdom of God unless they are born of water and the Spirit. [6] Flesh gives birth to flesh, but the Spirit gives birth to spirit. [7] You should not be surprised at my saying, 'You must be born again.'
>
> John 3:1–7 (NIV)

To be restored once again to a state of spiritual purity in the sight of God is the _purpose_ of baptism.

Ananias asked Saul:

¹⁴ "...what are you waiting for? Get up, be baptized and wash your sins away, calling on his name."

Acts 22:14 (NIV)

⁹ Since we have now been justified by his blood, how much more shall we be saved from God's wrath through him! ¹⁰ For if, while we were God's enemies, we were reconciled to him through the death of his Son, how much more, having been reconciled, shall we be saved through his life! ¹¹ Not only is this so, but we also boast in God through our Lord Jesus Christ, through whom we have now received reconciliation.

Romans 5:9–11 (NIV)

The Bible gives many examples of people in all walks of life submitting to baptism by immersion. Even though there was absolutely no need for Jesus to be baptized to wash away His sin, He was baptized to fulfill all righteousness. He led by example.

It is important to understand there is a direct parallel between Jesus' death, burial, and resurrection and the baptism of an individual who decides to submit to God's plan for spiritual cleansing from sin.

MESSAGE OF MOST IMPORTANCE

² By this gospel you are saved, if you hold firmly to the word I preached to you. Otherwise, you have believed in vain.
³ For what I received I passed on to you as of first importance: that Christ died for our sins according to the Scriptures, ⁴ that he was buried, that he was raised on the third day according to the Scriptures.

I Corinthians 15:2-4 (NIV)

JESUS' DEATH, BURIAL, AND RESURRECTION

Death

³⁴ One of the soldiers pierced Jesus' side with a spear, bringing a sudden flow of blood and water.

John 19:34 (NIV)

Burial

⁵⁹ Joseph took the body, wrapped it in a clean linen cloth, ⁶⁰ and placed it in his own new tomb that he had cut out of the rock

Matthew 27:59 (NIV)

Physical Resurrection

² There was a violent earthquake, for an angel of the Lord came down from heaven and, going to the tomb, rolled back the stone and sat on it. ³ His appearance was like lightning, and his clothes were white as snow. ⁴ The guards were so afraid of him that they shook and became like dead men.
⁵ The angel said to the women, "Do not be afraid, for I know that you are looking for Jesus, who was crucified. ⁶ He is not here; he has risen, just as he said. Come and see the place where he lay.

Matthew 28:2–6 (NIV)

Spiritual Resurrection

⁵¹ While he was blessing them, he left them and was taken up into heaven.

Luke 24:51 (NIV)

ARE SYMBOLIZED THROUGH

My Death, My Burial

⁴ We were therefore buried with him through baptism into death in order that, just as Christ was raised from the dead through the glory of the Father, we too may live a new life.

Romans 6:4 (NIV)

My Physical Resurrection while living on earth

> ⁵ For if we have been united with him in a death like his, we will certainly also be united with him in a resurrection like his.
>
> Romans 6:5 (NIV)

My Gift from God

> ³⁸ "And you will receive the gift of the Holy Spirit.
>
> Acts 2:38 (NIV)

God's Desire

> ¹³ May the God of hope fill you with all joy and peace as you trust in him, so that you may overflow with hope by the power of the Holy Spirit.
>
> Romans 15:13 (NIV)

Remember the light that was shed upon understanding the term "little child" as it is used in Matthew 19:14? The Greek meaning indicates that we are born as "immature Christians" in the sight of God.

The very fact that the new babe in Christ is given the gift of the Holy Spirit *immediately* after baptism emphasizes the newborn Christian's need for strength and guidance—beginning with day one in one's walk with Jesus. It is extremely important that the babe in Christ realizes the value of this gift.

My Spiritual Resurrection at the End of Time

¹³ Brothers and sisters, we do not want you to be uninformed about those who sleep in death, so that you do not grieve like the rest of mankind, who have no hope. ¹⁴ For we believe that Jesus died and rose again, and so we believe that God will bring with Jesus those who have fallen asleep in him. ¹⁵ According to the Lord's word, we tell you that we who are still alive, who are left until the coming of the Lord, will certainly not precede those who have fallen asleep. ¹⁶ For the Lord himself will come down from heaven, with a loud command, with the voice of the archangel and with the trumpet call of God, and the dead in Christ will rise first. ¹⁷ After that, we who are still alive and are left will be caught up together with them in the clouds to meet the Lord in the air. And so we will be with the Lord forever. ¹⁸ Therefore encourage one another with these words.

Thessalonians 4:13–18 (NIV)

When people are baptized by the authority of Christ, we have His reassurance:

¹⁸ So he came to them and said, "All authority in heaven and on earth is given to me. ¹⁹ So go and make followers of all people in the world. Baptize them in the name of the Father and the Son and the Holy Spirit. ²⁰ Teach them to obey everything that I have told you to do. You can be sure that I will be with you always. I will continue with you until the end of time."

Matthew 28:18–20 (ERV)

This closer examination supports the truth that spiritual baptism by immersion in water is done as the result of one recognizing his or her need for spiritual cleansing. It is a *personal* decision—not one made for me by others.

Now let's take a closer look in the book of Acts to understand that people from *all* walks of life who chose to follow Jesus were cleansed from their sins as their first step walking with Him. This same truth applies to us today.

Chapter Two

Examples Of Baptisms In The New Testament

Person:	Jesus
Position in life:	God's Son
Information given:	Came from Galilee to Jordan River to be baptized
	Jesus was baptized to fulfill all righteousness.
Deeper insight:	After coming up out of the water, the heavens opened; the Spirit of God descended from heaven lighting on him saying, "This is my Son, whom I love; with him I am well pleased."
Scripture:	Matthew 3:13–17 (NIV)

Examples Of Baptisms In The New Testament

Collectively the following Scriptures clearly show examples of people in all walks of life recognizing their need for baptism. Some responded after being taught the difference between being baptized as an indication of their repentance from sin and the forgiveness of sin.

After understanding their individual need, those believing in Jesus submitted to God's plan for salvation. Through baptism they entered the narrow gate. As a result, they were on the right road leading to heaven.

People:	General Public
Information given:	People came from Jerusalem and all Judea and the whole region of Jordan to hear John's message.
Deeper insight:	They had been baptized with water as an indication of their repentance for having sinned. It was not done to be cleansed from sin.
Time frame:	Immediately in the river Jordan
Scripture:	Matthew 3:5–6 (NIV)

༺꧂

People:	Jews
Position in life:	God's chosen people

Information given:	They were responsible for crucifying Christ.
Deeper insight:	People were in need of cleansing and forgiveness of sins. As the result of Peter's sermon on the Day of Pentecost, many Jews were convinced they were responsible for the death of the Son of God. They were cut to the heart. They accepted Peter's message and asked, "Brothers, what shall we do?" Three thousand were baptized.
Time frame:	Same day
Scripture:	Acts 2:36–41 (NIV)

Person:	Simon
Position in life:	A Sorcerer
Information given:	He thought he was someone great.
Deeper insight:	After his baptism, Simon became a close follower of Philip because he was astonished by the miracles Philip performed. Peter and John came to Samaria where Simon offered them money to buy the power of the Holy Spirit. He was

	condemned by Peter for his greedy attitude. Simon asked Peter to pray for him because of the wickedness in Simon's heart.
Time frame:	Same day
Scripture:	Acts 8:9–11, 8:18–24 (NIV)

People:	Samaritans (both high and low status in life)
Position in life:	They had been followers of Simon, the sorcerer.
Information given:	These people considered Simon to be "the divine power known as the Great Power."
Deeper insight:	However, they had been blinded from the truth of the "good news of the kingdom of God." After learning the truth, both men and women were baptized.
Time frame:	Same day
Scripture:	Acts 8:12 (NIV)

Person:	Eunuch
Position in life:	Government official
Information given:	He was in charge of the treasury of Candace, Queen of Ethiopia
Deeper insight:	The eunuch was an educated man. He had been to Jerusalem to worship. However, he felt the need to understand the Scriptures more clearly. He asked Philip to explain what he was reading in the book of Isaiah. The eunuch responded to Philip's teaching. He was baptized; then the Spirit took Philip away.
Time frame:	Same day
Scripture:	Acts 8:26–40 (NIV)

Person:	Saul
Position in life:	Criminal
Information given:	Saul persecuted Christians. He witnessed the stoning of Stephen
Deeper insight:	Because Saul was anti-Jesus, he threatened those people who were following Jesus. Saul asked high officials for permission to kill His' followers. While

	traveling to Damascus, the Lord's presence was made known to Saul. As a result, he lost his vision for three days. God gave Ananias the power to restore Saul's sight. Saul, the criminal, was baptized. Later Paul, (his name after accepting Christianity) became an apostle and took the gospel of Christ to the Gentiles.
Time frame:	Immediately after hearing Ananias' message
Scripture:	Acts 7:57–58; Acts 9 (NIV)

Person:	Cornelius
Position in life:	Military officer
Information given:	Gentile
Deeper insight:	He was a *good* man—a devout, God-fearing, generous man who prayed regularly. His attitude toward God was right, yet he was lacking complete knowledge. Cornelius clearly recognized an angel as being sent by God. He immediately sent three men to Joppa. God sent Peter to

Cornelius; he and the hearers were baptized in the name of Jesus Christ.

Time frame:	Immediately after hearing Peter's message
Scripture:	Acts 10 (NIV)

Person:	Lydia
Position in life:	Business woman
Information given:	Worshiper of God
Deeper insight:	She was a dealer in purple cloth. The Lord opened her heart to respond to Paul's teaching. She was baptized, along with members of her household.
Time frame:	Immediately after hearing Paul's message
Scripture:	Acts 16:11–15 (NIV)

Person:	Crispus
Position in life:	Synagogue ruler
Information given:	Believed in the Lord

Deeper insight:	Crispus, along with his entire household and many other Corinthians, believed the gospel teaching and were baptized.
Time frame:	Immediately
Scripture:	Acts 18:7–9 (NIV)

※

People:	About 12 men
Position in life:	Followers of God
Information given:	Wrong understanding of baptism
Deeper Insight:	These 12 had not been taught about the Holy Spirit. They had received John's baptism unto repentance, not baptism for the forgiveness of sins. After being instructed to believe in Jesus, they were baptized again into the name of Jesus.
Time frame:	Immediately after hearing the message
Scripture:	Acts 19:1–5 (NIV)

It is *extremely important* to understand that baptism alone does not ensure our eternal salvation. The Bible does not teach "once saved, always saved." The following verses support this truth.

* The one who endures to the end will be saved.   Matthew 24:13 (NIV)

- We will reap if we do not grow weary.   Galatians 6:9 (NIV)
- We will be presented holy, if we continue in the faith.   Colossians 1:21-23 (NIV)
- Some will fall away from the faith.   I Timothy 4:1 (NIV)
- We are to take care not to fall away from the living God.   Hebrews 3:12 (NIV)
- If we are overcome by the world again we are worse off.   II Peter 2:20 (NIV)
- Be on your guard lest you fall from your own steadfastness.   II Peter 3:17 (NIV)
- Watch out so you don't lose what you have worked for.   II John, v 8 (NIV)

After being reconciled back to God through Christ, we are to remain faithful to Him. This goal is accomplished as we express our love for God through our obedience to His commandments. Following Jesus will provide us with the protection from Satan who will continually try to pull us back into the world.

God's Retirement Plan for His faithful followers is heaven. It is certainly worth any sacrifices we may make.

Praise God for His grace and mercy.

Onward

to

Higher Ground

Chapter Three

As The Result Of Baptism

When we submit to God's commandments in accordance with His will, we can be assured that we are spiritually safe as His children!

> [12] Yet to all who did receive him, to those who believed in his name, he gave the right to become children of God— [13] children born not of natural descent, nor of human decision or a husband's will, but born of God.
>
> John 1:12-13 (NIV)

What makes our submissive obedience to God worthwhile?

> [4] But when the set time had fully come, God sent his Son, born of a woman, born under the law, [5] to redeem those under the law, that we might receive adoption to sonship. [6] Because you are his sons, God sent the Spirit of his Son

into our hearts, the Spirit who calls out, *"**Abba**, Father."* ⁷ So you are no longer a slave, but God's child; and since you are his child, God has made you also an heir.
Galatians 4:4–7 (NIV)

By way of reminder, this powerful teaching is *filled* with encouragement:

⁵ And hope does not put us to shame, because God's love has been poured out into our hearts through the Holy Spirit, who has been given to us.
Romans 5:5 (NIV)

We must *allow* the Spirit to do His work.

¹ So now anyone who is in Christ Jesus is not judged guilty. ² That is because in Christ Jesus the law of the Spirit that brings life made you free. It made you free from the law that brings sin and death. ³ The law was without power because it was made weak by our sinful selves. But God did what the law could not do: He sent his own Son to earth with the same human life that everyone else uses for sin. God sent him to be an offering to pay for sin. So God used a human life to destroy sin. ⁴ He did this so that we could be right just as the law said we must be. Now we don't live following our sinful selves. We live following the Spirit.
⁵ People who live following their sinful selves think only about what they want. But those who live following the Spirit are thinking about what the Spirit wants them to do. ⁶ If your thinking is controlled by your sinful self, there is spiritual death. But if your thinking is controlled by the Spirit,

there is life and peace. ⁷ Why is this true? Because anyone whose thinking is controlled by their sinful self is against God. They refuse to obey God's law. And really they are not able to obey it. ⁸ Those who are ruled by their sinful selves cannot please God.

⁹ But you are not ruled by your sinful selves. You are ruled by the Spirit, if that Spirit of God really lives in you. But whoever does not have the Spirit of Christ does not belong to Christ. ¹⁰ Your body will always be dead because of sin. But if Christ is in you, then the Spirit gives you life, because Christ made you right with God. ¹¹ God raised Jesus from death. And if God's Spirit lives in you, he will also give life to your bodies that die. Yes, God is the one who raised Christ from death, and he will raise you to life through his Spirit living in you.

¹² So, my brothers and sisters, we must not be ruled by our sinful selves. We must not live the way our sinful selves want. ¹³ If you use your lives to do what your sinful selves want, you will die spiritually. But if you use the Spirit's help to stop doing the wrong things you do with your body, you will have true life. ¹⁴ The true children of God are those who let God's Spirit lead them. ¹⁵ The Spirit that we received is not a spirit that makes us slaves again and causes us to fear. The Spirit that we have makes us God's chosen children. And with that Spirit we cry out, "*Abba*, Father." ¹⁶ And the Spirit himself speaks to our spirits and makes us sure that we are God's children. ¹⁷ If we are God's children, we will get the blessings God has for his people. He will give us all that he has given Christ. But we must suffer like Christ suffered. Then we will be able to share his glory.

Romans 8:1–17 (ERV)

And *added to this delightful, never-ending benefit package is the fact that the Holy Spirit is available as our Prayer Partner!*

[26] In the same way, the Spirit helps us in our weakness. We do not know what we ought to pray for, but the Spirit himself intercedes for us through wordless groans. [27] And he who searches our hearts knows the mind of the Spirit, because the Spirit intercedes for God's people in accordance with the will of God.

Romans 8:26–27 (NIV)

There are many additional Scriptures in the Bible identifying how the Holy Spirit *actively* works in the lives of Christians on a daily basis. Allowing Him to guide us will be absolute ensurance that we will no longer suffer the consequences of living the cheated life experienced in the past.

A full life in Christ is guaranteed as long as we accept God and Jesus as Final Authority for righteous living and choose to follow them.

Onward

to

Higher Ground

Chapter Four

My New Home On Earth

Now as a part of our "Child of God Benefit Package," our attention will be focused upon the tremendous blessings received as the result of God adding us to *His* church—*His* "family." His family cannot be found outside of His church. We can only become a part of it by responding to *His* gospel in accordance with *His* plan. As individual people respond to *God's* plan of salvation, *He* adds them to *His* church. It is <u>not</u> an organization that can be "joined."

> ⁴¹ Those who accepted his message were baptized, and about three thousand were added to their number that day.
>
> Acts 2:41 (NIV)

One of the many purposes of the body of Christ—the family of God—is to protect, comfort, and nurture those who have suffered heartache after heartache after heartache as the result of being lured into one or more of Satan's many traps.

Several teachings within Scriptures speak very clearly to the truth that the church is not a physical building, but rather it is comprised of true followers of Jesus.

Remember we learned in Colossians 1:18 that "Jesus, the Son of God, is the head of the body, which is the church." Acts 2 describes when and how the church was established after the death of Christ.

> [22] And God placed all things under his feet and appointed him to be head over everything for the church, [23] which is his body, the fullness of him who fills everything in every way.
>
> Ephesians 1:22–23 (NIV)

The word "the" indicates one church of which Christ, the Son of God, is the head. The origination of all other religious groups can be traced back to a human being!

It is the desire of every physical father for the members of his family to be identified through his last name—i.e., Smith, Jones, etc.

Have you given any thought to why this is true? This is another way that a physical father bears the "image" and "likeness" of his spiritual father. Thus, it is very important to God that His church wears a name that identifies its membership as being part of Him.

Let's look at the names revealed through Scripture that are used to identify the "members," "flock," and "believers" within His Church. More than one name for the church that Jesus established is identified.

*	"My church"	Matthew 16:18 (NIV)
*	"the church of God"	Acts 20:28 (NIV)
*	"church of Christ"	Romans 16:16 (NIV)
*	"church of the firstborn"	Hebrews 12:23 (NIV)
*	"church of the living God"	I Timothy 3:15 (NIV)

All of these names have one common thread; each of them indicates *ownership*—God and Jesus. They are the same—God, the Father, and Jesus who was God living on earth in human form. Each of them points to the *founder* of the church that God lives in. Also as we read these verses, it is important to notice the strong words used, "pillar" and "foundation," which indicate the strength upon which the church has been built.

It is important to understand that, although a religious group may have one of these names above the door, it is dangerous to assume that what is taught therein is in keeping with God's Word.

Below is a suggested screening process.

- First, learn whether or not the group has founding fathers, an "earthly" headquarters or controlling body.
- This information can be gained by typing into Google the name of the religious group and reviewing the what information given.
- Another filter that can be used is to simply ask members of the group their origination and type of worship service.
- If you actually attend one of their religious meetings, observe what you see. Are idols worshipped? Can the teachings presented be easily understood as they should be?
- Be certain of the source of information from which lessons are presented. Classes or sermons are not to be presented through a creed book or catechism.
- Compare what is being taught with Bible teaching. If they do not agree, God's Word must be accepted as truth. A good Bible concordance will help in achieving this goal.

Knowing the guidelines for worship that identify the Lord's church will be most helpful as you proceed with the filtering process.

> [23] Yet a time is coming and has now come when the true worshipers will worship the Father in the Spirit and in truth, for they are the kind of worshipers the Father seeks. [24] God is spirit, and his worshipers must worship in the Spirit and in truth."
>
> John 4:23–24 (NIV)

Bible-authorized qualifications for both elders and deacons are specified within the Bible. Guidelines for their wives are also given. Women are to occupy supportive roles in the Lord's church *under* the leadership of men.

- * Male leadership in the Lord's church:
    - * Elders are to be overseers of the flock for the purpose of support and guidance in spiritual matters.
    - * Deacons are assistants to the elders in many ways.
    I Timothy 3:1-13 (NIV)

    Each congregation is autonomous in that it is not guided or controlled by a board of directors or national headquarters.

- * Male ministers are to preach the word
    II Timothy 4:1-5 (NIV)

- * Regular attendance to worship God and encourage one another.
    Hebrews 10:25 (NIV)

* Observance of the Lord's Supper:
  * On the first day of the week we came together to break bread.
    Acts 20:7 (NIV)

Certainly an appropriate question would be, "What is the Lord's Supper?"
It is a simple meal consisting of a small piece of *unleavened* bread (communion bread), representing Jesus' body, and a small container of *grape* juice, representing His bloodshed on the cross.
Matthew 26:26–28 (NIV)
Luke 22:14–20 (NIV)

* It is to be done in remembrance of His death.
  Corinthians 11:24–25 (NIV)

* Acappella Singing:
  Ephesians 5:19 (NASB)
  Colossians 3:16 (NIV)

Another appropriate question: "What is acappella singing?"
It is singing without instrumental music.

Although several types of musical instruments are mentioned in the Old Testament, there are none in the New. The early church did not use instrumental music.

* Contribution:

II Corinthians 9:7 (NIV)

* Prayer:

James 5:16 (NIV)
I Thessalonians 5:16 (NIV)

After making a comparison between teachings received and Bible truth, you will be able to make a decision regarding your religious affiliation based upon the Word of God.

May God guide each searching soul through this process!

It is important to remember that when and if we choose to submit to God's teaching and become a member of His church, this is not a stopping place but a beginning point for a new life in Christ.

In no way is it meant to be our retirement plan but only the beginning of a new life of service to Christ. We serve Him in appreciation for what He has done for us.

Christians are Jesus' hands and feet to reach out, teach, and guide others to Him. This is one of many missions we are given as Christians.

Onward

to

Higher Ground

Chapter Five

My New Family On Earth

It is not uncommon for people who have chosen to follow Jesus to be disowned by their physical families. Indeed, this results in heartache and frustration known only to the people who have made this sacrifice as the result of obeying the gospel of Christ.

Through God's wisdom, His church was established to provide a spiritual home for His children while living on earth. In this way His followers are brought back to where we are meant to live in peaceful union, one with the other.

> [19] Consequently, you are no longer foreigners and strangers, but fellow citizens with God's people and also members of his household, [20] built on the foundation of the apostles and prophets, with Christ Jesus himself as the chief cornerstone.
>
> Ephesians 2:19–20 (NIV)

The Bible gives us several descriptive terms to help us understand His spiritual body—the church.

> ⁴ For just as each of us has one body with many members, and these members do not all have the same function, ⁵ so in Christ we, though many, form one body, and each member belongs to all the others.
>
> Romans 12:4–5 (NIV)

> ²⁷ Now you are the body of Christ, and each one of you is a part of it.
>
> I Corinthians 12:27 (NIV)

In other words, we become part of a spiritual family.

It is important to remember there are some components of our inner beings that baptism will not wash away. Experiencing them does not mean we have not been spiritually cleansed and reunited back with God through Christ. This must be understood lest the devil is successful in his efforts to pull us back into the world.

These components include:

* *The root from which our sins come!*
  This may appear to be an unrelated thought until we understand the name of the root—free choice. It is not

taken away when we rise up from the waters of baptism. God allows us to exercise this gift throughout our lives.

* *Temptation!*
  The fact that Satan attempted to pull Jesus, the Son of God, away from His Father should certainly serve as a very strong warning for us that we are *not* exempt from these same satanic efforts!

In keeping with his reputation, Satan will use our times of weakness and discouragement to continually tempt us. He will always be prowling around looking for ways to discourage or destroy us. Whether we are young or old, we can be assured that Satan's efforts to pull Christians back into the world will intensify after our decision to follow Jesus. This will continue to be true until the end of time.

Certainly this is not a time to engage in "independent thinking." It is impossible to overcome Satan's influence in our lives without God's guidance.

Always be on guard! As Christians, we *must continually be alert* to his schemes. And when we are being attacked, it is critically important that we ask for help from our Christian family so that we may stand firm. Remember God's warning and promise:

> [12] So, if you think you are standing firm, be careful that you don't fall! [13] No temptation has overtaken you except what

is common to mankind. And God is faithful; he will not let you be tempted beyond what you can bear. But when you are tempted, he will also provide a way out so that you can endure it.

I Corinthians 10:12–13 (NIV)

* *The need for ongoing forgiveness!*

It is equally important for Christians to understand that we will continue to make wrong choices (sin) after becoming a child of God. However, more importantly, we must remember that—through prayer, repentance, and asking for forgiveness of our sins—the blood of Jesus will *continually* restore us into the right relationship with Our Father. This Scripture assures us that as long as we remain in Christ, God will continually forgive our sins!

> [21] At one time you were separated from God. You were his enemies in your minds, because the evil you did was against him. [22] But now he has made you his friends again. He did this by the death Christ suffered while he was in his body. He did it so that he could present you to himself as people who are holy, blameless, and without anything that would make you guilty before him. [23] And that is what will happen if you continue to believe in the Good News you heard. You must remain strong and sure in your faith. You must not let anything cause you to give up the hope that became yours when you heard the Good News.
>
> Colossians 1:21–23 (ERV)

Is there anything more frustrating than being asked to do something without being told or shown how to do it? God is not that type of father. As always, He provides positive direction when trying to comfort others.

> ³ Praise be to the God and Father of our Lord Jesus Christ, the Father of compassion and the God of all comfort, ⁴ who comforts us in all our troubles, so that we can comfort those in any trouble with the comfort we ourselves receive from God.
>
> II Corinthians 1:3–4 (NIV)

Within your new family, you will find many members who have experienced numerous temptations, emotional scars, and needs for forgiveness. They have "been there, done that," but have remained faithful to Christ despite the challenges set before them. Based upon their experiences, your new brothers and sisters in Christ can provide strength and encouragement to you in your efforts to grow forward in Christ.

As adjustments are made in your new family, it is critically important that strong effort is put forth into overcoming attitudes of independence. Holding on to them will inhibit, prevent, or completely stop future spiritual growth. God's family is here on earth to share in times of sorrow, illness, depression, financial problems, death—any and all issues of life.

For God's plan to succeed, we must allow others to help us. Without our cooperation, His plan is thrown completely out of balance. Refusing others help in our time of need is another of Satan's cunning ways to control our thinking. He does not want us to maintain a close relationship with our spiritual family.

These words are spoken from experience. My husband and grandson died six hours apart on the same day. It was only through Christ and His church that I was able to survive. That was three years ago. Today I still turn to my spiritually minded brothers and sisters for encouragement when Satan tries to pull me back. God intends for His church to be a family!

As the Apostle Paul teaches, *we cannot grow forward in Christ while looking backward*! It's absolutely impossible!

Onward

to

Higher Ground

Section Eleven

How to Overcome Evil with Good

Prelude

How do you react when someone tells you that the task at hand is simply too large for you to do?

A strong motivator to get someone to do something is to tell them that they cannot do it! Then they adopt a "I will show them" attitude and go on with meeting the challenge using their own strength.

With this thought in mind, why is it, when God asks us to do something, we engage in negative thinking by saying the job is too big for us? Again, we must ask ourselves "How much thought do we give to the truth that we can do far more than we can possibly imagine with God's strength and power?"

Of course, everyone knows that it is impossible for *one* person to change the whole word. We must look at the positive influence we could have collectively on the whole world when each person does their part.

How to overcome evil with good is another area of life that God provides ample instruction for. The ones that follow are only a few of the whole.

Onward

to

Higher Ground

Chapter One

How To Help Turn The Tide

As we begin, remember Jesus' statement in Matthew 24:12 that, "because of the ongoing increase of sin in the world, the love within the hearts of most will grow cold!"

Follow this with the Apostle Paul's reassurance that *evil can be overcome with good.*

Therefore, the logical questions could be:

* If I do not want to be personally overcome by evil and coldness of heart, what can I do to prevent it from happening?
* If my heart has already grown cold, what steps must be taken to correct "hardening of the hearteries" within me?

As part of the Apostle Paul's appeal to Timothy to remain faithful to God, this counsel was given:

How To Help Turn The Tide

> ⁶ For this reason I remind you to fan into flame the gift of God, which is in you through the laying on of my hands. ⁷ For the Spirit God gave us does not make us timid, but gives us power, love and self-discipline.
>
> II Timothy 1:6–7 (NIV)

Certainly it is important to remember that, as the result of the Holy Spirit living within us, we can have a positive attitude that will develop into the confidence that we can make a difference in this world. As Christians, if we allow the small flame within us to grow into a fire, great good will be accomplished as the result of the Spirit's work.

When we put God's recipes into practice and direct them toward *self-improvement,* we have tremendous prescriptions for recovery from any negative thinking that may be creeping into our hearts and minds.

Another necessary spiritual attitude is one of humility. We cannot be arrogant if we are to be successful in influencing others in a positive way.

Foundational to success is one's personal decision to have the right attitude of heart toward life in general. If I do not accept the circumstances within my own life with a positive mind-set, it will be difficult to overcome evil with good.

God's Word reveals several "recipes" teaching us how to strive toward this goal. Following them will certainly help to change the path our world is following today. Here is one of them:

How to Overcome Evil with Good

¹³ Hold them in the highest regard in love because of their work. Live in peace with each other. ¹⁴ And we urge you, brothers and sisters, warn those who are idle and disruptive, encourage the disheartened, help the weak, be patient with everyone. ¹⁵ Make sure that nobody pays back wrong for wrong, but always strive to do what is good for each other and for everyone else.
¹⁶ Rejoice always, ¹⁷ pray continually, ¹⁸ give thanks in all circumstances; for this is God's will for you in Christ Jesus.
¹⁹ Do not quench the Spirit. ²⁰ Do not treat prophecies with contempt ²¹ but test them all; hold on to what is good, ²² reject every kind of evil.
²³ May God himself, the God of peace, sanctify you through and through. May your whole spirit, soul and body be kept blameless at the coming of our Lord Jesus Christ.

I Thessalonians 5:13–23 (NIV)

Often it is easier to get the impact of a verse through direct meditation upon what is in the verse. Because understanding how to overcome evil with good is so very important, the messages within these verses will be itemized to help us to focus on the complete message.

Within his counsel, Paul guides us to warn the idle; warn the disruptive; encourage the disheartened; help the weak; be patient with everyone; do not pay back wrong for wrong; *always* strive to do good for everyone (including Christians and non-Christians); rejoice always; pray continually; give thanks in *all* circumstances; do not quench the Spirit; hold on to what is good; reject every kind of evil.

Could it be that the reason people are idle and disruptive is because they have never had anyone to help them identify with their talents? This frustration alone could lead to one feeling useless, idle, and disruptive. If you know people with these feelings, certainly evil could be overcome with good by helping them to both identify and develop the skills that *you* see God has placed within them.

Encouraging the disheartened and weak is a gift second to none. We have absolutely no way of knowing what factors have led someone to this attitude of mind. However, if we allow the Spirit to work within us, we will be guided as we work with these individuals.

Being patient with *everyone* is a tall order indeed. However, it can be done. One of the major factors that must be put on the shelf is the attitude of selfishness that may be within my heart. We want others to be patient with us; with God's help we can do the same for them.

There is no place for revenge. God teaches us that He will repay those that bring harm to Christians.

Sometimes we find it challenging to do good to everyone in the Lord's church. Paul's teaching expands the horizon to *everyone* in the world. We are called to show God's love to all we meet.

It is vitally important that we *pray continually*, without ceasing. Jesus wants us to ask for His guidance every step of the way as we go out into the world to make a change. We are instructed not to quench the Spirit of God. We simply must *allow* the Holy Spirit to work within us.

Rejoice in the fact that God will guide and that He has honored every Christian by providing multiple opportunities to show

His love on a daily basis. Indeed, we should consider it an honor to be called into His service in this way.

If we are to be successful in serving others with *God's love*, it is important that we understand how to develop it within us. How do we do this? Another of God's Recipes!

Peter's Directive for Developing God's Love within Us!

Faith + Goodness + Knowledge + Self-Control + Perseverance + Godliness + Brotherly Kindness
bring forth
LOVE

Interesting math—all additions, no subtractions!

Certainly this same principle can be applied when attempting to bring positive change into today's society.

How to Disperse God's Love to Everyone We Know

When considering how to reach those lost from Christ—those deeply angered and troubled—a change in *my thinking* with regard to how I feel about them will come as I apply Paul's guidance in how to share the love God has given to me with others! Ask the Holy Spirit to guide you as you think about ways to put these words into action.

- Think about <u>*whatever is true*</u> in relationship to others!
  - Everyone, like me, was created in the "image" and "likeness" of God.
  - This alone gives *everyone* value!
- Think about <u>*whatever is honorable*</u> or noble in relationship to others!
  - Remember, reaching out to the lost—despite how deeply their lives are drenched in sin—is what Christ would have me do.
- Think about <u>*whatever is right*</u> in relationship to others!
  - Help these people in whatever healthy way possible.
  - Speak with gentleness.
  - Provide physical help.
  - If they offer, *allow them to help you.*
  - If they do not offer, <u>ask</u> them to help you. This will help to build their confidence and feel accepted.
- Think about <u>*whatever is pure*</u> in relationship to others!
  - Do not be hypocritical or judgmental when talking with or thinking about the lost.
  - Apply the Golden Rule!
  - Try to put yourself in their positions.
  - How would you react?

- Be sincere.
- Show love!
- Think about <u>whatever is beautiful</u> or lovely in relationship to others!
  - Look to a future in Christ for this person's life.
  - Think of what he or she can *become* in Christ if you allow God to use you as an instrument of peace while working toward the goal of reaching this person for Him.
- Think about <u>whatever is respectable</u> in relationship to others!
  - Encourage these individuals in what they do right.
  - Focus on their positives, not the negatives.

How to Overcome Evil with Good
God's Directive

[9] Your love must be real. Hate what is evil. Do only what is good. [10] Love each other in a way that makes you feel close like brothers and sisters. And give each other more honor than you give yourself. [11] As you serve the Lord, work hard and don't be lazy. Be excited about serving him! [12] Be happy because of the hope you have. Be patient when you have troubles. Pray all the time. [13] Share with God's people who need help. Look for people who need help and welcome them into your homes.
[14] Wish only good for those who treat you badly. Ask God to bless them, not curse them. [15] When others are happy,

you should be happy with them. And when others are sad, you should be sad too. ¹⁶ Live together in peace with each other. Don't be proud, but be willing to be friends with people who are not important to others. Don't think of yourself as smarter than everyone else.

¹⁷ If someone does you wrong, don't try to pay them back by hurting them. Try to do what everyone thinks is right. ¹⁸ Do the best you can to live in peace with everyone. ¹⁹ My friends, don't try to punish anyone who does wrong to you. Wait for God to punish them with his anger. In the Scriptures the Lord says,

"I am the one who punishes;
 I will pay people back."

²⁰ But you should do this:
"If you have enemies who are hungry,
 give them something to eat.
If you have enemies who are thirsty,
 give them something to drink.
In doing this you will make them feel ashamed."
²¹ Don't let evil defeat you, but defeat evil by doing good.

Romans 12:9–21 (ERV)

The Importance of Allowing This Growth to Happen

Remember,
⁸ If all these things are in you and are growing, they will help you never to be useless. They will help your knowledge of our Lord Jesus Christ make your lives better.

II Peter 1:8 (ICB)

And, regardless who we are sharing with,

> [29] When you talk, do not say harmful things. But say what people need—words that will help others become stronger. Then what you say will help those who listen to you. [30] And do not make the Holy Spirit sad. The Spirit is God's proof that you belong to him. God gave you the Spirit to show that God will make you free when the time comes. [31] Do not be bitter or angry or cross. Never shout angrily or say things to hurt others. Never do anything evil. [32] Be kind and loving to each other. Forgive each other just as God forgave you in Christ.
>
> Ephesians 4:29–32 (ICB)

With all of the encouragement to overcome evil with good that is provided within God's Holy Word, may we step out in faith with the armor of love as our clothing and reach out to the world.

Onward

to

Higher Ground

Chapter Two

Forgiveness
It Is Both Possible And Necessary

Forgiving others when they have wronged us is probably one of the most difficult things we encounter in life. It is possible. Again, the Apostle Paul gives us this reassurance:

> ¹³ I can do all things through Him who strengthens me.
>
> Philippians 4:13 (NASB)

Now it is important to understand *why* we must forgive others. ¹⁴ Yes, if you forgive others for the things they do wrong, then your Father in heaven will also forgive you for the things you do wrong. ¹⁴ But if you don't forgive the wrongs of others, then your Father in heaven will not forgive the wrong things you do.

> Matthew 6:14–15 (ICB)

※

²⁵ And when you stand praying, if you hold anything against anyone, forgive them, so that your Father in heaven may forgive you your sins."

Mark 11:25 (NIV)

※

²¹ Then Peter came to Jesus and asked, "Lord, how many times shall I forgive my brother or sister who sins against me? Up to seven times?"
²² Jesus answered, "I tell you, not seven times, but seventy-seven times.

Matthew 18:21–22 (NIV)

※

³ So watch yourselves.
"If your brother or sister sins against you, rebuke them; and if they repent, forgive them. ⁴ Even if they sin against you seven times in a day and seven times come back to you saying 'I repent,' you must forgive them."

Luke 17:3–4 (NIV)

※

With positive thinking through Jesus, we know we can endure the hardships of life because He is our source of power. The following verse attempts to express His physical appearance. However, in no way do they come close to expressing His pain!

> ¹⁴ Just as there were many who were appalled at him—
> his appearance was so disfigured beyond that of any human being and his form marred beyond human likeness—
> Isaiah 52:14 (NIV)

Despite all of the physical and verbal abuse imposed upon Him by His enemies, what was Jesus' response? The Bible explains:

> ³³ When they came to the place called the Skull, they crucified him there, along with the criminals—one on his right, the other on his left. ³⁴ Jesus said, "Father, forgive them, for they do not know what they are doing." And they divided up his clothes by casting lots.
> Luke 23:33–34 (NIV)

His example speaks volumes!

Yes, rather than desiring revenge, Jesus prayed to God on behalf of those who had so brutally mistreated Him!

Consider these thoughts.

* What if Jesus had rebelled against His Father's plan for Him to shed His blood and die on the cross so that mankind could be forgiven and cleansed of their sins?

* Where would that leave you and me? Certainly we would be left without hope of an eternity with God!

Meditate upon these thoughts.

MY FORGIVENESS OF OTHERS IS VERY SERIOUS BUSINESS IN THE SIGHT OF GOD

How will He respond to those who refuse to follow His teaching?

> [32] "Then the master called the servant in. 'You wicked servant,' he said, 'I canceled all that debt of yours because you begged me to. [33] Shouldn't you have had mercy on your fellow servant just as I had on you?' [34] In anger his master handed him over to the jailers to be tortured, until he should pay back all he owed.
> [35] "This is how my heavenly Father will treat each of you unless you forgive your brother or sister from your heart."
> Matthew 18:32–35 (NIV)

ANOTHER PURPOSE FOR FORGIVENESS

The Apostle Paul said:

> [5] If anyone has caused grief, he has not so much grieved me as he has grieved all of you to some extent—not to put it too severely. [6] The punishment inflicted on him by the

majority is sufficient. ⁷ Now instead, you ought to forgive and comfort him, so that he will not be overwhelmed by excessive sorrow.

II Corinthians 2:5–7 (NIV)

How do we receive our forgiveness?

God's plan of salvation for man has been clearly explained. When we have been reunited with God, our Father, through Christ, we have these promises:

> ⁷ He made known his ways to Moses,
>   his deeds to the people of Israel:
> ⁸ The Lord is compassionate and gracious,
>   slow to anger, abounding in love.
> ⁹ He will not always accuse,
>   nor will he harbor his anger forever;
> ¹⁰ he does not treat us as our sins deserve
>   or repay us according to our iniquities.
> ¹¹ For as high as the heavens are above the earth,
>   so great is his love for those who fear him;
> ¹² as far as the east is from the west,
>   so far has he removed our transgressions from us.
> ¹³ As a father has compassion on his children,
>   so the Lord has compassion on those who fear him;
> ¹⁴ for he knows how we are formed,
>   he remembers that we are dust.

Psalms 103:7–14 (NIV)

≈≈≈

⁴³ All the prophets testify about him that everyone who believes in him receives forgiveness of sins through his name."

Acts 10:43 (NIV)

≈≈≈

³⁸ "Therefore, my friends, I want you to know that through Jesus the forgiveness of sins is proclaimed to you.

Acts 13:38 (NIV)

≈≈≈

⁶ But I want you to know that the Son of Man has authority on earth to forgive sins." So he said to the paralyzed man, "Get up, take your mat and go home."

Matthew 9:6 (NIV)

≈≈≈

⁹ If we confess our sins, he is faithful and just and will forgive us our sins and purify us from all unrighteousness.

I John 1:9 (NIV)

BLESSINGS RECEIVED WHEN WE FORGIVE

³⁷ "Do not judge, and you will not be judged. Do not condemn, and you will not be condemned. Forgive, and you

will be forgiven. ³⁸ Give, and it will be given to you. A good measure, pressed down, shaken together and running over, will be poured into your lap. For with the measure you use, it will be measured to you."

Luke 6:37–38 (NIV)

Another prime example of forgiveness is seen in the story of Joseph and the conflict within his family. His story begins in Genesis, chapter 37. In summary,

* Jacob and Rachel were his parents;
* Joseph was the eleventh of twelve boys;
* He was his father's favorite;
* His father, Jacob, gave him a very special robe;
* His brothers became very jealous;
* Joseph had the God-given ability to interpret dreams;
* He shared one interpretation with his father;
* His father kept the matter in mind;
* The ten older brothers were sent to care for Dad's sheep;
* Jacob asked Joseph to go see how they were doing;
* When Joseph was reunited with his brothers, they saw an opportunity to seek revenge;
* Except for Joseph's oldest brother, Reuben, his brothers wanted to kill him;
* Rather than killing Joseph, his brothers sold him to traveling merchants;

- They killed a goat, dipped the robe in the animal's blood, took it back to their father and told their father that Joseph was dead;
- Jacob grieved.

Without his family's knowledge, through the course of time, Joseph

- was placed in charge of everything Potiphar (an officer to the king) owned;
- was falsely accused of being sexually involved with Potiphar's wife;
- spent time in prison;
- was blessed by God while in prison;
- was befriended by the prison warden;
- made overseer of the prison.

The knowledge of his ability to interpret dreams became widespread to the point that the king called upon Joseph to explain the meaning of his dreams. Part of this was the prediction of seven years of ample food supply to be followed by seven years of famine. As the result of Joseph's interpretation of the king's dream, Joseph was put in charge of the whole land of Egypt!

His new responsibilities included oversight of the food supply. All of Egypt came to buy grain. Needless to say, "all of Egypt" included his father and brothers. When his ten brothers came to purchase food, Joseph recognized them; however, they did not recognize him. Without his brothers' knowledge, Joseph gave instructions for their money to be put back into their sacks along with their food. When they found it, "Their hearts sank and they turned to each other trembling and said, 'What is this that God has done to us?'"

As the story continues to unfold, Joseph's family was provided with ample food and gifts. Genesis, chapter 45, explains that Joseph made himself known to his brothers. What happened then? One would think that he would vent his anger toward them. Not so! Rather, Joseph

* wept loudly;
* asked about his father, Jacob;
* said to his brothers, "Come close to me. I am your brother, the one you sold into Egypt";

Genesis 45:2-4 (NIV)

Why would Joseph be so gracious? How could he be?

> [5] And now, do not be distressed and do not be angry with yourselves for selling me here, because it was to save lives that God sent me ahead of you. [6] For two years now there has been famine in the land, and for the next five years there will be no plowing and reaping. [7] But God sent me ahead of you to preserve for you a remnant on earth and to save your lives by a great deliverance.

> ⁸ "So then, it was not you who sent me here, but God. He made me father to Pharaoh, lord of his entire household and ruler of all Egypt.
>
> Genesis 45:5–8 (NIV)

After Jacob's death, the brothers became concerned that Joseph would then display a grudge toward them. This is evidence that they had not stopped being distressed.

> ¹⁵ When Joseph's brothers saw that their father was dead, they said, "What if Joseph holds a grudge against us and pays us back for all the wrongs we did to him?" ¹⁶ So they sent word to Joseph, saying, "Your father left these instructions before he died: ¹⁷ 'This is what you are to say to Joseph: I ask you to forgive your brothers the sins and the wrongs they committed in treating you so badly.' Now please forgive the sins of the servants of the God of your father." When their message came to him, Joseph wept.
>
> Genesis 50:15–17 (NIV)

This group of Scriptures shows that even though the brothers remained skeptical about how Joseph would respond to them, they did what their father asked them to do. They went to Joseph and asked him for forgiveness. Obviously they were afraid. However, we must focus upon the peace of mind that came to all as the result of obeying their earthly father.

This discussion cannot be left without asking,

- * WHAT IF Joseph had refused to be so gracious toward his family?
- * WHAT IF the brothers had refused to accept his forgiveness?

Either way, God would not have been glorified! Additionally, the unresolved resentment and jealousy within Joseph's brothers and the heartache within Joseph himself would have continued to increase over the years—indefinable heartache advancing throughout.

Also, needless to say, Jacob's heartache would have continued. He would have died a very distraught father knowing there was unresolved emotional turmoil among his children.

Thankfully these joyful outcomes occurred because the brothers communicated among themselves for the purpose of resolving the issues at hand.

This same principle is taught in the New Testament:

> [15] "If your brother or sister sins, go and point out their fault, just between the two of you. If they listen to you, you have won them over. [16] But if they will not listen, take one or two others along, so that 'every matter may be established by the testimony of two or three witnesses.' [17] If they still refuse to listen, tell it to the church; and if they refuse to listen even to the church, treat them as you would a pagan or a tax collector.
>
> Matthew 18:15–17 (NIV)

These examples are a clear demonstration of the fact that it is possible to forgive others regardless of how dire the circumstances. Doing it is a tremendous challenge for man.

Not only is forgiveness another key element of God's Plan for Man, it can also be a major factor in overcoming illnesses. Failing to forgive is certainly rooted in negative thinking. Remember Louise Hay's conclusion:

> "ingrained negative thoughts and negative feelings that are not released can cause cancer! Likewise, it can be *dissolved* through positive thinking."[1]

Onward

to

Higher Ground

References

[1] Hay, Ibid.

SECTION TWELVE

HOW TO DEVELOP MENTAL PEACE

PRELUDE

A life of mental turmoil is one of the many byproducts of lives that are will with the "rush and go, push and shove" mindset. We are exhausted in every way with no vision for peace of mind.

This is not God's will.

Peace of mind can become part of our daily living when we pursue a change in thinking--a positive change based upon putting into action the teachings in God's Word.

Although this chapter is very brief, the information becomes very powerful when it is allowed to change our thinking processes.

Onward

to

Higher Ground

Chapter One

Never Forget This Truth

In the eyes of God,
You are a
Valuable, **I**mportant, **P**erson!

Not only are you a "VIP"
but, more importantly, you are a "VBPP"
Very **B**eautiful **P**recious **P**erson

Why have these letters been chosen to describe you?

Certainly there are those who do not agree,
    but regardless of what others may say or do,
    or what <u>*you*</u> *may think about* <u>*you*</u>, it is true!
Please know this day

Never Forget This Truth

you *did not* grow forth from a blob of undefined source,
   Nor did you "evolve from a monkey," as some say,
   to throw you off course.
YOUR <u>beauty</u> was implanted deep within by the Master Designer.
   You were created in God's "image," in His "likeness,"
   long before you were sent to your parents to live on earth.
YOUR <u>preciousness</u> may not be seen in the sight of men but,
   in <u>His</u> sight, it will never end.
   After all, you are an <u>important</u> part of Him!

Indeed, as a person, *you* are the result of His workmanship,
   created for a purpose that He alone has in mind.
   By His plan and design,
   you are truly a <u>valuable person</u>, one of a kind.

Despite the problems of life,
   may these *truthful* thoughts of *value*
   bring *feelings of hope* to your soul.
Regardless of the stress and strife all around,
   may they give you
   a deeper feeling of being whole.
To believe anything else other than this *truth*
   is to help Satan destroy the relationship God desperately wants
   …for YOU to live with HIM forevermore!)

Chapter Two

God's Recipe for Recovery

Finally, be strong in the Lord and in his mighty power. Put on the full armor of God so that you can take your stand against the devil's schemes. For our struggle is not against flesh and blood, but against the rulers, against the authorities, against the powers of this dark world and against the spiritual forces of evil in the heavenly realms. Therefore put on the full armor of God, so that when the day of evil comes, you may be able to stand your ground, and after you have done everything, to stand. Stand firm then, with the belt of *truth* buckled around your waist, with the breastplate of righteousness in place, and with your feet fitted with the readiness that comes from the gospel of peace. In addition to all this, take up the shield of faith, with which you can extinguish all the flaming arrows of the evil one. Take the helmet of salvation and the sword of the Spirit, which is the word of God. And pray in the Spirit on all occasions with all kinds of prayers and requests. With this in mind, be alert and always keep on praying for all the saints.

Ephesians 6:10–18 (NIV)

[1] Therefore, as God's chosen people, holy and dearly loved, clothe yourselves with compassion, kindness, humility, gentleness and patience. Bear with each other and forgive whatever grievances you may have against one another. Forgive as the Lord forgave you. And over all these virtues put on love, which binds them all together in perfect unity.
Let the peace of Christ rule in your hearts, since as members of one body you were called to peace. And be thankful. Let the word of Christ dwell in you richly as you teach and admonish one another with all wisdom, and as you sing psalms, hymns and spiritual songs with gratitude in your hearts to God. And whatever you do, whether in word or deed, do it all in the name of the Lord Jesus, giving thanks to God the Father through him.

Colossians 3:1–17 (NIV)

God, through His Son, Jesus Christ, provides the opportunity to become a Christian. It is our responsibility to accept His offer.

Final Summary

* True peace of mind comes only through submission to God and obedience to His teachings. There is no other way.

* The purpose of life is to honor God by living in accordance with His will.

   As a Result,

Chapter Three

Heaven Will Be My Home For Eternity

The following words of encouragement were spoken by Our Savior:

> ¹ Jesus said, "Don't be troubled. Trust in God, and trust in me. ² There are many rooms in my Father's house. I would not tell you this if it were not true. I am going there to prepare a place for you. ³ After I go and prepare a place for you, I will come back. Then I will take you with me, so that you can be where I am.
>
> John 14:1–3 (ERV)

In contrast to the Bible-based description of hell given earlier, God's Word also provides words of beauty to describe heaven.

> ¹ Now I saw a new heaven and a new earth, for the first heaven and the first earth had passed away. Also there

was no more sea. ² Then I, John, saw the holy city, New Jerusalem, coming down out of heaven from God, prepared as a bride adorned for her husband. ³ And I heard a loud voice from heaven saying, "Behold, the tabernacle of God *is* with men, and He will dwell with them, and they shall be His people. God Himself will be with them *and be* their God. ⁴ And God will wipe away every tear from their eyes; there shall be no more death, nor sorrow, nor crying. There shall be no more pain, for the former things have passed away."

⁵ Then He who sat on the throne said, "Behold, I make all things new." And He said to me, "Write, for these words are true and faithful."

⁶ And He said to me, "It is done! I am the Alpha and the Omega, the Beginning and the End. I will give of the fountain of the water of life freely to him who thirsts. ⁷ He who overcomes shall inherit all things, and I will be his God and he shall be My son. ⁸ But the cowardly, unbelieving, abominable, murderers, sexually immoral, sorcerers, idolaters, and all liars shall have their part in the lake which burns with fire and brimstone, which is the second death."

The New Jerusalem

⁹ Then one of the seven angels who had the seven bowls filled with the seven last plagues came to me and talked with me, saying, "Come, I will show you the bride, the Lamb's wife." ¹⁰ And he carried me away in the Spirit to a great and high mountain, and showed me the great city, the holy Jerusalem, descending out of heaven from God, ¹¹ having the glory of God. Her light *was* like a most precious stone, like a jasper stone, clear as crystal. ¹² Also she had a great and high wall with twelve gates, and twelve angels at the gates, and names written on them, which are

the names of the twelve tribes of the children of Israel: [13] three gates on the east, three gates on the north, three gates on the south, and three gates on the west.

[14] Now the wall of the city had twelve foundations, and on them were the names of the twelve apostles of the Lamb. [15] And he who talked with me had a gold reed to measure the city, its gates, and its wall. [16] The city is laid out as a square; its length is as great as its breadth. And he measured the city with the reed: twelve thousand furlongs. Its length, breadth, and height are equal. [17] Then he measured its wall: one hundred *and* forty-four cubits, *according* to the measure of a man, that is, of an angel. [18] The construction of its wall was *of* jasper; and the city *was* pure gold, like clear glass. [19] The foundations of the wall of the city *were* adorned with all kinds of precious stones: the first foundation *was* jasper, the second sapphire, the third chalcedony, the fourth emerald, [20] the fifth sardonyx, the sixth sardius, the seventh chrysolite, the eighth beryl, the ninth topaz, the tenth chrysoprase, the eleventh jacinth, and the twelfth amethyst. [21] The twelve gates *were* twelve pearls: each individual gate was of one pearl. And the street of the city *was* pure gold, like transparent glass.

The Glory of the New Jerusalem

[22] But I saw no temple in it, for the Lord God Almighty and the Lamb are its temple. [23] The city had no need of the sun or of the moon to shine in it, for the glory of God illuminated it. The Lamb *is* its light. [24] And the nations of those who are saved shall walk in its light, and the kings of the earth bring their glory and honor into it. [25] Its gates shall not be shut at all by day (there shall be no night there). [26] And they shall bring the glory and the honor of the nations into it. [27] But there shall by no means enter it anything that

defiles, or causes an abomination or a lie, but only those who are written in the Lamb's Book of Life.

Revelation 21:1-27 (NKJV)

<u>Continuing on</u>:

And he showed me a pure river of water of life, clear as crystal, proceeding from the throne of God and of the Lamb. ² In the middle of its street, and on either side of the river, *was* the tree of life, which bore twelve fruits, each *tree* yielding its fruit every month. The leaves of the tree *were* for the healing of the nations. ³ And there shall be no more curse, but the throne of God and of the Lamb shall be in it, and His servants shall serve Him. ⁴ They shall see His face, and His name *shall be* on their foreheads. ⁵ There shall be no night there: They need no lamp nor light of the sun, for the Lord God gives them light. And they shall reign forever and ever.

The Time Is Near

⁶ Then he said to me, "These words *are* faithful and true." And the Lord God of the holy prophets sent His angel to show His servants the things which must shortly take place. ⁷ "Behold, I am coming quickly! Blessed *is* he who keeps the words of the prophecy of this book."
⁸ Now I, John, saw and heard these things. And when I heard and saw, I fell down to worship before the feet of the angel who showed me these things.
⁹ Then he said to me, "See *that you do* not *do that.* For I am your fellow servant, and of your brethren the prophets, and of those who keep the words of this book. Worship God." ¹⁰ And he said to me, "Do not seal the words of the

prophecy of this book, for the time is at hand. ¹¹ He who is unjust, let him be unjust still; he who is filthy, let him be filthy still; he who is righteous, let him be righteous still; he who is holy, let him be holy still."

Jesus Testifies to the Churches

¹² "And behold, I am coming quickly, and My reward *is* with Me, to give to every one according to his work. ¹³ I am the Alpha and the Omega, *the* Beginning and *the* End, the First and the Last."
¹⁴ Blessed *are* those who do His commandments, that they may have the right to the tree of life, and may enter through the gates into the city. ¹⁵ But outside *are* dogs and sorcerers and sexually immoral and murderers and idolaters, and whoever loves and practices a lie.
¹⁶ "I, Jesus, have sent My angel to testify to you these things in the churches. I am the Root and the Offspring of David, the Bright and Morning Star."
¹⁷ And the Spirit and the bride say, "Come!" And let him who hears say, "Come!" And let him who thirsts come. Whoever desires, let him take the water of life freely.

A Warning

¹⁸ For I testify to everyone who hears the words of the prophecy of this book: If anyone adds to these things, God will add to him the plagues that are written in this book; ¹⁹ and if anyone takes away from the words of the book of this prophecy, God shall take away his part from the Book

of Life, from the holy city, and *from* the things which are written in this book.

I Am Coming Quickly

[20] He who testifies to these things says, "Surely I am coming quickly."
Amen. Even so, come, Lord Jesus!
[21] The grace of our Lord Jesus Christ *be* with you all. Amen.
Revelation 22:1-21 (NKJV)

There

is

No Higher Ground!

APPENDICES

THE UGLY TRUTH WE CAN NO LONGER DENY OR IGNORE

There are many truths in life that we do not want to face. When this occurs, we are left with one or more choices. Healthy decisions with positive consequences come through the evaluation of all factors. Although it may be difficult, it is important that we do not allow negative emotions to control our thinking. The whole process requires time and energy. We cannot allow the busyness of life rob us of these two factors lest painful consequences come into view.

All too often the trivial activities of life have taken our focus off of the most important of all God's creation--people. Their needs are many times pushed aside in pursuit of personal needs, desires or goals.

These statements are not said to place blame but simply to emphasize the fact that the emotional needs of many are not being met on an ongoing basis. Consequently, the suffering individual reaches a point of what they considerer hopeless--no way out except to take their own life.

The statistics that follow reveal these truths. As you read them, please keep in mind the truths that have been revealed through the previous pages of this book.

Please know that by joining together we can help to significantly reduce these statistics while, at the same time, help those who have experienced the pain of having lost a loved one as the result of not being aware of not having put into practice a positive approach.

∽⃝⃝∾

Suicide Stats
SUICIDE STATS
from American Foundation for Suicide Prevention

FACTS AND FIGURES

After cancer and heart disease, suicide accounts for more years of life lost than any other cause of death.

AFSP's latest data on suicide is taken from the Centers for Disease Control and Prevention (CDC) Data & Statistics Fatal Injury Report for 2013.

Suicide Deaths

The Centers for Disease Control and Prevention (CDC) collects data about mortality in the U.S., including deaths by suicide.

In 2013 (the most recent year for which full data are available), 41,149 suicides were reported, making suicide the 10th leading cause of death for Americans In that year, someone in the country died by suicide every 12.8 minutes.

From 1986 to 2000, suicide rates in the U.S. dropped from 12.5 to 10.4 suicide deaths per 100,000 people in the population. Over the next 12 years, however, the rate generally increased and by 2013 stood at 12.6 deaths per 100,000

https://www.afsp.org/understanding-suicide/facts-and-figures

Suicide Statistics from WHO

Background

The **World Health Organisation** (WHO) estimates that each year approximately one million people die from suicide, which represents a global mortality rate of 16 people per 100,000 or one death every 40 seconds. It is predicted that by 2020 the rate of death will increase to one every 20 seconds.

The **WHO** further reports that:

* In the last 45 years suicide rates have increased by 60% worldwide. Suicide is now among the three leading

causes of death among those aged 15-44 (male and female). Suicide attempts are up to 20 times more frequent than completed suicides.

* Although suicide rates have traditionally been highest amongst elderly males, rates among young people have been increasing to such an extent that they are now the group at highest risk in a third of all countries.
* Mental health disorders (particularly depression and substance abuse) are associated with more than 90% of all cases of suicide.
* However, suicide results from many complex sociocultural factors and is more likely to occur during periods of socioeconomic, family and individual crisis (e.g. loss of a loved one, unemployment, sexual orientation, difficulties with developing one's identity, disassociation from one's community or other social/belief group, and honour).

THE <u>WHO</u> ALSO STATES THAT:

* In Europe, particularly Eastern Europe, the highest suicide rates are reported for both men and women.
* The Eastern Mediterranean Region and Central Asia republics have the lowest suicide rates.

* Nearly 30% of all suicides worldwide occur in India and China.
* Suicides globally by age are as follows: 55% are aged between 15 to 44 years and 45% are aged 45 years and over.
* Youth suicide is increasing at the greatest rate.

⁂

In the US, the **Centre of Disease Control and Prevention** reports that:

* Overall, suicide is the eleventh leading cause of death for all US Americans, and is the third leading cause of death for young people 15-24 years.
* Although suicide is a serious problem among the young and adults, death rates continue to be highest among older adults ages 65 years and over.
* Males are four times more likely to die from suicide than are females. However, females are more likely to attempt suicide than are males.
  http://www.befrienders.org/suicide-statistics

⁂

OTHER FACTORS TO BE CONSIDERED

Certainly it would be both unfair and biased to say that the depression, anger, erratic behavior, Alzheimer's, cancer, ADD, and many other factors that can contribute to suicidal thoughts are *solely caused* by a broken relationship with Christ. Some people may even believe that these maladies of man are imposed upon society by God. This is very dangerous thinking, to say the least. In fact, quite the opposite is true. They are the consequences of the devil working non-stop to contaminate all of God's precious creations brought into existence for man's enjoyment.

Regardless of what Satan uses to distort our thinking, God can bring us closer to Him for guidance and comfort. It will become reality if we allow it.

On the other hand, it is possible for us to separate from God if we *blame* Him for all of mankind's dilemmas. This truth cannot be overlooked. The result comes down to whether we choose to view these life situations through positive or negative lenses?

Satan has used mankind to bring into existence many factors that are capable of creating adverse circumstances within our physical bodies. Understanding this truth is very important. When considered in a positive light, it will help us to think of God more realistically.

Words of Encouragement to Pursue the Research

Several suggestions for the possible causes of our physical, emotional, and mental disorders are provided for your consideration. This is done for the purpose of guiding us to a better understanding of the potential power within each of them to destroy our inner beings at various levels. Hosea's statement—"my people are destroyed from the lack of knowledge" (Hosea 4:6)—is not only true from a spiritual viewpoint but also from a physical one. Our lack of knowledge regarding food additives in commercially prepared food, effects of chemical drugs taken, and a multitude of other factors in life can contribute heavily to physical and mental well-being.

Please do not adopt the attitude that says, "What I don't know won't hurt me I won't want to know," etc.

Taking the attitude that "when it is our time to go, we will go" may be a cop-out. The truth may be that God wants you to take a more proactive approach to regain your health. In reality, it is possible that early death may not be the result of His plan for you but rather, the result of Satan's deception regarding your health care.

Obviously, all possible sources of illnesses mentioned here may not apply to each person's specific circumstances. Hopefully, they will be some benefit to everyone.

Remember, effective change is slow. Nonetheless, it is *very* important. As research is done, the fact will be well established that the cause of many of man's misfortunes come as the result of Satan working through man's desire for convenience, quick fixes, and emotional release.

In an effort to provide hope for those seriously ill, I will share my personal story with you. Today I am not plagued with any of them. Therefore, my pathway to recovery is being shared with you in an effort to help you in your efforts to gain improved health. Pray to God asking Him for guidance.

> In 1989 doctors projected that I would live another five to ten years if my lifestyle did not change. Eight diagnoses, including bipolar disorder (manic depression), were laid before me. One of them was a sinus infection. To overcome it, the medical community gave me five prescriptions of antibiotics (thirty each). They did not work. This was followed by one shot of cortisone. As a result, my total sleep during the next eight days equaled fifteen hours. This was followed by twelve days in a psych hospital.

I asked the doctor, "Did I have a nervous breakdown?"

"No," he answered, "you have a chemical imbalance in the brain!"

Duh. Wonder why? It was at that point that a personal commitment was made to divorce pharmaceutical drugs!

Obviously, change was necessary. Where to begin? Through God's guidance, several books were made available to me. I recommend them for your personal research.

The first one was *The Food Pharmacy*, by Jean Carper. This book was tremendously helpful in teaching me how to overcome a deeply embedded sinus infection through the use of honey.

Beating the Food Giants, by Paul Stitt, was another of the early books added to my library. A real eye-opener! It helped me to understand what is being done to our food by the food giants.

At one point, Barbara Stitt worked closely with a juvenile court in Ohio. After convincing the judge about the effect of diet on crime, the juveniles were "sentenced" to her healthy diet program. Those who followed it never returned to their previous lifestyles.

For further learning, research any of Barbara Stitt's books. They are very informative regarding the effect of hypoglycemia on our health.

Please pay close attention to this as some doctors do not test for hypoglycemia, which can be a forerunner of diabetes.

You will find any books by these three authors to be very helpful.

Continuing along this same thought supporting the truth that there can be a relationship between diet and crime, visit this website:

* http://www.crimetimes.org/contact.htm provides relevant information regarding the connection between diet and crime.

Suggestions for Personal Research

Pertaining to health hazards in our food

It is important not to overlook the effects of GMO (Genetically Modified Organisms) on our health. Great insight will be gained as you learn how the seeds are treated before our commercial food supply is grown. Begin here:
* http://blogs.ei.columbia.edu/2013/07/30/the-intensifying-debate-over-genetically-modified-foods/

As your research expands, you will learn Japan and other countries have stopped buying wheat from the United States because of the grain contamination.

* http://articles.mercola.com/sites/articles/archive/2013/11/06/washington-gmo-labeling.aspx
  Washington State Votes to Label GMO Foods—Very informative. Grow your own food! This gives guidelines on how to do this even in small spaces!
  http://globalresearch.ca
  Monsanto is a Ticking Time Bomb for U.S. Agriculture: Japan Halts Imports of U.S. Wheat after USDA's Finding of Genetic Pollution from GMOs
  End of GMO foods in sight
* http://articles.mercola.com/sites/articles/archive/2013/09/01/gmo-eradication.aspx
  A wide variety of information is available online. Dig deep and then resolve to improve your diet. Don't allow Satan to lead you into negative thinking—"No way," "It can't be done," etc.

Websites that help us to understand how foods affect our mental health

* http://www.chatelaine.com/health/diet/how-to-improve-your-mood-by-avoiding-food-additives/
* http://www.shape.com/blogs/shape-your-life/13-banned-foods-still-allowed-us

Several years ago, it was a privilege to interact with a young man who, at the age of 15, was heavily involved with drugs. After becoming a Christian, he became deeply engaged in the process of withdrawal.

He was blessed with a doctor who took an active interest in helping him achieve his goal. As they worked together, the fact was established that one food additive in Thousand Island dressing triggered drug cravings.

Be certain to research every possible crack in the wall through which these supposedly meaningless, innocent factors can creep into your life. Remember, your present health and quality of life can be improved by watching your diet more closely. No sacrifice should be too great to achieve these goals.

OF SPECIAL CONCERN TO PARENTS OF SMALL CHILDREN

* http://EzineArticles.com/2378794

Since the 1990s there has been a dramatic increase in the use of anti-depressant medications, including for young children, and including 3000 prescriptions to babies under 12 months of age in the USA alone!

There has been a 10 fold increase in major depression since 1945.

Since the 1970s rates of autism are thought to have increased 10 fold in the USA.

* http://livingbetterwithfewerchemicals.blogspot.com/2009/02/beware-of-banned-food-additives-in.html

Here is another word of caution for parents. When an ingredient is banned for use in food, it is not automatically banned for use in other areas, such as medicine. According to an <u>expose' by the British Food Commission</u> last year, food additives that have already been banned for use in food and beverages are still used in a majority of pediatric over-the-counter medicines.

Their survey found that *all but one out of the forty-one medicines contained an additive that had been banned.*

* http://articles.mercola.com/sites/articles/archive/2008/07/29

Food Dyes and Preservatives That Make You See Red

The issue of whether or not food additives such as artificial colors contribute to behavioral problems in children has been disputed for many years. However, the tide is finally turning.

A carefully designed, randomized, double-blind, placebo-controlled study published in the journal *The*

Lancet last year (for a free PDF of the full study see this link) concluded that a variety of common food dyes, and the preservative sodium benzoate – found in many soft drinks, fruit juices and salad dressings – do cause some children to become measurably more hyperactive and distractible.

The study also found that the E-numbered food dyes do as much damage to children's brains as lead in gasoline, resulting in a significant reduction in IQ.

The results of this study have prompted the British Food Standards Agency (FSA) to issue an immediate advisory to parents, warning them to limit their children's intake of additives if they notice an effect on behavior. They're also advising the food industry to voluntarily remove the six food dyes named in the study by the end of 2009, and replace them with natural alternatives if possible.

The U.S., however, has not followed suit in issuing any similar warnings to American parents.

This is another important point to be considered. If an expectant mother allows food dyes to become a part of her diet, a high risk is being taken that her child's brain can be adversely affected. Exposing a child's brain to food dyes is like exposing them to lead in gasoline.

Therefore, it is critically important that all ingredient panels are read! Recently I read one panel listing ten different food dyes in *one* very popular product.

OTHER ADVERSE EFFECTS OF CARBONATED AND SPORTS DRINKS ON OUR HEALTH

* http://www.mindconnection.com/library/health/softdrinks.htm
  This website shows the connection between osteoporosis, cancer, diabetes, etc., and carbonated drinks as the result of our bodies being robbed of vital nutrients
* http://www.webmd.com/diet/news/20121116/more-deaths-illness-energy-drinks
  "Nov. 16, 2012—The FDA has posted adverse-event reports for two more energy drinks: 40 illnesses and five deaths linked to Monster Energy, and 13 illnesses and two lasting disabilities linked to Rockstar Energy."

<u>Pertaining to dyes of various kinds</u>

Websites explaining the connection between hair dyes or colorings and suicide:

* http://www.ncbi.nlm.nih.gov/pmc/articles/PMC2700586/
* http://business.highbeam.com/409604/article-1G1-200348706/hair-dye-poisoning-and-developing-world
* http://newindianexpress.com/cities/chennai/Is-it-hair-dye-or-poison/2013/07/11/article1677191.ece
* http://articles.mercola.com/sites/articles/archive/2013/11/20/nanoparticles-tattoo-

Websites explaining the connection between hair dyes or colorings and cancer:

* www.nyrnaturalnews.com/article/the-hair-dyecancer-connection
* www.cancer.gov/cancertopics/factsheet/Risk/hair-dyes
* www.cancer.org/.../intheworkplace/hair-dyes?sitearea=PED
* www.hairboutique.com/tips/articles.php?f=tip622.htm
* www.hairboutique.com/tips/tip622.htm

Websites showing the connection between hair dyes and heavy metal poisoning (mercury, lead, cadmium, etc.)

* www.copperwiki.org
  These harmful heavy metals are contained in varying concentrations in most permanent hair dyes.

Websites explaining other factors that can lead to depression and suicidal thoughts or completed suicide

These websites offer very helpful information:

Diet deficiencies

* http://ezinearticles.com/?Suicide,-Depression-and-Magnesium-Deficiency&id=4020422
* http://www.mgwater.com/rod19.shtml
* http://www.suicide.org/depression-and-vitamins.html

Vitamins for Depression

* http://depression.about.com/cs/diet/a/vitamin.htm

A Good Vitamin Supplement Could Be Just What the Doctor Ordered
By Nancy Schimelpfening
Updated August 6, 2013
Did you ever wish that you could take a vitamin for depression? Well, for some it may be just that simple. There are a variety of vitamin deficiencies that can lead to depression symptoms.

Prescription drugs

* http://www.foxnews.com/story/2008/09/02/connection-between-prescription-drugs-suicide-studied/
* http://beforeitsnews.com/health/2012/09/government-ignores-link-between-prescription-drugs-and-suicides-2449192.html
* http://wp.rxisk.org/rxisk-asks-are-prescription-drugs-causing-suicides/
* http://www.wisegeek.com/what-is-the-link-between-prozac-and-suicide.htm
* www.flcv.com/depress.htm
  Depression and other Neurotransmitter Related Conditions-the mercury connection by B. Windham (Ed.)

Factors to be considered regarding alcoholism

* http://www.bouldermedicalcenter.com/articles/Alcohol_Nutrition.htm
* http://psuvanguard.com/news/portland-state-professor-investigates-connections-between-suicide-alcohol/

SOURCES OF HEAVY METAL POISONING

* www.evenbetterhealth.com/heavy-metal-poisoning-sources.php
  Lead Metal Sources: Lead is found in dyes, gasoline
  Cadmium Metal Sources: Cadmium is contained in cigarettes

MY PERSONAL EXPERIENCE REGARDING HEAVY METALS

After returning from a short trip in early 2013, I became very ill. The Lord led me to a nutritionist with training in Nutritional Response Testing.

Although these practitioners are not large in number, you can learn if there is one in your area by contacting:

OTHER FACTORS TO BE CONSIDERED

Ulan Nutritional Systems, 1170 NE Cleveland St., Clearwater, FL 33755 (727) 442-7101.

All testing is non-invasive. Muscle testing is a major tool for diagnosis and it is totally painless. It is absolutely amazing what medical issues can be identified through this methodology. The so-called "medication" for correcting the problems comes in the form of herbal formulas.

After a few visits with my nutritionist, it became apparent that my lungs were a definite area of concern. As the Lord guided me, I learned from a national newscast that there was an increased rate of lung cancer among women who had never smoked.

I was in that category. An Internet search showed that mercury was the cause. Hmm! That set me to thinking. My doctor tested me for heavy metal poisoning only to learn that I had a very high concentration of mercury in my body. Immediately I was given a homeopathic product to detox my body. It was several weeks coming, but after taking it for over two months, the mercury concentration had almost disappeared.

As improvement continued, I shared with my doctor what I learned from the newscast. After doing the research and putting two-and-two together, I concluded that I was a very high-risk candidate for lung cancer.

Because he was not a medical doctor, he could not say yes, but what he did say was enough—"Could be."
During our many conversations, he shared with me that those who identify health issues through this specialized training have concluded that many with cancer have heavy metal poisoning within that organ.

With this insight, anyone dealing with cancer can ask Google, "What heavy metal is connected to _____ cancer?" Fill in your type of cancer.

Then pursue further research to determine how to remove it from the body.

Proactive approach to avoid Alzheimer's

* http://articles.mercola.com/sites/articles/archive/2013/11/07/peanut-butter-coconut-oil-alzheimers-detection Two Exciting Alzheimer's Advances: A Novel Early Detection Test Using Peanut Butter, and a Study Evaluating Coconut Oil

How to overcome food cravings

* http://upwave.com/diet/food-cravings-explained

OTHER FACTORS TO BE CONSIDERED

HOW TO CHANGE FROM PROCESSED TO NATURAL FOODS

* http://articles.mercola.com/sites/articles/archive/2010/07/01/wean-yourself-off-processed foods in 7 steps.aspx

SUGGESTIONS FOR FURTHER GOOGLE SEARCHES

The following is a list of questions that can be typed into Google as the beginning points of your personal research. It is important to become proactive in successful effort to eliminate problems influencing depression, suicide, and other adverse behaviors in man.

Of course the questions can be adapted based upon the specific health issues of the individual.

* connection between asthma medications and diet pills with depression and suicidal tendencies
* connection between nail polish, hair spray, perm chemicals and depression or suicide
* connection between depression and carbonated drinks
* connection between gluten and suicide or depression
* connection between junk food and drug addictions
* connection between acne medication and suicide
* connection between junk food and gambling
* connection between alcohol and suicide

Suggested sites for parental research (search Google with these words or phrases)

* http://www.lebmetal.com/2009/05/heavy-metal-encourages-teen-suicide/
* http://comp.uark.edu/~ches/CountryMusic_Suicide.pdf

Other interesting facts regarding music

* http://teddy031.blogspot.com/2012/07/psychology-of-music-studies-indicate.html

Other factors that may contribute to depression and suicide

* http://www.blogher.com/there-connection-between-social-media-and-suicide
* http://bullying.about.com/od/Effects/a/How-Strong-Is-The-Link-Between-Bullying-And-Suicide.htm
* http://healthland.time.com/2013/01/17/study-reveals-how-concussions-can-trigger-depression/

OTHER FACTORS TO BE CONSIDERED

Even after years of personal research, it is alarming to learn the multiple facets that can lead to severe disease, depression, and suicide in today's world. Nonetheless, it is necessary if causes of individual health issues are to be identified. Please press on. With each day of research and applying what you learn to your personal life, encouragement will be gained to move past the negative toward a more positive outlook on life.

Although all of this information can overwhelming, it has been provided for several reasons.

(1) To provide guidelines which will lead to improved health.
* The first rule to recovery is, despite what the doctors may tell you, DO NOT ROLL OVER AND DIE. When my doctor's forecast for my lifespan was five to ten years, my answer was, "Not if there's something I can do about it."
* Never fail to sincerely ask God for guidance. It may come in the form of a flyer advertising a good health book, counsel from a friend who has walked a path similar to yours, a bit of information picked up from watching a health show on TV, etc. Just be alert and watch for the guidance that will come.
* It is important to remember that this will not be accomplished as a one-man mission. When we reach out

to Him in a manner in accordance with His will, He will guide us step by step, laying the path we are to follow.

(2) To help us understand the terrible price we are paying in the names of "convenience" and "saving time," remember there are ways to provide healthier foods for your family—and save money—at the same time. Make it a family effort.
   * A Crock-Pot is a great beginning.
   * Freeze small amounts of leftover meats and vegetables in one container. When it is full, make soup or a potpie.

   If your attitude has been "it's too much work to cook," ask yourself,

   "What is more work—learning to cook properly or fighting a deadly, diet-related disease for years on end only to lose the battle to death."

(3) To provide encouragement for those who are truly seeking help in overcoming depression and suicidal thoughts. Hopefully, the websites given will save you time as you do your own research, you may find other sites that are more effective in meeting your personal needs. The important goal is that you gain viable information that, when put into practice, will result in a much brighter future.

(4) A terrible price is also carried over from the emphasis placed upon personal appearance, manicured nails, hair color, etc., without giving thought to the chemicals that are being ingested within.

(5) All too often we are very angry with God as the result of blaming Him for all of the negatives man has suffered. All too often, we turn our backs on God because we fail to realize the true cause of life's heartaches—Satan.

(6) To help each of us to understand that there are several avenues we can travel to turn the tide from negative to positive. To think and do otherwise is allowing Satan to win!

Again, we must ask ourselves,

"How long will it be before we become angry with Satan rather than God?"

MY PERSONAL PLEA

In today's world, violence is right around the corner if not right in front of our faces. First responders in all categories, hospital workers, social workers, workers in the medical field at various levels, and people with memories of active involvement in war zones are just a few of those who face emotionally devastating circumstances that are beyond the average person's comprehension.

Also let's not forget the families (children included) that are left behind while a father or mother, husband or wife participates in military action.

Memories of these occasions remain with them day after day, week after week. Although we may think of them as being bionic or having nerves of steel, the reality is they are human. They have emotional limitations like anyone.

Therefore, it is critically important that all people be recipients of our ongoing efforts offering special emotional support and encouragement.

Earlier this year it was my privilege to attend a suicide prevention seminar. Several times emphasis was placed upon this statement: "Those who commit suicide do not want to die. They are trying to end the pain."

Therefore, prIt is important not to become so busy that we fail to do everything possible to provide what others *need*. Nothing will ever take the place of a warm handshake or a light touch on the shoulder as you stand beside the person. A listening ear or a walk in the park with them may be the best possible gift you could bless them with. Looking at life through *their eyes* will help us to develop these skills.

Equally important, let us be very careful in our choice of words as we minister to people we know. We have absolutely no way of knowing what they have experienced in their lives, what has brought them to their present-day mind-set.

When these guidelines are honored, unrealistic goals for recovery will not be placed upon them. Emotional scars can take years to overcome. We simply must be patient. What a tragic mistake it is to put a time frame on someone else's healing process.

God will guide us as we keep the needs of others in the forefront of our minds rather than focusing on our own personal needs to the detriment of another's mental health!

Even though you may not appreciate their actions, tell people you know, "I appreciate you because you are a creation of God."

May each of us diligently strive to continually walk toward higher ground through daily living.

MY PERSONAL PLEA

Never doubt that a small group of
thoughtful, committed people can change the world.

Indeed,
It is the only thing that ever has.
Margaret Mead

※

Coming together is a beginning;
Keeping together is progress:
Working together is success.
Author Unknown

※

Tis' the human touch in this world that counts,
Tis the touch of your hand and mind
Which means far more to the fainting heart,
Than shelter and bread and wine.

For shelter is gone when night is over
But the touch of the hand and the sound of a voice
Sings on in the soul of man.
E. G. Billingsley

Made in the USA
Charleston, SC
08 August 2015